Jamaica
and
Voluntary Laborers from Africa
1840-1865

Jamaica
and
Voluntary Laborers from Africa
1840-1865

Mary Elizabeth Thomas

A Florida State University Book

The University Presses of Florida
Gainesville

Contents

Introduction

THE ISLAND OF JAMAICA IN THE MID-NINETEENTH century was in dire need of laborers who would work for hire. Largest of the British West Indies and having a continuous growing season, the island had been for decades the major sugar producer of the British Empire.[1] As its pre-eminence was challenged, however, first by the island of Mauritius, then by the newer sugar colonies of British Guiana and Trinidad, the market price for Jamaica's sugar declined. During this crucial time, in 1834, Great Britain abolished slavery throughout the empire; four years later she brought an end to the system of apprenticeship which had served as a transition from slavery to complete freedom. Consequently the supply of labor available for use on the sugar estates dwindled to the point where it became necessary to curtail the acreage planted in sugar cane. Planters of Jamaica tried to meet the emergency by importing particularly from Africa laborers who would come freely and voluntarily. They would be unusual immigrants to the island, but it seemed essential to find new sources of labor. Recruiting of foreign labor could be pursued, however, only if it was not opposed by the imperial government.

The efforts made by Jamaica to secure free and voluntary immigrants from Africa provide an important chapter in the history of the colony's

1. Jamaica is not large, approximately 150 miles in length and 50 miles at its greatest width.

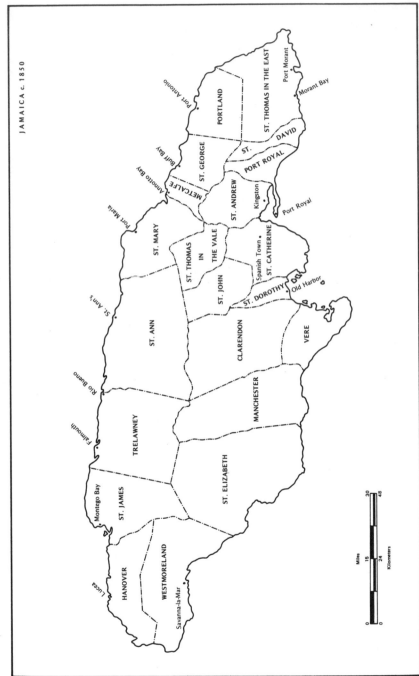

JAMAICA c. 1850

Port Morant
ST. THOMAS IN THE EAST
Morant Bay
PORTLAND
Port Antonio
ST. DAVID
ST. GEORGE
Buff Bay
PORT ROYAL
METCALFE
Annotto Bay
ST. ANDREW
Kingston
Port Maria
Port Royal
ST. MARY
ST. THOMAS IN THE VALE
Spanish Town
ST. CATHERINE
ST. JOHN
ST. DOROTHY
Old Harbor
St. Ann's
ST. ANN
CLARENDON
VERE
Rio Bueno
MANCHESTER
Falmouth
TRELAWNEY
Montego Bay
ST. JAMES
ST. ELIZABETH
HANOVER
Lucea
WESTMORELAND
Savanna-la-Mar

Miles
0   15   30
Kilometers
0   24   48

relations with West Coast Africa and the Colonial Office. Those efforts are the subject of this book.

Jamaica as a colony had limited control over its own affairs. The Legislature was composed of a House of Assembly, chosen by less than one percent of the population,[2] and an upper house, or Council, appointed by the governor. He, in turn, was appointed and instructed by Her Majesty's government. While measures adopted by the Legislature were subject to approval by the governor, final disposition lay with the ministry in London, where decisions concerning Jamaica were usually made by the Colonial Office, though often in consultation with other departments.

The capital of Jamaica was at Spanish Town, inland some twelve miles from Kingston (the largest town of the colony), and about twenty miles from the naval base of Port Royal. The terrain of Jamaica rises sharply from the sea to form an island of many mountains and valleys, the highest elevation being over 7000 feet. Communication over the island was slow, as it was with London. More than three weeks often were required for a despatch from the governor to arrive at a desk in the Colonial Office; weeks, and sometimes months, elapsed before a formal reply was placed in the mail for Jamaica. The delays were frustrating, and Jamaica frequently considered that her interests were unrecognized or neglected by the mother country.[3]

Slowness of communication sometimes, however, enabled the Legislature to maneuver for a temporary advantage under these circumstances. For instance, a measure passed by the Legislature and signed by the governor in Jamaica might be treated immediately as operative, only to be disallowed months later by the imperial government. During the interval, Jamaica had been able to proceed as if the measure were the law of the land. There were other means, too, by which Jamaica could circumvent the imperial government. Revenue and appropriation measures were introduced by

2. It was estimated in 1838 that a total of 1796 votes were cast in the election for members of the House of Assembly in that year. Sir Lionel Smith to Lord Glenelg, Dec. 25, 1838, no. 42 in "Papers on the Condition of the Labouring Population, West Indies," *Parliamentary Papers,* 1838, XXXV:175 (hereinafter cited as *PP*). Although there was no exact count of the population, at the time of emancipation the black population was given as 311,700; the white was estimated as 30,000, and the free colored as 70,000, thus making a total estimated population of 411,700. See "Remarks on Emigration to Jamaica," by Alexander Barclay, Commissioner of Emigration for Jamaica, in Jamaica, *Votes of the Honourable House of Assembly of Jamaica* (St. Jago de la Vega, 1840-1865), 1841-1842, Ap.5 p. 50 (hereinafter cited as *Votes*).

3. For a discussion of the Colonial Office, see Paul Knaplund, *James Stephen and the British Colonial System, 1813-1847* (Madison, Wis., 1933), pp.42-45.

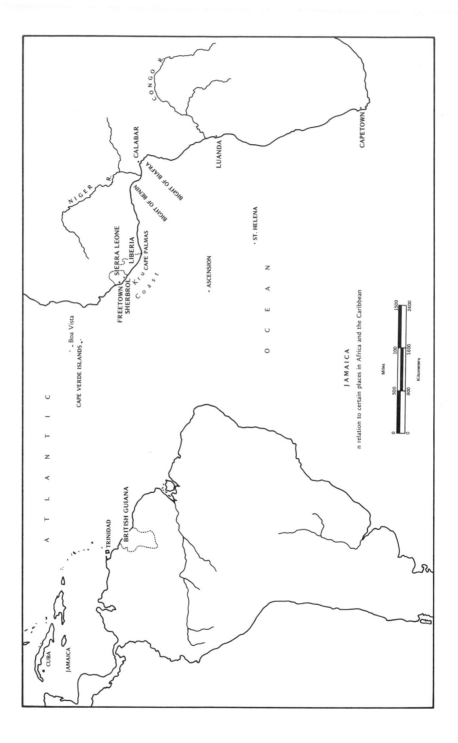

JAMAICA

in relation to certain places in Africa and the Caribbean

individual members of the assembly, rather than after certification by the governor. By this means the governor was prevented from initiating financial measures wanted by Great Britain but objectionable to Jamaica. Furthermore, a device known as the Commission of Public Accounts enabled the assemblymen to exercise continuing control over finances; all of the members of the assembly were ex-officio members of this commission and retained their power when the assembly was not in session. Nothing interrupted their authority to meet and act.[4] This extraordinary power of the Legislature was of no moment as long as that body was satisfied with the policies of the imperial government. But when it was displeased with those policies, it could (and did) use these means to emphasize the colony's displeasure, even if its action affected the immigration of much-needed laborers.

Jamaica's influence in London had been reduced with the passage of the Parliament Bill of 1832, for with an end to the "purchase" of seats in the House of Commons, the West Indian interests were no longer able to maintain themselves in the imperial parliament. Shortly thereafter slavery was ended and the planters' troubles mounted. In order to preserve the plantation system and the Jamaica economy, the estate owners tried to find some means whereby they might recover influence over imperial legislation. From this effort came the Association of Jamaica Proprietors, organized in London in May, 1838, to serve as a propaganda agency. The organization considered itself as representing all of the Jamaica proprietors resident in Great Britain and as having the confidence of those resident in Jamaica.[5]

The Legislature itself had a London agent through whom it could conduct business with members of the imperial government. So definitely did the agent represent the Legislature that instructions were given to him only as authorized by a meeting of a Committee of Correspondence of Jamaica. This committee, composed of all of the members of the House of Assembly and all of the members of the Council, met when the Legislature was not in session, and enabled the members to exercise continuing influence within Jamaica. In addition, by working through the agent in London, they could bypass the governor if they wished to communicate

4. Earl Grey, *The Colonial Policy of Lord John Russell,* 2 vols. (London, 1853), 1:175-176.
5. "Memorial Addressed to Lord Melbourne through the Marquis of Normanby, May 30, 1839, by the Planters, Merchants, and others interested in Jamaica," CO 137/246.

informally with the imperial government. Conversely, the agent could serve as a channel for suggestions from the imperial government to the colonial legislature. He might also keep that body alerted to contemplated changes in imperial policy. Sometimes it was the agent's task to communicate unofficially to the Colonial Office the views of Jamaica's residents.[6]

A different approach was followed, however, if either the Legislature or bodies of citizens wished to communicate officially with the imperial government. On such occasion it was necessary to draw up memorials, which were presented formally through the governor, and only through him. He could, of course, include his own interpretation of the problem. In short, in the late 1830s Jamaica was in a position to voice approval or dissatisfaction, but how clearly she would be heard in London remained uncertain.

6. William Burge to the Marquis of Normanby, July 10, 1839, no.1767 Jamaica in CO 137/249; "An Act for Appointing an Agent in the United Kingdom of Great Britain and Ireland, for Appointing Commissioners of Correspondence, and for Other Purposes," no. 3316 Jamaica in CO 137/377.

1

Jamaica's Problem of "Continuous Labor"

JAMAICA WAS BESET BY LABOR PROBLEMS AFTER 1834 and blamed the situation on the British parliament. "An Act for the Abolition of Slavery Throughout the British Colonies," passed by the imperial parliament in 1833 to become effective August 1, 1834, had immediately freed all slaves below the age of six; others were to serve an apprenticeship—in the case of praedial workers,[1] until August 1, 1840; non-praedial workers, until August 1, 1838. Abolitionists, convinced of the inability of ex-slaves to fend for themselves, demanded the appointment of officials to protect them; but these same abolitionists refused to entrust the task to the regular local officials of Jamaica, whom they distrusted as members of the ruling class. Reformers were influential in high places of government, and they had their way. Special officials, stipendiary magistrates, usually non-Jamaican, were appointed by the imperial government to oversee the apprentices, settle disputes between employer and apprentice, and ensure good treatment.[2]

Because the Colonial Office decided in 1838 to classify certain non-field workers as non-praedial and free as of August 1, 1838, the Jamaican

1. The term "praedial" was imprecise, but it included field laborers and others associated in various ways with field work.
2. William L. Burn, *Emancipation and Apprenticeship in the British West Indies* (London, 1937), pp.196-312.

7

assembly provided that all apprentices should become free on that date.[3] Thus Jamaica suddenly found itself deprived of two of the years anticipated for accomplishing the transition from apprenticeship to free labor on the estates. There followed a dispute between the imperial government and the governor on the one hand, and the House of Assembly on the other, over Jamaica's policies with regard to the Negroes. It culminated in 1839 in a threat to suspend the colony's constitution; but instead, Parliament empowered the governor-in-council to revive by proclamation annual laws which the assembly had permitted to expire. As a result, it was hoped that never again would a recalcitrant assembly be able to leave the colonial treasury without funds.[4]

The labor problem was aggravated by the condition of the sugar market. The island's sugar, along with that of the other West Indian colonies, lost its preferential treatment within the empire[5] when the differential rate on sugar was abandoned in 1836. By 1840 Jamaican sugar was feeling the pinch of competition with sugar from Mauritius as well as from the newer sugar colonies. In the foreign market Jamaica was totally unable to compete with the slave-grown sugar of such areas as Cuba, Puerto Rico, and Brazil. Against this confused and confusing background Jamaicans who were politically and economically conscious and active were trying desperately to halt the plunge toward total ruin. The wealth of the island had been based primarily on sugar cane, the cultivation of which required a large supply of laborers, particularly at certain stages of growth. Before emancipation, when a "continuous" supply of labor was a certainty, laborers were available at all times and could easily be shifted from less essential to more essential tasks. With apprenticeship, laborers often were not available when needed, especially at crop time. Nonetheless, under the apprenticeship system, it was possible to continue reasonably well with cane production.

After August 1, 1838, the situation changed. When apprenticeship ended, laborers all over the island simply quit work. Cultivation was almost entirely suspended. The agricultural outlook was dismal. Canes were ripe and spoiling on the ground. Untended cattle destroyed the canes, and canes for

3. J. Holland Rose, A. P. Newton, and E. A. Benians, eds., *Cambridge History of the British Empire,* 8 vols. in 9 (Cambridge, 1929-1959), 2(1940):490 (hereinafter cited as *CHBE*).

4. *CHBE,* 2:491; Marquis of Normanby to Sir Charles T. Metcalfe, Aug. 6, 1839, no.3 in "Papers Relative to the West Indies, Jamaica," *PP,* 1840, XXXV:2.

5. Burn, *Emancipation and Apprenticeship,* p.87.

the next crop were not planted.[6] Late in September some laborers drifted back to work, but the total was far short of the old number. A planter who had fifty percent of his former gang of field hands was fortunate; more often the turnout was no more than twenty-five percent. Because of lack of a labor force, much of the 1838 crop was lost, and little of the 1839 crop was planted; because of decreased income from the 1838 and 1839 crops, the planter was sharply limited as to the wages he could offer.

In Britain, however, it was the heyday of the humanitarians. Missionaries and other zealous reformers, though often not eyewitnesses of the conditions they depicted, had besieged both the country and the Colonial Office with accounts of the mistreatment of slaves by their masters, and had totally rejected efforts of the proprietors to present evidence in refutation of these charges. Efforts of Jamaican planters to present their cause in Britain fell on deaf ears. James Stephen, who as Permanent Undersecretary of State for the Colonies (1836-1847) occupied one of the most influential posts in the Colonial Office, was busy improving the efficiency of that department and in some instances strengthening Colonial Office direction of individual colonies; Charles Grant, Lord Glenelg, was Secretary of State for the Colonies (1835-1839); and Sir Lionel Smith was governor of Jamaica (1836-1839). To a large degree all three reflected the point of view of the missionaries and humanitarians, and gave scant or slighting attention to Jamaican efforts to present any other picture. William Burge, Jamaica Agent in London, complained that Sir Lionel Smith, as governor of Jamaica, absolutely would not forward to the Colonial Office any evidence presented in support of the proprietors.[7]

The planters could and did offer explanations for the plight of the estates. While Jamaica did not have ungranted lands, it had much unoccupied land, and many of the former slaves simply took to the mountains where as squatters they maintained themselves merely by cultivating the soil. Some of the ex-slaves who had prospered bought small plots of ground and became small farmers. On the other hand, some of the newly freed Negroes would not leave the homes and grounds to which they were accus-

6. Enclosures in William Burge to the Marquis of Normanby, Feb. 20, 1839, *PP*, 1839, XXXV:1-79; Burge to Normanby, Apr. 1, 1839, *PP*, 1839, XXXV:80-93; Statement by Burge in "Report from the Select Committee on the West Coast of Africa," Ap.24, *PP*, 1842, XII:469; "A Return of the Staple Exports of Jamaica, 1839," *PP*, 1840, XXXV:188.
7. Burge to Normanby, Mar. 18, 1839, *PP*, 1839, XXXV:32-33.

tomed; during slavery and apprenticeship they had been entitled to a house and grounds, and they now could not understand that with freedom they no longer had this claim. They refused either to work for the owner or to pay rent. The planters were further handicapped when the Law Offices of the Crown decided that these Negroes could not be dispossessed until the expiration of three notices to quit. Consequently, only by the use of notice-to-quit could the employer place himself in a situation whereby the Negroes occupying house and grounds on his estate had to recognize him as the owner of the land that they occupied.[8]

If a tenant still would not work, pay rent, or leave voluntarily, the planter's only recourse was to evict him. Evictions brought charges of cruelty from the missionaries. If laborers did go to the fields, many worked for only a few days, then quit until they again needed money. It was impossible to cope with the situation: if the proprietor paid a high wage, the laborer accumulated enough money to stop work for a while; if the proprietor did not pay the high wage, the laborer decided not to hire himself out at all, but to cultivate a plot for his own use. The planters asserted that for a variety of reasons the wages offered were the highest they could afford. They had lost heavily even before the passage of the abolition act because the market value of slave property had dropped sharply from the moment in 1823 when Buxton introduced his resolution for abolition. Compensation for slave property, as provided by the imperial government, was heavily weighted in favor of owners in the newer sugar colonies, hence discriminated against those in Jamaica. Complete financial ruin was close at hand. If the trend toward this desperate condition was to be halted, the planters would have to find a supply of continuous labor, because in their eyes Jamaica had an "insufficient" supply of labor, and it was imperative to find at once some means for increasing the availbliity of labor.

Governor Sir Lionel Smith, however, did not agree with the conclusions of the planters. There was no shortage of labor, he wrote to the Colonial Office; the Negroes would work if only they were dealt with in a fair and liberal spirit and given adequate remuneration. Accounts of the stipendiary magistrates were of the same tenor. In fact, Smith's conclusions were based in part on information provided by these officials, who were

8. "Copies of Communications Addressed to the Secretary of State by the Agent for the Island of Jamaica Relative to the Conduct of the Negro Population of the Island," *PP*, 1839, XXXV:7.

both appointed and paid by the imperial government to watch over the newly freed Negroes. Their reports, along with those of Smith, were accepted by Glenelg as beyond question.[9]

Jamaicans complained that the governor, unable to make the fatiguing journey necessary to see conditions for himself, had trusted the reports of missionaries and stipendiary magistrates, who had deceived him.[10] They not only defended the rate of wages (1s. to 1s. 8d.), but implied that Jamaica had been victimized by imperial economic policy. They were sharply critical when they stated:

> When Her Majesty's Government take leave to object to this rate of wage as inadequate, they should remember that by an ill-timed submission to the remonstrances of interested persons and theorists in equalizing the duties upon East and West Indian sugar, and withdrawing the bounty upon the exportation of refined sugar, they themselves precluded the West Indian proprietors from being more liberal to their laborers.[11]

Statements made to the Colonial Secretary by stipendiary magistrates, they asserted, were garbled, biased, and at variance with those of proprietors and managers resident in the colony.[12] Much of the trouble in the island, they charged, was due to the conduct of stipendiary magistrates, who caused the Negroes to distrust their employers and to demand unreasonable wages. Furthermore, these same officials led the Negroes to expect adjudication favorable to them in any difference between them and their employers.[13]

The Committee of Correspondence of Jamaica attributed the cessation of labor to interference by stipendiary magistrates and Baptist missionaries, who by press, sermon, and oration urged the Negroes not to accept the wages offered.[14] As neither group seemed amenable to control by island government, some in Jamaica became convinced that only the imperial authority could effect their restraint. Acting on such a premise, the Committee of Correspondence directed the colonial agent to impress upon the Colonial Office the wisdom of exercising imperial authority on the side of

9. Burge to Normanby, Feb. 20, 1839, in "Copies of Communications," ibid., pp.4-5.
   10. Extract from Cooke to Burge, Jan. 17, 1839, ibid., p.13.
   11. "Copies of Communications," ibid., p.4.
   12. Ibid., p.6.
   13. Ibid., p.8.
   14. Copy, Burge to Normanby, Feb. 20, 1839, ibid., p.1.

moderation.[15] Burge and a delegation from the Association of Jamaica Proprietors obtained a conference with the Prime Minister (Lord Melbourne) and the Colonial Secretary; but their objective was not secured, for nothing could shake Glenelg's confidence that Governor Smith's reports presented the true picture of Jamaica. As these continued the theme of abundant labor, if proprietors would only give fair pay and kind treatment, the planter interests increasingly regarded themselves as victims of bias.[16]

When the Marquis of Normanby became Secretary of State for the Colonies, February, 1839, planter interests had some hope of improvement. Perhaps the new Colonial Secretary would place less emphasis upon stipendiary magistrate reports as the only accurate source of information on labor conditions in Jamaica. But those hopes were soon dispelled. Although papers relative to Jamaica were presented to Parliament, March 16, they merely sustained the old charges against the planters. Burge, while protesting to Normanby their erroneous impression, pointed out that, with one exception, the governor had forwarded the stipendiary magistrates' reports of inadequate wages and exorbitant rents, but had withheld communications which disproved the accuracy of the officials. Such action by the governor, declared Burge, not only was unjust to the proprietors, but unfair to the government and public. But when the colonial agent applied to Normanby to have his own report placed before parliament in refutation, he found the Colonial Secretary unyielding.[17]

Jamaica had the further misfortune to be made an issue in British party politics. Charges made by a stipendiary magistrate against a Jamaica planter were laid before parliament; eventually refutation of those charges also was placed before parliament. Within a year the controversy was recognized as mere House of Commons tactics which had served the momentary purpose. The injustice was admitted, and it was agreed with Burge that in the future all charges against individuals would be suppressed until the accused party had had an opportunity to deny their accuracy. The damage to Jamaica proprietors had been done, however, for the original charges, not the refutation, tended to remain in men's minds.[18]

15. "Papers Relative to the Conduct of the Negro Population," ibid., pp.1-2.
16. Burge to Normanby, Feb. 20, 1839, in "Copies of Communications," ibid., p.3-5.
17. Burge to Normanby, Mar. 18, 1839, ibid., pp.32-33.
18. Minute by James Stephen, June 1, 1840, no.934 Jamaica Separate, April 1, 1840, CO 137/248.

A few months later Smith was replaced as governor by Sir Charles T. Metcalfe (1839-1842). While Metcalfe was en route to Jamaica, Normanby was succeeded at the Colonial Office by Lord John Russell. The new Secretary of State for the Colonies, who studied reports of both Sir Lionel Smith and the stipendiary magistrates, professedly saw no cause for discouragement about the ultimate prospect for agriculture in the island. Nonetheless he directed the new governor to impress upon the planters and proprietors in general that Parliament and the people of the United Kingdom would never permit a return to compulsory labor or award any further compensation for its abolition.[19]

When Metcalfe arrived at his new post in Jamaica, September 26, 1839, he was struck with the cordiality displayed by the Negro population to the departing governor who had been so sympathetic with their complaints. Proprietary interests could only hope for something better.

Although Metcalfe himself had little optimism for his chances of conciliating the antagonistic factions in Jamaica,[20] his reports presented a picture unlike the one his predecessor had so imprinted on the public mind in Britain. Part, though not all, of the cause for friction he ascribed to the stipendiary magistrates and their invariably blaming the managers when anything went wrong; but the greatest hindrance to prosperity was lack of cheap and continuous labor—a by-product of the "house and grounds" policy. In his effort to determine the origin of the policy and to analyze its role in proprietor-labor antagonisms, Metcalfe went far beyond earlier reports. The facts revealed by his investigation led to conclusions somewhat at variance with those usually reported to the Colonial Office. Both as slave and as apprentice, the laborers traditionally had had the use of a house and provision grounds, whose surplus he could sell; when this was not withdrawn immediately upon termination of apprenticeship, rumor among the Negroes, noted the governor, foretold a law from England to give them possession of what they currently occupied. Meanwhile, by continuing to use free of charge the house and market-garden owned by someone else, the Jamaica Negro was able, for the most part, to be independent of wages and to hold out for terms to his liking. Under such conditions, explained Metcalfe, when the laborer would not work on the estate, the owner charged

19. Lord John Russell to C. T. Metcalfe, Sept. 9, 1839, no.10 in "Papers Relative to the West Indies, Jamaica," *PP*, 1840, XXXV:19.
20. Metcalfe to Normanby, Sept. 30, 1830, no.26 in "Papers Relative to the West Indies, Jamaica," ibid., p.64.

him rent in order to provide an incentive to work for wages, and thus prevent the Negro from confining his efforts to cultivation of provisions for himself and for local sales. As a consequence there had been much irritation and litigation. Laborers were anxious to obtain leases for their houses and grounds; proprietors were willing to give them, if the laborer would enter into engagements to work for the same period; but laborers were averse to any contract relating to work, and proprietors, explained the governor, were reluctant to relinquish what they regarded as their only control over the laborers—that of keeping them tenants-at-will. But "house and grounds" was not the only cause of the wage controversy, which had reached something of an impasse.

Metcalfe reported that Baptist missionaries had encouraged discontent among the Negroes. They brought their parishioners together in large assemblies where they dwelt upon the concept of a wicked legislature which deliberately adopted measures injurious to laborers; they preached the intransigence of the local government; they proclaimed their own unique influence as the only means of securing redress of grievances from the imperial government. By their tactics the Baptist missionaries had made themselves peculiarly obnoxious to the proprietors, for they seemed to thrive on promoting ill-will toward the Europeans. In fact, concluded Metcalfe, by their interference they might possibly have prevented a settlement equally favorable to both parties.[21]

From mid-February until mid-March, 1840, Metcalfe toured the island to gain first-hand information. He not only visited coastal towns easily accessible by ship, but, riding horseback because of bad roads, went over much of the interior. On this relatively wide tour, the governor observed dissatisfaction between landlords and tenants all over the island. It was still impossible for a proprietor to secure continuous labor, particularly at the time when assistance was needed for the crop. Laborers seldom worked more than a four-day week, yet not even then could they be relied upon from one week to the next. The tour strengthened Metcalfe's earlier opinion that shortage of labor stemmed from two causes—too small a laboring class

21. Metcalfe to Normanby, Oct. 16, 1839, no.32 in "Papers Relative to the West Indies," ibid., p.71-74; Metcalfe to Normanby, Mar. 30, 1840, *Selections from the Papers of Lord Metcalfe,* John William Kaye, ed. (London, 1855), pp.337-338. Baptist missionaries were among the first to work among the Negroes. There are frequent references to their influence and their urging refusal of the wages offered by the planters. The missionaries presumably believed the planters could afford to pay higher wages.

and the ease with which the population could support itself without working in the service of others. Clearly, kind treatment of the laborers was not a remedy. But what was?[22]

Immigration seemed the most logical answer to Jamaica's need for rapid and appreciable increase of laborers. There was already an extensive immigration from Europe to North America and Australia and some emigrants were leaving Asia. A flow of laborers might well be directed toward Jamaica. Most Jamaicans who favored the project, however, did not want European laborers, for proprietors who had sponsored their introduction had found them ill-adapted to work in the hot and sultry lowlands of the island. One group of laborers located on an estate in the highlands was prospering, as was a group of Scots, but three townships of European immigrants had failed. Immigrants from Europe, warned the governor, could succeed only in the highlands, only if accommodations had been readied for them, and only if they were willing to advance themselves by work. European immigrants left in seaports would be subject to a dreadful mortality rate.[23]

Planting interests, who were vitally concerned with the island's economy, favored bringing in free Africans as the people best suited to work in the lowlands, where most of the cane estates were then located. Less desirable as field laborers, but still acceptable were Asiatics. Jamaicans fully realized there would be many objections in Britain to the introduction of laborers from Africa or Asia, but past experience with immigrants from Europe did not warrant any expectation of relief from that source. Negroes from North America would fit well into the life and economy of the island, but there was little hope of their coming because they received higher wages there than could be paid in Jamaica.[24] It seemed wise, however, to seek immigrants from any source even though the most wanted were Africans.

From all over the island came assertions of need for an increase in the supply of labor. Although a proprietor occasionally imported a family or individual immigrant, results were negligible and costs were high. Seemingly some overall planning was needed; if the colonial government took up the project with organizational and financial assistance to individuals, perhaps enough laborers might be recruited for continuing cultivation of the crops

22. Extract, Metcalfe to Russell, no.50, Mar. 30, 1840, CO 137/248.
23. Metcalfe to Russell, Mar. 30, 1840, *Papers of Metcalfe,* pp.340-342.
24. Extract, Metcalfe to Russell, no.50, Mar. 30, 1840, CO 137/248.

so long of vital importance to Jamaica. Planter interests, which dominated the Legislature, demanded action.[25] Consequently, the House of Assembly took up the problem and soon produced a bill acceptable to the governor and signed by him in April, 1840.

The Act to Encourage Immigration, 1840, was noteworthy for drawing upon the island government for funds and organization to promote immigration. It undertook to establish a network of agents to recruit and transport immigrants from North America, Great Britain, or "elsewhere." It empowered the governor to appoint: (1) an agent-general of immigration, together with such subordinate officials as might be needed in the island, and (2) a commissioner, who should go to the United States and from there to Great Britain or "elsewhere." The commissioner was directed to appoint agents in the recruitment areas and to initiate steps for recruiting suitable immigrants. Any Jamaican who wished to secure the services of immigrants should make written application in which he stated the number wanted, location and type of work, rate of pay, and any other perquisites such as provision grounds or medical attendance.[26]

Applications and information from the planters were to be forwarded to a recruiting agent, upon whom was placed tremendous responsibility. His duties were varied, and included the obligation to see to it that the immigrants were healthy and fully aware of the distance to Jamaica, as well as the difficulty of return. Immigrants must be accepted at the ratio of one female to two men. Furthermore, the agent must make certain of the seaworthiness of the ship designated to bring these people to Jamaica and its compliance with the minimum standards for provisions and water. For each statutory adult there had to be a minimum of five gallons of pure water and seven pounds of breadstuff for each week of the voyage. The voyage from the USA was estimated to require five weeks; from Great Britain or Ireland, nine weeks; from the coast of Africa north of Cape Palmas, seven weeks; from the coast of Africa south of Cape Palmas, eleven weeks; from Malta or other Mediterranean ports, nine weeks; and from any place east of the Cape of Good Hope, twenty-one weeks.[27]

25. Metcalfe to Russell, Mar. 30, 1840, *Papers of Metcalfe,* pp.340-342.
26. An Act to Encourage Immigration, Jamaica no.3346, CO 139/77.
27. An Act to Encourage Immigration, Jamaica no.3346, CO 139/77. (The paragraphs of the rather lengthy act are unnumbered.) Barclay, while in the United States, stated that Jamaica was sixteen days' passage and 1400 miles from New York. "Remarks on Emigration to Jamaica," by Alexander Barclay, in *Votes,* 1841-1842, Ap.5, p.50.

Certain regulations were set for the voyage. The number of passengers should be in proportion to the tonnage of the vessel, with a requisite of at least ten superficial feet of lower deck space per person and five and one-half feet between decks. There could be no more than two tiers of berths. In counting passengers, all persons fourteen years of age or more were classified as adults; two children between the ages of three and fourteen were considered as the equivalent of one adult; three children between the ages of one and three, as one adult; infants less than twelve months of age were not to be counted.[28]

When an immigrant transport arrived in Jamaica, the master of the ship must notify the agent-general of immigration (the AGI) or the sub-agent, who should inspect both ship and passengers to make certain of compliance with all requirements. Not until then could the immigrants debark, and the receiver-general, on warrant of the AGI, pay the cost of transporting the passengers. Once landed, the immigrants were at liberty to indent themselves to the person whose proposals were approved by the subagent; but if an immigrant refused so to indent himself, he must repay the expenses of his passage. The customary term of indenture was expected to be three years; yet in instances where the employer reimbursed the AGI for approximately half the cost of the immigrant's transportation, there seemingly was no restriction as to length of indenture.[29]

With the Act to Encourage Immigration, 1840, Jamaica in its own way was adhering to the nineteenth-century concept of assisted migration. Financial assistance would come from the island treasury; centralization of control and of direction would be provided by agents of the Jamaica government. By such means, it was hoped, the island would secure from some place the free laborers it so desperately needed.

28. An Act to Encourage Immigration, Jamaica no.3346, CO 139/77.
29. Ibid.

2

Jamaica's Solution: Voluntary Immigration from Africa

IF JAMAICA'S ECONOMY WAS TO BE SAVED BY IMMI-
grant labor, there was no time to be lost. While awaiting formal sanction by
Her Majesty's government, Jamaica proceeded as if its Act to Encourage
Immigration were actually law. Alexander Barclay was the man chosen to
implement the project. A member of the House of Assembly as well as a
planter with extensive interests in the eastern part of the island, he was well
qualified to represent those who needed estate labor. As commissioner of
immigration for Jamaica he was given broad responsibility for recruiting
immigrant laborers and appointing whatever subordinate officers might be
needed in North America, England, and Africa.[1] While for more than a year
Barclay moved about in search of laborers, the progress of immigration to
Jamaica was closely linked with his travels and work.

North America was the logical starting point. The Negro population
there, more than in any other place, had the agricultural skills which could
be of vital importance to the economy of Jamaica. Furthermore, according
to a rumor widely believed in Jamaica, the white population of the United
States not only wanted the free Negroes to leave the country, but in some
states would not permit an owner to free his slaves unless they would agree
to emigrate. As these people were free only in Canada and in certain regions

1. Metcalfe to Russell, July 24, 1840, *PP,* 1842, XIII:554.

of the United States, recruitment efforts needed to be concentrated in those regions if labor was to be secured from North America.[2]

Immediately after his appointment, the commissioner set out on his mission to recruit labor for Jamaica, but the route which he took to reach the Baltimore area is illustrative of the difficulties of communication between his country and the United States. He sailed from Port Royal to Trinidad, from there to Cienfuegos, Cuba, and then on to Havana, where he boarded a small American steamer which called at Savannah, Charleston, and finally at Wilmington, North Carolina. From Wilmington, Barclay continued his journey by railroad as far as Norfolk, Virginia, where he transferred to steamer for the trip up Chesapeake Bay to Baltimore, which he reached on June 24.[3]

In Baltimore Barclay found that agents had already arrived for the colonies of Trinidad and Demerara, which were also trying to augment their labor force. In the course of their discussions he became aware of certain difficulties he would encounter in recruiting. In the first place, Trinidad was paying higher wages than Jamaica could possibly offer; in the second place, Jamaica's system for reckoning wages was too complicated for easy explanation to people totally unfamiliar with it. Although the free Negro in the United States was in too good a position economically to be attracted to the West Indies by wages, Jamaica had something to offer which might be more persuasive than money. Barclay emphasized this when he was able to arrange meetings with a few free Negroes, presumably ones who were influential among their own people. Seizing upon the theme of personal status, he used the term "coloured" in a way which could be misleading to anyone in the United States. In Jamaica, where "white," "coloured," and "black" were used for purposes of classification by race, "coloured" referred to those whose ancestors were from both the white and black races. Possibly unaware that in the United States the word was not so understood, in his promotional activities Barclay failed to define "coloured." Intent upon convincing his audience of a better life awaiting them in Jamaica, he emphasized that free coloured, no matter how well educated and respected, could not give evidence in a United States court; by contrast, in Jamaica they would enjoy the rights and privileges of free men denied to them in the

2. Metcalfe to Russell, Aug. 8, 1840, CO 137/249.
3. Barclay to Captain Higginson, Baltimore, June 29, 1840, in *Votes*, 1841-1842, Ap.5, p.47.

United States. His audience, however, remained unconvinced; the best response he could get was merely a suggestion that he invite some of them to visit Jamaica for first-hand investigation. They could draw their own conclusions about the merits of Jamaica and then report to their countrymen.[4]

As he continued his efforts to recruit free Negro immigrants, Barclay made a circuit from Baltimore to Philadelphia to New York to Philadelphia to Baltimore. When he discovered that the people whom Jamaica wanted to attract knew nothing about the colony, he tried to inform them of its many advantages, both material and social—but particularly the latter. His pamphlet, entitled "Remarks on Emigration to Jamaica: Addressed to the Colored Class of the United States," was published in New York just one month after he arrived in the United States. It set forth at length the advantages of Jamaica as well as its plans for assisting immigrants. The Jamaica legislature had appropriated a large sum of money to provide immigrants with a free and comfortable passage along with protection until they found employment in Jamaica. Barclay, as the commissioner appointed by the governor, was authorized to meet with the free Negro residents of the United States and to make arrangements for any who wanted to emigrate to Jamaica. To help them in making a decision, he gave information as to: size, distance from New York, and the climate of the island; crops, both major and minor; and livestock. Small farming was one of many occupations open to industrious persons from the United States, particularly those who could take a little capital with them. Furthermore, the U. S. coloured person would feel at home immediately in Jamaica where the ratio of coloured to white was fourteen to one.

Because plantation labor was carried on in many different ways, it was impossible to give specific information about the rate of pay. By way of illustration, he wrote, pay for cutting cane was by daily wages, by the cart, by a given quantity of cane juice per day, or by the acre; in the claying of cane fields, some worked by the day, some by the task, while more commonly one man contracted to do the field at from $2 to $5 per acre, then found his own hands to do the work. In general, a laborer could easily earn $ 0.375 to $ 0.50 per day, with free house, garden, and medical care. Although the rate might seem small in the United States, the work was constant rather than seasonal, and wants were more easily supplied than where winters were cold. "Every visitor to Jamaica," he proclaimed, "has admitted

4. Ibid.

that the comforts enjoyed by the laboring class of Jamaica are exceeded by none in the world."[5]

Although it was immigrants for field labor whom Jamaica wanted, in his efforts to secure them Barclay continued to stress political privilege and social status. In contrast with their inability to participate in political affairs in the United States, the coloured class in Jamaica had already attained high rank, good education, and considerable property. As proof of ideal conditions in the island, Barclay quoted extensively in his pamphlet from an account by two travelers whose journal was published by the American Anti-Slavery Society. They stressed the complete "intermingling" in the schools, in business, in the courts, in parish meetings, and in all political and civil bodies throughout the island. Coloured merchants were numerous, including druggists, grocers, and general importers, dealers in dry goods, crockery, and glassware.[6] Barclay's pamphlet might well have been misleading to his readers, for it contained nothing to indicate a distinction in the term "coloured" as used in the United states and in Jamaica. Great stress, however, was placed upon the offer for a limited number of U. S. Negroes to make a cost-free experiment of living in Jamaica; if they succeeded, many more were expected to follow; if they failed, the distance from the United States was not so great as to prohibit return.[7]

The commissioner assured his readers of his colony's interest in any class of immigrant, whether American or European, and its intent to make the immigration act satisfactory by correcting any defects which might appear. He warned quite sternly, however, against idle, improvident, and intemperate habits which would lead to destitution in Jamaica just as elsewhere; on the other hand, sober, frugal, and industrious men could make themselves comfortable and independent in the "favored island," and could do so with comparative ease.[8]

Barclay was able to meet with the free Negroes, but he secured no volunteers. Yet despite lack of interest on the part of the U. S. laborers, he made arrangements for transportation of any who might decide to accept the offer. He authorized three firms—Aymar and Company of New York,

5. Barclay, "Remarks on Emigration to Jamaica," in *Votes,* 1841-1842, Ap.5, p.53.
6. James A. Thome and I. Horace Kimball, *Emancipation in the West Indies: A Six Months Tour in Antigua, Barbados, and Jamaica in the Year 1837* (New York, 1839), as quoted in *Votes,* 1841-1842, Ap.5, p.56.
7. Barclay, "Remarks on Emigration to Jamaica," ibid.
8. Ibid., p.57.

Bevan and Humphrey of Philadelphia, and Howell and Sons of Baltimore—
to provide free passage for any emigrants to Jamaica.[9] Even though each
firm was located in a city presumably convenient for the Negroes' departure, there was no response. When the Jamaica commissioner met with
agents of Demerara and Trinidad to discuss recruiting problems, all three
agreed as to the improbability of enlisting even a moderate number of North
American emigrants; their conclusion was not immediately communicated
to the Colonial Office, however, because the Demerara delegate objected.

Jamaica's initial efforts to establish government-directed immigration
had not been productive. Barclay, as the man charged with designing and
implementing the program, suggested a number of reasons for the failure to
attract the free Negroes of North America. In assessing causes and reporting
to his government, he touched only lightly upon a natural reluctance to
leave one's homeland, and the rate-of-wages factor; at the same time he
pointed an accusing finger at societies whose objectives were diametrically
opposed to his own. Although no specific incident was cited, the Colonization Society, composed of some U. S. citizens interested in sending freed
U. S. Negroes to Liberia, was named as important in preventing people from
going to Jamaica. Furthermore, said the commissioner, many owners freed
their slaves on the express condition of departure for Africa. Seemingly,
however, it was the abolitionists, themselves opponents of the Colonization
Society, who were the major obstacle to Barclay's efforts. Controlling a
press with wide circulation and powerful influence among the Negroes, they
reportedly demanded that those who were free remain at home in order to
support the cause of their brethren still in bondage.

Clearly, Jamaica's economy, in need of immediate labor, would not
acquire it from the United States. As Barclay was responsible for setting up
the entire recruiting program, it seemed wise for him to spend no more time
in North America but to proceed to England, the next stage of his
assignment.[10]

Perhaps, for both imperial and international relations, it was well he
had failed. The imperial government had not been aware of Jamaica's plans
until the commissioner was in the United States and actively involved in
recruiting. As such procedure could be very embarrassing to diplomatic
relations between Britain and the United States, the Colonial Office ex-

9. Ibid.
10. Barclay to Higginson, New York, July 31, 1840, ibid., pp.47-50.

pressed disapproval of the project.[11] But so long was the time span necessary for the Colonial Office to learn of Barclay's efforts in the United States, then have its letters of disapproval arrive in Jamaica, that the commissioner, completely unaware of Colonial Office attitude, had already become discouraged and prepared to embark for England. Force of circumstances had saved him from possible rebuke. Anticipating better results from the eastern side of the Atlantic, he sailed on August first.[12]

Barclay was going to London not with much hope or desire of enlisting British immigrants, but rather of gaining permission to recruit free Negroes along the west coast of Africa, particularly at Sierra Leone. When the commissioner arrived in London in mid-August, however, the Colonial Secretary, Lord John Russell, was in Scotland. Not until a fortnight later was Barclay received by that official.[13]

Although absence from town was reason enough for the Colonial Secretary not to see Barclay immediately upon his arrival, there were probably two additional considerations. First he needed time to weigh an impassioned despatch received from Governor Metcalfe shortly before the commissioner's arrival. Dissatisfied with the proceedings of the island Legislature, Russell had, in April, professed finding it difficult not to disallow some of the acts as oppressive and unjust. The governor promptly took exception to the tone of the despatch, and warned against inflicting a wound not easily healed. Moreover, he stated, it would strengthen the hand of a few mischief-makers who, by exciting the Negro population against the local legislature, were "laying the foundations of incalculable evil."[14] The European population and their descendants (of both pure and mixed blood) he described as loyal, warmhearted, well disposed, anxious to meet the wishes of Her Majesty's government and secure the good opinion of the mother country. Patience and conciliation, he emphasized, were the wisest policies with a colony whose interests and affections were united with those of the parent state. He further warned:

> The Community of Jamaica are at the same time sensitive, and there is a general resentment among them at the calumnious

---

11. Metcalfe to Russell, Aug. 8, 1840, no.1810 Jamaica, CO 137/249.
12. Barclay to Higginson, New York, July 31, 1840, in *Votes,* 1841-1842, Ap.5, pp.47-50.
13. Barclay to Russell, London, Sept. 5, 1840, ibid., pp.60-61.
14. Metcalfe to Russell, June 11, 1840, in no.1338 Jamaica, CO 137/249.

opinions expressed of them by numbers in England. Nothing I
conceive could tend more to wound their feelings than to find
that Her Majesty's Ministers gave countenance to such injuries,
or entertained suspicions which are known to be unjust.

He concluded with an assurance of complete absence of oppression for the
Negro population and the flat assertion, "Your Lordship may be certain
that whatever else may be in jeopardy in the state of Jamaica, her Negro
population are as free as any people in the world under civilized Government!"[15]

Although consensus at the Colonial Office was that Metcalfe was
needlessly irritated,[16] Her Majesty's government had arrived at no final
decision with regard to the Jamaica immigration act; the governor's implications may have given Russell pause to consider the entire problem. Certainly
he was not then in a position for an interview with the commissioner.

In the second place, British humanitarians had created unforeseen
complications. At the very time when Jamaica was seeking Negro labor, the
British government was trying by diplomacy and by use of the Royal Navy
to end the slave trade on the west coast of Africa.[17] Sierra Leone, by now a
crown colony, had been established by English philanthropists late in the
eighteenth century as a haven for Negroes freed within the British Isles.[18]
As it was the location of both a Vice-Admiralty prize court and a Court of
Mixed Commission, slavers taken as prize by ships of the Royal Navy were
usually taken there for adjudication.[19] Both ship and slave cargo might be
condemned before one of these courts and confiscated. Africans "liberated"
from slave ships were maintained for a time by the British government; but
they tended to become a problem to both the colony and themselves, as
well as a charge on the British treasury.

Sierra Leone itself was poor. The Negroes in the area of Sierra Leone
were divided into three categories: "settlers," or descendents of those
English Negroes colonized in Sierra Leone by a philanthropical society in
England; "tribe," or people native to the area; and the "liberated" or re-

15. Ibid.
16. Minutes by James Stephen, Vernon Smith, and Lord John Russell, Metcalfe
to Russell, June 11, 1840, ibid.
17. For a detailed account of the campaign which the Royal Navy waged
against the slave trade off West Coast Africa, see W. E. F. Ward, *The Royal Navy and
the Slavers* (New York, 1969).
18. *CHBE,* 2:209-212.
19. Christopher Lloyd, *The Navy and the Slave Trade* (New York, 1949), p.16.

captured Africans. Small farmers found little market for their produce and jobs were scarce. The settler population was too small and the liberated Africans too numerous for any but a limited number to be apprenticed in the colony.[20] Because the liberated slaves believed there was no opportunity to improve their position in Sierra Leone, they were inclined to return to their native areas where it might be possible to recover their former status. They hoped by traveling in large numbers to avoid being captured again for the slave trade.[21]

On the other hand, many of the Maroon[22] and settler population wanted to take their families and leave for the West Indies, where, according to rumor, labor by free African immigrants was in such demand that wages were many times higher than in Sierra Leone. Colonel Richard Doherty, governor of Sierra Leone, assumed the Colonial Office would not oppose the departure of these free Africans; but he was uncertain of its attitude toward liberated Africans, who were regarded as, to some degree, wards of Her Majesty's government. Quite possibly they might wish to follow the example of the free settlers and go to the West Indies. Their departure from the colony would certainly decrease unemployment, but the governor needed to know the official attitude toward any would-be emigrant. To this end he queried the Colonial Office for instructions.[23]

The office was sympathetic to the project, but replied that before any decision could be made it would be necessary to know definitely the attitude in the West Indies and to gain a clearer knowledge of opportunities available there. Subsequently, Lord John Russell circularized the governors of Jamaica, Trinidad, and Demerara.[24] As replies had not been received from the West Indies when Barclay reached London, Russell was not then in a position to engage in a practical discussion.

At this juncture it seemed as if British philanthropical and humanitarian activities might inadvertently assist Jamaica's efforts to save its own economy, for the unemployed African who posed a problem for Sierra

20. Barclay to J. M. Higginson, Mar. 16, 1841, *PP*, 1842, XII:466; same to [same], May 21, 1841, *Votes*, 1841-1842, Ap.5, p.89; *PP*, 1842, XII:468.
21. R. Doherty to Russell, Mar. 20, 1840, *PP*, 1842, XIII:553-554; Barclay to [Higginson], May 21, 1841, *PP*, 1842, XII:468.
22. The Maroons were slaves who escaped to the mountains of Jamaica and in the eighteenth century rose against the British. Some of them were transported to Nova Scotia, from where they eventually went to Sierra Leone.
23. Doherty to Russell, Mar. 20, 1840, *PP*, 1842, XIII:553-554.
24. Russell to Light, June 9, 1840; Russell to Doherty, June 17, 1840, ibid.

Leone could well be the exact solution to the demand for labor in the West Indies. The reply of Jamaica's governor reflected the attitude of the planters as well as his own—any Africans, but liberated Africans most of all—would be very welcome in Jamaica, and would find employment, good wages, and food in abundance. As proof of the island's receptive mood, he cited the new (April, 1840) immigration act, which was designed by the Jamaica assembly to create a veritable network of agents to speed recruitment and distribution of immigrant laborers to Jamaica, yet at the same time to afford them protection from exploitation.[25] Immigrants were, of course, to indent themselves, but the term could not legally exceed three years.[26]

Great Britain, however, was of no mind to accept casually anything so important as the Jamaica immigration act; rather, the act was subjected to suspicion and careful scrutiny, with attention focused sharply on the clause pertaining to place and duration of contract. The Colonial Land and Emigration Commission,[27] to whom the Colonial Office had referred the act for review, recognized that a colony which paid for passage of laborers should be able to ensure their presence long enough to compensate for the cost of transportation; nonetheless, it wondered if the objective could not be accomplished without infringing on the principle, laid down by Her Majesty's government, of invalidation of contracts if made outside the colony where the immigrant was to be employed. Perhaps, it suggested, the bargain could be made immediately after the immigrant arrived in the new land.[28] Russell meanwhile advised Jamaica of his decision to recommend disallowance of the act unless the contract-for-service was limited to twelve months, or, if more than twelve months, was terminable by either party with three months' notice.[29] There must not be, he stressed, any possibility of the revival of compulsory labor.[30]

Relations between the imperial government and Jamaica were not the

25. Metcalfe to Russell, July 24, 1840, ibid., p.554.
26. An Act to Encourage Immigration, Jamaica no.3346, CO 139/77.
27. The Colonial Land and Emigration Commission was officially recognized in January 1840. Its members were Thomas F. Elliot, Robert Torrens, and E. E. Villiers. The Commission was given charge of the sale of land in the colonies and of emigration from Britain. Among their other assignments were those of supervision and regulation of immigration to Jamaica. See Fred H. Hitchens, *The Colonial Land and Emigration Commission,* (Philadelphia, 1931).
28. T. F. Elliot, Robert Torrens, Edward F. Villiers to James Stephen, July 29, 1840, enc. in no.47, "Papers Jamaica," CO 137/249.
29. Russell to Metcalfe, July 14, 1840, no.99, ibid.
30. Russell to Metcalfe, Sept. 16, 1840, no.47, ibid.

smoothest at the time Commissioner Barclay was attempting to carry out the second part of his assignment. Difficulties of communication had prevented him from being warned of opposition to the service contract as provided by the immigration act. When, after a considerable lapse of time, he was granted an interview with Russell, he asked if the benefits of the Jamaica Act to Encourage Immigration could be offered to the British settlements on the coast of Africa, whose population was suited to Jamaica's lowlands. In reality, he wanted not merely permission but official support, and implied that written authorization for the governor of Sierra Leone to support the undertaking would be of inestimable importance. His hopes, he said, were for the two governments to work "hand in hand" in solving Jamaica's labor problem. He also hoped there would be official encouragement for the government in Canada and in Malta to support recruiting of laborers for Jamaica.[31]

Barclay soon discovered that the general prejudice in England against a long apprenticeship was a serious obstacle to his plan.[32] While a three-year period did not seem long in Jamaica, it did in Great Britain, where it might be branded as slavery in disguise. Consequently it was essential to proceed with caution: anti-slave trade societies and similar organizations in Britain must have no ground for clamoring against the project; at the same time the commissioner must conciliate Russell, whose adamant opposition to the three-year term of apprenticeship was revealed during the first interview.[33] The commissioner, too, warned that the immigration act would not be allowed if the three-year apprenticeship were retained. Any change in the act would have to wait, of course, until the Jamaica Legislature convened in October, as it normally did. Russell, meanwhile, despatched another message to the governor. Timed to arrive in Jamaica about the date for the Legislature to convene, it made dire predictions as to the fate of those who then dominated Jamaica. The Negro laborers and artisans, he forecast, might soon acquire a powerful and perhaps predominant influence in electing representatives of the people; it was important to treat them well in order to forestall their becoming oppressors at some future date.[34] Russell's mes-

31. Barclay to Russell, Sept. 5, 1840, *Votes,* 1841-1842, Ap.5, pp.60-61.
32. Barclay to Higginson, Aug. 27, 1840, ibid., pp.57-59.
33. Barclay to Higginson, Sept. 10, 1840, ibid., pp.59-60.
34. Russell to Metcalfe, Oct. 5, 1840, no.40, "Papers Jamaica," CO 137/249. Written at a time when in England few people below the middle class could vote, these seem strange words from Lord John.

sages failed to hasten action by the assembly. Not until December did that body, bowing to the inevitable, reduce the term of indenture to only twelve months. The amended act was approved by Her Majesty's government.[35]

In the meantime, while action by the assembly of Jamaica was still pending, Barclay continued his efforts to elicit imperial authorization for the colony to recruit labor from West Coast Africa. Seemingly he was successful, for in the course of an interview at the Colonial Office, Russell observed that as white people could not stand the climate, Jamaica would have to look to the black population. When the Secretary further agreed to Jamaica's sending an agent to Africa immediately, Barclay interpreted this as tantamount to official permission for recruitment there. He promptly set about traveling over Britain to make arrangements for a ship and the necessary equipment.

Although his plans focused principally on steps to procure African labor, Barclay was unwilling to discount entirely the possibility of adding to the white population despite uncertainty about the suitability of Europeans to the climate of the lowlands. Enquiries with regard to Malta were discouraging, however, for emigrants from there would be expensive and not adapted to Jamaica's needs. As several of the West India proprietors believed that a circular would be useful in England, Barclay had copies made both of the immigration act and of his pamphlet addressed to the coloured people of America. These he distributed in Britain.[36] The response was disappointing: in Ireland, popular clamor against the project was so violent that in one incident (at Limerick) a police force was necessary to protect the "slaveship" from being destroyed.[37] Convinced there would be no appreciable number of European immigrants, Barclay concentrated on Africa.

After several weeks spent in hiring a ship in England, the commissioner returned to London with the expectation of securing permission from the Colonial Office and then going to Sierra Leone; to his chagrin, however, he now found Russell unwilling to give formal sanction to the project—apparently because of opposition from the powerful abolition party.[38] Instead of conceding defeat, Barclay tried to enlist support and cooperation

35. An Act to Repeal and Amend an Act Entitled "An Act to Encourage Immigration," no.3382, CO 139/78; Russell to Metcalfe, April 20, 1841, *Votes,* 1841-1842, pp.46-47.

36. Barclay to Higginson, Sept. 10, 1840, *Votes,* 1841-1842, Ap.5, p.59; same to same, Sept. 28, 1840, ibid., p.63.

37. Barclay to Higginson, Jan. 1, 1841, ibid., p.66-67.

38. Barclay to Higginson, Dec. 1, 1840, ibid., p.64.

from the opponents themselves. For this purpose, in interviews with such abolitionists as Sir Thomas F. Buxton and Dr. Stephen Lushington, he depicted emigration from Africa as the only measure which would enable the colonies to recover the prosperity "every right thinking man would wish them to have in their new state of freedom."[39]

Reportedly Sir Fowell felt some repugnance to the scheme because of its resemblance to the slave trade. Barclay stressed to the abolitionist the calamities which would befall the entire island unless additional labor could be procured. As Buxton seemed willing to support the West Indian colonies only if they made common cause with him and his friends, the commissioner warned his government that if Jamaica wanted emigration it would be advisable to adopt a policy of opposition to slavery and the slave trade.[40]

When the imperial government sent an agent to investigate conditions on the Gold Coast and to report upon the state of Sierra Leone settlements, Barclay took some hope from the move because the agent, an abolitionist, had asked for copies of the commissioner's American pamphlet, which the agent planned to circulate during his investigations in Africa.[41] As time passed and no response came from the Colonial Office, it became obvious Russell had decided not to approve the project. Barclay's efforts to discuss the question at greater length were unsuccessful, and Russell left town in late December without any further interview or commitment.[42]

When more than a fortnight passed without any further communication from the Colonial Office, Commissioner Barclay reviewed the situation: there had not been approval, yet neither had there been disapproval; he would proceed accordingly. As Trinidad proprietors were about to send out a ship, he became anxious to push along in order to be ahead of them. He had no information as to the type of reception he could expect in Sierra Leone—whether the governor would be cooperative and the people eager to accept his offer, or whether he would have to institute a sales campaign to persuade them to go to Jamaica. In view of such uncertainty his plans had to be flexible. He chartered one vessel in England and hoped to engage a second if he found a very large number of people wanting to emigrate. On the other hand, if the people were reluctant to depart, he planned to get a

39. Ibid., p.65.
40. Barclay to Higginson, Dec. 15, 1840, ibid., p.65.
41. Ibid.
42. Edward Hammond to Barclay, Dec. 28, 1840, *Votes,* 1841-1842, Ap.5, p.67; Barclay to Higginson, Jan. 1, 1841, ibid., p.66.

few of them to accompany him as delegates to see Jamaica and take a report back to Sierra Leone. The commissioner had been instructed by the island Legislature to further the removal of Africans from Sierra Leone to Jamaica: as there had not been official prohibition by the imperial government, he sent notice to Russell on January 1, 1841, that he anticipated no objection to emigration from Sierra Leone to Jamaica and had engaged the ship *Hector* for transporting those who wished to go.[43]

While the Colonial Office had not opposed recruitment of free emigrants in Africa, the Royal Navy on patrol along the West Coast could be a serious obstacle. In her efforts to end the slave trade, Great Britain frequently exercised the right of visitation and search. Any ship found with unusually large stores of food and water was likely to be suspected of intent to carry slaves and seized. In the case of ships chartered to transport free emigrants from Africa to the West Indies, something was clearly needed to protect them from such interference. A certificate of character and purpose would be the solution, and through the efforts of the Colonial Office, Commissioner Barclay obtained such a document from the Admiralty. He was further supported by letters of introduction from Russell, from the brother of the Secretary of War, and from a member of the Mixed Commission, and from the Secretary of the Wesleyan Society.[44] Although Barclay had not received the official approval he had hoped for, the assistance from those in high office clearly constituted at least quasi-approval.

So armed, Barclay arrived in Sierra Leone in March, 1841, and called on the new governor there, Sir John Jeremie, in order to outline his plans. Jeremie seemingly was sympathetic, but adhered to the official attitude in London and refused to give formal approval.[45] He did, however, proclaim the Transatlantic Passengers Act in effect in Sierra Leone. Enacted by Parliament, that measure was designed to protect from unscrupulous shipping interests any immigrant whose passage to North America originated in a port of the United Kingdom. Among its regulations were those fixing the minimum daily allowance of water and requiring specific items of food; these were to be calculated by multiplying the per-day ration by the total number of adults on ship and by the estimated number of days for the

43. Barclay to Russell, Jan. 18, 1841, ibid., p.77.
44. Barclay to Higginson, Jan. 29, 1841; Barclay to Russell, Jan. 18, 1841; R. Vernon Smith to Barclay, Jan. 26, 1841; Barclay to Higginson, Feb. 10, 1841, ibid., pp.76-78.
45. Barclay to Higginson, April 5, 1841, ibid., p.79; *PP*, 1842, XII:466-467.

voyage. As welfare of passengers and crew depended upon a correct estimate of the probable duration of the voyage, various officials familiar with the route, including some at the Admiralty, were consulted; only then was the estimated length of the voyage from Sierra Leone to the West Indies officially stated as eight weeks.[46]

The commissioner began his campaign by a well-calculated appeal to the people of Sierra Leone, be they Maroon, settler population, or liberated African. He announced that he had come to offer a free passage to all Africans in Sierra Leone who might wish to go to Jamaica—that is, as many as the ship *Hector* would carry—and he promised to arrange passage at a later date for those who could not be accommodated on the first ship. This broadside was addressed to all who might wish to become settlers in Jamaica; in addition to free passage, it offered such inducements as transportation for "furniture" (a loose term for cooking utensils, gourds, mats, etc.), payment of good wages, and perfect freedom to choose their employer in a plantation village. At the end of one year, the indenture was terminable upon three months' notice given by either party to the agreement of indenture. The immigrant could then remain on the island or return to Sierra Leone.[47]

Many local regulations proved to be obstacles. A Sierra Leone law that required persons intending to leave the colony to post their names for ten days in the secretary's office resulted only in delay and confusion because of similarity in the Africans' names. A passport was required; as many of the laborers could not afford the required fee, Barclay paid it, thus adding to the cost of the project. While it was hoped these provisions would soon be withdrawn, they were a distinct hindrance to the first voyage. Another difficulty was the Jamaica requirement of one female immigrant to every two males,[48] for the women in Sierra Leone were not as eager to emigrate as were the men. As if there were not enough obstacles in getting emigration under way, further complications seemed likely when two additional ships, one from Trinidad and one from Demerara, anchored alongside the *Hector*.

46. An Act to Extend to the Colony of Sierra Leone . . . An Act of the British Legislature . . . ; Proclamation by His Excellency Sir John Jeremie, *Votes*, 1841-1842, Ap.5, pp.81-83; *PP*, 1842, XXXI:467.

47. Notice to Emigrants for Jamaica, by A. Barclay, Commissioner for Immigration for Jamaica, *PP*, 1842, XIII:593-594; Barclay to Higginson, April 5, 1841, *Votes*, 1841-1842, Ap.5, pp.80-81.

48. An Act to Repeal and Amend an Act Entitled "An Act to Encourage Immigration," paragraph 24, no. 3382, CO 139/78.

With three ships waiting in port to carry them away, the Africans might easily conclude there was some sinister plan, perhaps even that of taking them into slavery. To forestall such erroneous ideas, Commissioner Barclay resorted to his original plan of employing delegates. In other words, it was expected that eyewitness reports by satisfied Africans who had been to Jamaica and *returned* would provide the best possible encouragement for emigration and would successfully refute any derogatory rumors. Accordingly, when a small prize brig in good condition came on the market, Barclay bought it to transport a few influential persons to Jamaica so they could see for themselves, then go back to Sierra Leone, presumably to spread the word of the island's great advantages.[49]

As soon as the brig was acquired, Barclay launched his effort to recruit delegates. Circulars, similar to those already released, depicted the advantages of emigrating to Jamaica and invited one or two headmen of certain villages to make an expense-free round trip to Jamaica in order to see for themselves; in addition, as they would be paid for the trip, in part in advance, their families would not lack support during their absence. The circulars were sent to some thirteen villages, some close to Freetown, some relatively distant. The response was good, and nine headmen, each from a different village, were recruited as delegates.[50] Insofar as possible, they were selected from the most numerous tribes so that when they returned they would have a wide influence.[51] Presumably, once migration was started, it would gain momentum merely from frequent and favorable reports by satisfied immigrants.

Meanwhile, Barclay was quite uncertain as to the effectiveness of his propaganda campaign to attract emigrants. Two weeks before the day scheduled for departure, the outcome of the venture was still uncertain. The project had been expensive as well as time-consuming; moreover, he feared that many of the would-be emigrants might change their minds before boarding time.

But this initial undertaking was far more successful than anticipated. For the most part, the first applicants were from Freetown and the sur-

49. Barclay to Higginson, April 5, 1841, *Votes,* 1841-1842, Ap.5, pp.79-80.
50. Copy of Barclay's Address to the Headmen of the Villages of Sierra Leone, April 12, 1841; copy of Barclay's Engagement with the Headmen of the Villages, Going to Jamaica, April 17, 1841, ibid., pp.86-88; *PP,* 1842, XII:567.
51. Two were Ebo, two Ackoo, one Cusso, one Funcho, one Calibar, and one Kru. Copy of Barclay's Engagement with the Headmen of the Villages, Going to Jamaica, April 17, 1841, *Votes,* 1841-1842, Ap.5, p.88.

rounding villages, but Krumen, too, were among them. As word of the project spread, it caught the fancy of the people who, neglecting their ordinary pastimes, discussed excitedly the advantages of this new opportunity and seemed to vie with one another for the privilege of migrating to Jamaica.[52] Consequently, with much palaver, the response was so overwhelming that even with the addition of the brig, less than half the applicants could be accommodated for the first crossing. They had been promised that at the proper time and when the ship was ready, boats would be provided to put them on board; but in their determination to be sure they were not overlooked or replaced by a rival, the applicants hired canoes to put themselves aboard. All told, there were 267 emigrants—64 Maroons; 16 Krumen, including one headman, who were to be sent back at the end of twelve months, if they wished; 8 headmen as delegates; and 179 liberated Africans—as many as the two ships could possibly carry, since without a surgeon for the brig, it could take no more than 100. The emigrants also included the women and children of the black troops recently sent from Sierra Leone to Jamaica. As these were not "soldiers' wives" in the common parlance, but held a respectable place in the Sierra Leone community, their going to Jamaica would inevitably influence others to do the same.[53]

All of these people were voluntary emigrants, taking with them their possessions to establish themselves in a new environment. Since they managed to get aboard before shipboard preparations had been completed, there was confusion in finding their places, in stowing away the luggage, and in assignment of sleeping space. There were difficulties during the passage: cooking and cleaning were done by the passengers, whom it was necessary to divide into groups for those tasks; regulations had to be developed to minimize fire hazards; stealing by the passengers became a nuisance. Tribal difficulties became evident: the Maroons had an exhalted opinion of their own importance and seemingly expected deferential treatment from the other passengers—who of a certainty did not share the Maroons' views. The brig was slowed to the speed of the ship, and both arrived at Port Royal, Jamaica, on May 21, 1841, just thirty-two days after leaving Sierra Leone. So generous had been the provisions of food and water that there was still a

52. Report from the Select Committee on the West Indian Colonies, Ap.1, *PP*, 1842, XIII:600.
53. Barclay to [Higginson], May 21, 1841, *Votes*, 1841-1842, Ap.5, P.92; *PP*, 1842, XII:88, 469.

large supply of both.[54] Despite the confusion and the many problems, the voyage was made without a single death or accident—a notable achievement in a day when the mortality rate on immigrant ships was commonly high.[55]

With demand for labor far greater than supply, there was no difficulty in finding employers for the African immigrants. Initial reports from employers all over the island were favorable; in general, good conduct; no offenses requiring court action; good workers, with liberated Africans working reasonably well, and no longer "useless creatures" as in Sierra Leone; Krumen adapting to agricultural work—all of this without any control except the general laws of the island. The immigrants were engaged at the rate of one shilling per day, plus free lodging, rations, and medical attendance. They were described as cheerful, happy, and industrious, and so well satisfied that they were inviting their friends to come to join them.[56]

The entire undertaking had been something in the way of a pilot project; 267 voluntary African immigrants had been introduced to Jamaica. It was an excellent beginning, but if the flow of Africans from Sierra Leone to Jamaica was to continue, it would be necessary for the island to have an agent in Sierra Leone. This agent, if he continued the procedures initiated by Barclay, must carry on recruitment, oversee many details, and assume responsibility for certifying ship compliance with standards set by the Act to Encourage Immigration. Before his departure with the emigrants, Barclay had found a suitable agent in the person of John Charles Cathcart, a colored Jamaican resident in the African colony, to whom he gave a commission and some instructions.[57]

Because Commissioner Barclay was the only official who had had personal experience on an immigrant ship as well as in recruiting, it seemed wise for him, before relinquishing his official duties, to give to Jamaica the benefit of his knowledge for use in subsequent voyages. So it was that after his arrival in Jamaica, Barclay sent back additional information for the Jamaica agent in Sierra Leone. This included copious advice and many

54. Barclay to Cathcart, July 6, 1841, *Votes,* 1841-1842, Ap.5, pp.95-96.
55. Barclay to [Higginson] , May 21, 1841, ibid., p.89; *PP,* 1842, XII:467.
56. Extract from the Stipendiary Magistrate's Reports, *PP,* 1842, XIII:603; Extract from Metcalfe's speech to the Legislature of Jamaica, Oct. 26, 1841, ibid., p.602; Report of John Ewart, Agent-general of Immigration, Sept. 30, 1842, *Votes,* 1842-1843, Ap. 7, p.74; Barclay to Ewart, Sept. 21, 1842, ibid., pp.77-79; Barclay to Cathcart, July 6, 1841, *Votes,* 1841-1842, Ap.5, pp.96-97.
57. Barclay to Cathcart, Apr. 18, 1841, *Votes,* 1841-1842, Ap.5, p.83; Barclay to Higginson, May 21, 1841, ibid., p.93.

regulations. He warned: as experience had proved that Maroons and Africans did not mingle well, every effort should be made to get the former to make up a complement for a vessel; the only alternative would be to divide the ship's hold across from side to side with an open railing to permit free circulation of air, but each group (Maroon and African) should have its own hatch for entrance and exit. The brig was too small to divide, so in the future it should take only one class of people. In Sierra Leone, when the people entered their names in the registry for passage, they had insisted upon a ticket—something they could display—and again on paying for a passport. All of this required additional work on the part of the emigration official, and to ease the situation, as well as to stimulate interest in emigration, the commissioner devised a form for each procedure—a ticket printed on fancy colored paper, and ornamented with the royal arms. This would distinguish the "Jamaica Book" from all others, and would have a favorable influence on the people.[58]

Barclay gave advice, too, with regard to comfort of the passengers and avoidance of confusion: there should be one or two good headmen for every vessel, and they should assist in stowing away the luggage and in showing people to their proper places. At the time fixed for embarkation, sailing preparations should have been completed, and passengers should be conveyed to the ship so quickly that the merely curious and friendly would not have time to crowd on board and confuse proceedings. It was difficult to regulate the passengers' sleeping place on an emigrant ship. Barclay suggested that the women should be attended to first, and they were to be assigned the most airy and best lighted part of the main deck—and kept together as much as possible. The men who preferred to sleep on deck should be encouraged to do so, and they could be provided with a mat and bed blanket. If the ship had good height between decks, hammocks could be provided, but they would have to be tied up in the daytime to keep the place open and comfortable for all.[59]

The commissioner also directed that certain rules pertaining to the welfare of all must be kept constantly before the immigrants. There should be no mingling of seamen and passengers, thus minimizing occasion for quarrels; disagreements should be settled by headmen, the captain, or the agent; and persons guilty of violence should be subject to confinement and,

58. Barclay to Cathcart, July 6, 1841, ibid., pp.95, 97-98.
59. Instructions for Embarking Emigrants at Sierra Leone, ibid., pp.101-102.

if necessary for the peace and safety of the ship, kept there until the ship reached port, when the case would be turned over to the authorities; if the passengers were in the way of the working of the ship and the officer on deck ordered them below, they were to obey immediately; when the candles were lit at night, the women were to retire below; the men who remained on deck must keep out of the way of the crew. Because of fire hazard, no palm oil should be used in cooking, and no cooking of any kind should be done after dark; no fire should be taken below in the ship, and smoking should be permitted only on deck. It should be the task of the headman to see that the several messes, in turn, performed the necessary duties of cooking, scouring the coppers, washing the deck below, and the water closets.[60] Finally, in the hope of deterring stealing, immigrants should be warned that on landing in Jamaica everyone's box, bag, and basket might be opened by the Queen's customhouse officer.[61] For health and comfort on an immigrant ship, especially in the tropics, cleanliness was imperative, and there had to be proper facilities for washing. For the morale of the passengers and the good impression upon the people of Jamaica, the immigrants should be encouraged to wash their clothing and be in good order when they landed; anyone who needed clothes should be provided with a couple of light suits a day or so before the ship was expected to reach port.[62]

It was planned to return both the delegates and the set of regulations by the brig, which could give the project further publicity by displaying the Jamaica colors in port at Sierra Leone. To make certain that the delegates would be enthusiastic about Jamaica, each one was given a new suit and promised pay for spreading the good word about Jamaica in the villages. In addition, a few large yams and coconuts were sent along to prove the advantages of agriculture in Jamaica as contrasted with Sierra Leone, which was plagued by drought, locusts, and crop-stealing.[63] In short, well-selected agricultural products would give concrete evidence of the productivity of Jamaica's soil; well-dressed delegates would provide further visual proof of advantages in Jamaica. These delegates, highly respected men in their native villages, would relate to their people the good care provided for emigrants on the South Atlantic crossing, and the advantages awaiting all who emi-

60. Rules to be Observed on Board of Ships Carrying Emigrants from Africa to Jamaica, ibid., pp.102-103.
61. Barclay to Cathcart, July 6, 1841, ibid., p.98.
62. Instructions for Embarking Emigrants . . . , ibid., p.102.
63. Barclay to Cathcart, July 6, 1841, ibid., p.99.

grated to Jamaica. Frequent communication between the island and Sierra Leone would prevent any slackening in the wild enthusiasm for emigration displayed by the Africans in April.[64]

The brig sailed in July for the return voyage, as was planned. Barclay warned the new captain that as the vessel was heavily rigged, in the event of squalls he must take special precaution to make everything secure until the danger was over.[65] Yet disaster struck soon after departure. The brig was lost although, more importantly, the passengers were not. There was delay, however, in acquiring a new ship; and even though eventually the delegates were again on their way, the fact that they did not arrive on schedule and were not even heard from for days provided ample cause for rumor and suspicion to become rife in Sierra Leone. This growing uneasiness among the Africans was not immediately realized, however, by the emigration authorities.

The planters, who wanted voluntary laborers from Africa, had gone to great length not only to encourage but to protect them and thereby to avoid antagonizing the humanitarians. The voyage conducted by Commissioner Barclay and described by one official as an "outpouring" that threatened to depopulate the colony of Sierra Leone,[66] had set off such a wild clamor by those who wanted to emigrate to Jamaica that hopes for floods of free African immigrants went soaring. In reality, in the form of better wages, more employment, and better growing conditions, Jamaica actually had much to offer these people. But the delegates had not returned as scheduled. Only slowly did the Island become aware of the ramifications of the loss of the brig *Commissioner Barclay.*

64. Barclay to Cathcart, July 6, 1841, ibid., p.95; Barclay to Messrs. Beckford and Ranken, ibid., pp.99-100.

65. Barclay to Captain Outerbridge, July 7, 1841, ibid., p.105.

66. Report of the Select Committee on the West India Colonies, *PP,* 1842, XIII:600.

3

An Experiment with "Assisted Migration"

THE FIRST YEAR OF JAMAICA'S PROGRAM OF ASSISTED migration seemed to indicate a successful beginning: 1417 immigrants were brought in from Africa, the British Isles, Europe, and North America during the period November 1, 1840-September 30, 1841. It is impossible to determine the precise number of Europeans and Africans, for the program was still in the introductory stage, and island agents, in process of developing a system for keeping records, were going about it in a somewhat casual way. The records note a "few" coloured Americans from Baltimore and Philadelphia, as well as Africans and Maroons brought in by Barclay via the *Hector* and the brig *Commissioner Barclay*. Presumably the remainder were white and were from Europe and the United States. Most of those from the United States were listed as Germans, Scots, English, or Irish, and on the whole a "bad selection." One ship from Scotland, one from Ireland, three from London brought chiefly Irish, but some English; one ship from Scotland brought all Scots.[1]

The entire concept of saving the economy by the labor of free people who would come as immigrants had been something new to Jamaica. It was so new, in fact, that details for procedure in the island had not been com-

1. John Ewart, Report on Immigration, Sept. 30, 1841, *Votes,* 1841-1842, Ap. 4, pp.30-31.

pleted before immigrants actually began to arrive. As the colony was un-accustomed to European immigrants, and little preparation had been made in anticipation of their arrival, they were kept crowded together in depots until indentured. Shelters were merely old stores or out-buildings located in port towns, and Europeans who had come from a temperate climate found themselves inadequately protected against heat and humidity, which were almost overpowering.

Although these immigrants were not the preferred laborers, Jamaica recognized the advisability of making some provision for their welfare if she was going to let them come. For that reason, when the assembly adopted an amended immigration act (December, 1840), it also authorized construction of model communities, or villages. Built at government expense, these were to be exclusively for European immigrants. Details of the plan suggest that someone closely associated with island government had been an astute stu-dent of proposals for an ideal society made by philanthropists outside Jamaica. Certainly they were contrary to the policies advocated by the Colonial Land and Emigration Commission (CL&EC), which had advised against free grants of land to immigrants. A person capable of making im-provements on property, they said, should be willing and able to pay a fair price for it; making free grants to the poorer class only withdrew them prematurely from the laboring class.[2]

Under provisions of the act adopted in Jamaica, the agent general of immigration (AGI) was given overall responsibility for the experiment. With approval of the governor, he was directed to purchase land for villages where each European immigrant might have a newly built cottage with an attached garden a half acre in size. The immigrant should be supported for two weeks, but thereafter must be self-sustaining, including payment of rent as fixed by the AGI, with the option of purchase.[3] In setting up these model communities, it was essential that some definite rules be observed. As one purpose was to get European immigrants out of the lowlands, all of these villages would be placed in the uplands where the climate was healthier. Furthermore, no parish could have more than two such villages; no more than four villages could be built per year for the entire island, with the maximum cost for each house set at fifty pounds. The total expenditure for

2. Extract from a Report from the CL&EC to James Stephen, April 8, 1841, *Votes*, 1841-1842, p.47; Russell to Metcalfe, April 30, 1841, ibid., pp.46-47.
3. No.3385, CO 139/78; "Correspondence Relative to Emigration: Jamaica," *PP*, 1842, XXXI:347.

construction of villages was limited to £6,000 per year. Finally, if there were as many as twenty cottages in the village, the AGI should appoint a schoolmaster, who would be provided with a rent-free cottage in addition to an annual salary of fifty pounds sterling. He must teach reading, writing, and arithmetic, with each student charged no more than three pence per week.[4]

Admittedly there were obstacles in the way of having the planned village actually awaiting European tenants; but such problems as obtaining title to land and transporting materials seemed outweighed by the advantages of being able to send European immigrants directly to the healthier uplands. Moreover, these immigrants might provide skilled labor for such industries as a "silk plant," which it was hoped would be established in close proximity. But even as an industrial employee, the immigrant would need a garden, which the AGI recommended should be fenced and well filled with provisions ready for use when the immigrant arrived. No one suggested that an immigrant who knew how to garden in Europe might not know how to do so in Jamaica. Despite the proposals, implementation of the planned-village program was slow. When John Ewart, whom Governor Metcalf appointed agent general for immigration, made his first official report in September, 1841, four villages were in the planning or development stage, but not one had been completed. Of these, two were in the parish of St. Ann, one in Manchester, and one in St. Elizabeth.[5]

The AGI emphasized that if a European immigrant was to be located on private property, it, too, must be in a healthy place in the interior, with a cottage and provisions similar to those of the village system. Provision grounds must be attached to the house, for if located at some distance, the plot would be of little use to an immigrant working five days a week for wages. As in the proposed village system, other considerations, such as a pig, chickens, and milk would go far in making for good relations between employer and immigrant. It was imperative, warned Ewart, for the European immigrant to be given these advantages, for in no other way could he exist on a wage of 1*s.* 6*d.* per day.[6]

In reality, the European laborers had come to Jamaica with expectations far too high; they neither prospered nor met the labor requirements of

4. Ewart, Report on Immigration, Sept. 30, 1841, *Votes,* 1841-1842, Ap. 4, pp.32-33.
5. Ibid., pp.31-35.
6. Ibid., p.37.

the island. They preferred the larger towns, which were in the lowlands where the climate was unsuited to Europeans; they did not like domestic service, and did not adapt to the fatigue of working in the cane fields in the lowlands. When they indentured and left the depot, many of them soon left their employer—some by mutual agreement, others by breaking their contract. Usually in debt when they quit, they then wandered about the countryside, only to make their way eventually to Kingston. There, without friends or funds, they applied for assistance and were sent to the public hospital, even when they were not ill.[7]

Incidence of illness and death was high among European immigrants. One group from a London ship was especially unsatisfactory. Many of them were ill; some died. Because they were malcontents, no one wanted to employ them. Twenty-seven were finally sent back to Britain. When these people charged the recruiting agent with deception, the West India Immigration Society asserted that if there was deception, it was on the part of the immigrants, who had claimed to be agricultural laborers, although it soon became evident they knew nothing of such work.[8]

Jamaica was becoming increasingly disenchanted with European immigrants and concluding that its long-standing preference for Africans was well warranted. Cost of living was less for an African than for a European. In Jamaica, each continued to need the same type of food and clothing he had used at home: those required by the African were obtainable rather cheaply in Jamaica; but those needed by the European cost about twice what they did in Europe, with medicine and medical attention about four times as expensive. Although wages paid in Jamaica were higher than in Africa, the Europeans did not earn more than they had at home. There was a growing conviction that while Africans adjusted to the climate and economy, European laborers did not, hence their immigration should not be encouraged.[9]

Stipendiary magistrates, who undertook to enquire into some of the cases of misfits, were regarded as meddlers whose activities almost always touched the interests of members of the assembly. One assemblyman considered himself injured by the conduct of some stipendiary magistrates and

7. Ibid., p.31.
8. Extract from Reports of Stipendiary Magistrates: Peter Brown, Parish of Portland, Port Antonio, Oct. 14, 1841; Thomas McCornock, St. Thomas-in-the-East, Sept. 1, 1841; Thomas Abbott, Savanna-la-Mar, June 8, 1841; Hall Pringle, Clarendon, Nov. 23, 1841; all in enc. no.4 of J. Stephen to CL&EC, Feb. 28, 1842, *PP*, 1842, XXXI:349-350.
9. Metcalfe to Stanley, Feb. 10, 1842, Jamaica no.72, CO 137/261.

the opinions of the attorney general. A committee, appointed from the House of Assembly for the purpose of taking evidence, broadened its assignment to consider the whole question of European immigration. The attorney general, who was a member of the Legislative Council, took the subject before that branch of the government, and secured the appointment of a second investigating committee. As a result of the activities of the two committees, time and attention of the legislative body was preempted for much of the session, although no formal report was made.[10]

By the latter part of 1841 there was very general dissatisfaction with the European immigrant and widespread conviction there was no place for him in Jamaica. Both assembly and governor believed the island's needs would be met more satisfactorily if attention should be directed principally to emigration from Africa, and no further government funds spent on European laborers.[11] Mortality among those immigrants, although not regarded as excessive when compared with the rate for the entire island, was used as indisputable justification for stopping their importation. Consequently, the governor officially directed the AGI to discontinue recruiting efforts in Europe.[12] The Legislature, reflecting the general attitude which had developed toward European immigration, prohibited the use of public funds for encouragement of immigration, and reduced to £20,000 (instead of £30,000 as previously provided) the appropriation for general purposes of immigration for the year 1842.[13] Individual Jamaican employers might import European laborers if they wished, but it would be at their own expense and without bounty (£6) until the European had been located successfully for a period of twelve months.[14] In short, except for possible bounty to the individual importer, the island would give no further assistance to immigration if Europe was the source.

Meanwhile, enquiries with regard to African immigrants had brought replies of general satisfaction with them as laborers. About sixty of the Africans brought in by Barclay were located on two estates in St. Thomas-

10. Address of the House of Assembly to the Governor, Oct. 29, 1841, *Votes,* 1841-1842, p.30.
    11. Metcalfe to Stanley, Feb. 10, 1842, Jamaica no.72, CO 137/261.
    12. Extract of the Votes of Moneys for Purposes of Immigration, Aug. 1, 1834-Apr. 15, 1843, Ap. D of Report by C. H. Darling, AGI, Oct. 24, 1843, *Votes,* 1843-1844, Ap. 4, p.190.
    13. Metcalfe to Stanley, Feb. 10, 1842, Jamaica no.72, CO 137/261.
    14. Extracts from the Stipendiary Magistrates. Reports as to the State of the Africans from Sierra Leone, no.37 in Appendix to the Reports from the Select Committee on West Indian Colonies, *PP,* 1842, XIII:603.

in-the-East, and doing well.[15] Captured Africans brought to Port Antonio and liberated in the parish of St. George had become as "industrious and civilized" as Creole Negroes on the island. There were similar reports from Savanna-la-Mar.[16] Unquestionably, Jamaicans agreed, Africans were the best suited for field cultivation in the Jamaica climate and were of great help.[17] From all over the island the clamor was for more African immigrants; yet convinced as they were that salvation for Jamaica's economy depended upon Negro immigration, planters and Legislature still failed to attach any long-range significance to the fate of the brig *Commissioner Barclay.* They continued to regard its loss as unfortunate but not disastrous. For several weeks mere authorization for importing laborers was the basis for assumption of their prompt arrival.

In accordance with his plan for frequent voyages, Barclay had already arranged with a London firm (Messrs. Beckford and Ranken) for four ships to go to Sierra Leone, one each on August 15, September 30, November 15, and December 30, to bring immigrants to Jamaica. Responsibility for equitable distrubution of laborers fell to the busy AGI; he directed the first ship to discharge its passengers at Savanna-la-Mar, in the western part of the island; the second at Annotto Bay, in the northeast; the third at Lucea, in the northwest; and the fourth at Kingston, in the south. The brig *Herald,* on its return, would go to Port Morant, in the extreme southeast. The West India Society of London, authorized by Ewart to send five hundred Africans to Savanna-la-Mar, had chartered two vessels whose arrival was expected momentarily. In addition, Cathcart, at Sierra Leone, was directed to purchase a small, fast-sailing vessel for regular communication between Jamaica and the African colony.[18] All of these transactions, conducted in the full tide of optimism which followed Barclay's initial voyage, were expected to serve the dual purpose of maintaining frequent communication between Jamaica and Sierra Leone and conveying many laborers.

But despite Jamaica's heavy financial involvement in government-conducted immigration, results were falling short of expectations. There was no flood of immigrants; on the contrary, ships were arriving with far less

15. Ibid.
16. Extract from Sir C. Metcalfe's speech to the Legislature of Jamaica, Oct. 26, 1841, no.36, ibid., p.602.
17. Ewart, Report on Immigration, Nov. 1840-Sept. 1841, *Votes,* 1841-1842, Ap. 4, pp.36-37.
18. Extract from a despatch by Governor McDonald, May 7, 1842, enc. in Stanley to Elgin, Aug. 17, 1842, *Votes,* 1842-1843, p.117.

than their capacity of passengers; one ship arrived with only seven immigrants. Reports from Sierra Leone were disappointing. The harbor, where once the Negroes had vied with each other to get aboard, was crowded with emigrant ships now waiting in vain for a full load of passengers.[19]

Jamaica had too much invested in this project and was too dependent on it as a solution for the labor problem to let it die; therefore, a study of cause and method for correction was made. Information provided by Barclay seemed to indicate fear of enslavement as the chief reason for the Africans' refusal to emigrate. The problem, then, was to remove such fear. But how? As return of delegates and frequent communication would keep before the Africans a picture of prosperity and free life in Jamaica, the answer was more frequent voyages, which meant more ships. Conveyance via ships owned and operated by the government of Jamaica seemed to offer the surest means of achieving the island's objective, so the AGI, with the consent of Governor Metcalfe, spent £3,000 for purchase of a second brig.[20] Renamed, it became the *Treasurer,* and together with the *Herald* (bought earlier for £1,000 to replace the brig lost by storm), was expected to establish regular communication with West Coast Africa. According to estimate, the two vessels could make three round trips per year to Sierra Leone and bring in a total of approximately seven hundred laborers.[21]

Securing a tide of African migration depended, also, upon the treatment received by the early arrivals; yet as long as planters were uncertain of immigrants, they were reluctant to incur any large expense to prepare for them. On the other hand, when they were able to obtain indentured laborers, it was often almost impossible to secure immediately enough carpenters to build the cottages. One proposed remedy called for applying the planned-village system to African immigrants. These villages, to be located in different parishes and close to work, would provide a place to which the newly arrived African could be taken at once instead of being crowded into a depot. Although costly, such a system would save the island maintenance costs of the depots and would immediately establish good relations between the employer and the immigrant.[22]

19. Sketch Account, in Report of the AGI, Sept. 30, 1842, *Votes,* 1842-1843, Ap. 7, p.76.
20. Ewart, Report, Sept. 30, 1842, ibid., p.73.
21. Ewart, Report on Immigration, Sept. 30, 1841, *Votes,* 1841-1842, Ap. 4, p.37.
22. Ewart, Report, Sept. 30, 1842, *Votes,* 1842-1843, Ap. 7, pp.70,73,76; Report of C. H. Darling, Oct. 24, 1843, *Votes,* 1843-1844, Ap. 4, p.183.

Immigration increased somewhat during 1842, and the report of September 30, 1842 noted the arrival of 1798 immigrants: of these, 393 were whites sent from Boston and London before expiration of the 1840 immigration act; 18 were Africans from the United States; 10 were Africans from Upper Canada; 582, Africans from Sierra Leone; 404, from St. Helena; the others, from the Bahamas, were for the most part liberated Africans. With a total expenditure of almost £33,000, the cost was just over £12 per person—considerably above Barclay's estimate of less than £7 for a thirty-one day voyage.[23]

In the course of the year 1842 Jamaica had received an unexpected but important windfall from St. Helena, where the liberated African population had been building up for several months and had become a problem. Slave cargoes were sometimes liberated in that small island, which had no need for them. In February, 1841, Her Majesty's brig *Brisk* captured a Portuguese schooner well filled with slaves. Although the schooner had left the coast of Africa just a fortnight earlier, 82 of its 420 captives had died of smallpox and dysentery.

Unlike Jamaica, St. Helena needed fewer laborers, not more. Of 737 captured Africans brought into St. Helena during the period June 11, 1840—March 1, 1841, only 24 had been apprenticed.[24] Liberated Africans, for whom there was no work, were a burden upon the imperial treasury and the society. These same people, who were a plague to St. Helena,[25] could become a blessing if sent to the West Indies as immigrant laborers. As their departure would have the additional advantage of absolving St. Helena and the imperial government of any further financial responsibility for them, the Colonial Office authorized Governor Middlemore of St. Helena to send them to any British colony that would pay transportation costs.[25] Moreover, it pledged "every possible encouragement"—but not compulsion—to induce these people to migrate from St. Helena to the West Indies where they would find employment.[26]

23. G. W. Hope to Burge, Jan. 27, 1842, in "Correspondence Relative to Emigration, St. Helena," *PP*, 1842, XXXI:540-547.

24. "A Return of the Number of Africans who have arrived, June 11, 1840-March 1, 1841," signed by John Young, Collector of Customs, enc. no.3 in "Correspondence Relative to Emigration, St. Helena," ibid., p.476.

25. Russell to Governor Middlemore, May 8, 1841, in "Correspondence Relative to Emigration, St. Helena," ibid., p.541.

26. G. W. Hope to Burge, Jan. 27, 1842, in "Correspondence Relative to Emigration, St. Helena," ibid., pp.540-547.

Not until January, 1842, however, was Burge (in London) officially given permission to take emigrants from St. Helena. He then communicated with the agents of Trinidad and Demerara so that the three colonies, the only ones interested or able to utilize the offer, could coordinate their efforts and avoid the fruitless expense of competition and ignorance of each other's proposed arrangements. One of the major questions was whether the three colonies should share a single transport or maintain a separate one for each colony. Expediency, as well as colonial pride, produced the decision to use a separate ship for each colony.

London shipping firms, however, were reluctant to cooperate in the venture. Because they had met with ill fortune in securing passengers in Sierra Leone, they had become wary of African emigration in general. Agents soon found it impossible to charter a ship unless they agreed to certain terms, namely, a monopoly for transporting liberated Africans from St. Helena; a directive for the governor to encourage embarkation on these vessels; and relaxation of certain provisions of the Passengers' Act. Agents of the colonies could not accede to modification of rules unless the Colonial Office approved. In this instance the imperial government was agreeable, for it was eager to get these people onto their own resources. As there were few females among the Africans brought to St. Helena, it was decided to relax the requirements of one-third females to two-thirds males. There was one stipulation, however: such relaxation was permissable only so long as it did not result in leaving a disproportionate number either of males or females in St. Helena. It was also emphasized that a ship must not tarry in harbor.

If the shipowners had reservations about the project, so did the colonial agents. The mortality rate had been high among the Africans at St. Helena and no colony wanted immigrants who were unable to work. In order to judge whether these people would be a benefit to the West Indies, the agents needed to know the cause of the high death rate as well as the state of health of the survivors. The sugar islands had no desire to introduce either an epidemic or sickly persons who would be an expense to the government. Agents were assured through the Colonial Office of no cause for concern—by quarantine and other regulations liberated Africans with contagious diseases were customarily kept separate from the rest of the island.[27] The assurance, it may be stated parenthetically, was curiously in contradiction to that of the governor of St. Helena.

27. Ibid.

But securing Colonial Office permission to recruit immigrants and hiring a vessel were only a part of what was entailed in sending out a ship to convey passengers from St. Helena. Supplies of foodstuffs and water for transatlantic voyages were always major problems. In this instance as both provisions and water casks had to be loaded before the ship left England, it was impossible to leave an estimate of days-on-voyage to the governor at the port of embarkation.[28] No one in Britain seemed to know the time required for sailing from St. Helena to the West Indies; it was a route seldom used, and as few emigrants had made the voyage, expert guidance was unavailable. By now the Colonial Land and Emigration Commission (CL&EC) had begun to accumulate extensive information on many parts of the empire although in this case its records were of no help.[29] The problem was passed on to the Lords Commissioners of the Admiralty, who fixed duration of the voyage from St. Helena to Jamaica as eight weeks, to British Guiana and Trinidad as seven weeks.[30]

Even with an official estimate of days-on-voyage, lack of experience posed a problem when it came to determining provisions, and again there was referral to the CL&EC. That body, in studying the scale proposed for St. Helena, found it varied only slightly from the one proclaimed at Sierra Leone on April 1, 1841. Nonetheless, the CL&EC recommended certain modifications, and recommendation by the CL&EC was tantamount to mandate; as an allowance of coffee and sugar was currently received by the Africans at St. Helena, it should be continued; an allowance of lime juice and of vinegar should be made as a precaution against scurvy.[31] Certain other comforts, such as mats for sleeping, spoons for eating, and other mess utensils were to be provided on the ship.[32] For protection of the immi-

28. Burge to Lord Stanley, Jan. 20, 1842, ibid., p.546, enc. no.9.
29. T. F. Elliot and Edward E. Villiers to James Stephen, Jan. 31, 1842, ibid., p.483.
30. S. Walcott, Secretary to CL&EC, Feb. 19, 1842, in no.10, "Correspondence Relative to Emigration, St. Helena," ibid., pp.548-549.
31. The daily allowance per adult: 1 qt. or 2 lbs. rice, or 1 lb. biscuit; ½ lb. salt beef, or salt pork, or salt fish (the salt fish not to be issued more often than on alternate days); ½ oz. coffee or cocoa; 1¼ oz. sugar; 1 oz. lime juice; ¾ oz. sugar (for mixing with the above); 1/3 gil palm oil; ¼ gil or oz. salt; 3 qts. water. To be allowed weekly: a half pint of vinegar. "Children in proportion." "Scale of Diet for Male and Female Liberated Africans from St. Helena to the West Indies," in T. F. Elliot and Edward E. Villiers to J. Stephen, Jan. 31, 1842, no. 10, "Correspondence Relative to Emigration, St. Helena," ibid., p.485.
32. S. Walcott, Secretary to CL&EC, to the Agents Employed in Sending Liber-

grants' health, the vessel was required to carry a surgeon and a "proper" medicine chest, where supplies must include a half hundredweight each of sago and of chloride of lime.[33] As the ship was fitted out in England, it fell to the government emigration agent at the Port of London to make the final inspection and certify the number of passengers that the ship was equipped to carry.[34]

The South Atlantic crossing was cold, and immigrants had to be protected; responsibility for issuance of proper clothing for the voyage rested with the governor of St. Helena. Each passenger, directed the Commissioners, must be supplied, before embarkation, with at least two blankets (or one blanket and one rug) in addition to two guernseys for each male and two woolen frocks for each female. Since these items were unavailable in St. Helena, they, too, were sent out from England—a total of a thousand blankets or rugs, and a thousand guernsey frocks, some large, some small.[35]

St. Helena, the Colonial Office, and the West Indies all wanted the liberated Africans moved across the Atlantic, but only after careful planning were they sent. Although reports of their embarkation at St. Helena are not available, their arrival in Jamaica was carefully noted. A total of 404, most of them children, debarked in July.[36]

Arrival of the St. Helena immigrants served to bolster Jamaican hopes of a real migration from Africa. Planters became quite jealous of the privilege of employing them. Again, Ewart, as AGI, tried to recognize the general demand and bring about some sort of equitable distribution. It would have been easy, of course, to permit ships from Africa to discharge passengers at the first port of call in the eastern part of the island. But to avoid a charge of favoritism to the eastern planters, the AGI undertook to set up a system of rotation by directing the transports to different parts of the island. With most of the planters wanting more immigrants than they were receiving, there was great interest in the selection of ports for debarkation.

As the man who had planned and personally directed the pilot voyage, apparently an outstanding success, Barclay doubtless felt well qualified to

ated Africans from St. Helena to the West Indies, Feb. 11, 1842, "Papers Relative to Emigration, St. Helena," ibid.

33. Same to same, ibid.

34. T. F. Elliot and Edward E. Villiers to James Stephen, Feb. 10, 1842, no.11 in "Correspondence Relative to Emigration, St. Helena," ibid., p.486.

35. Ibid.; Lord Stanley to the Governor of St. Helena, Feb. 12, 1842, no.12 in "Correspondence Relative to Emigration, St. Helena," *PP,* 1842, XXXI:550.

36. Ewart, Report, Sept. 30, 1842, in *Votes,* 1842-1843, Ap. 7, p.73.

point out flaws in subsequent plans, particularly if he thought his own eastern region was being slighted. Ignoring the loss of the brig *Commissioner Barclay* and the impact of that loss on Sierra Leone, he suggested that the flow of immigrants from there would have been greater if the direct tie with Port Morant had been maintained. He feared the system currently followed, of landing them in various parts of the island and scattering them about, would break the link with Africa. The former commissioner firmly insisted that debarkation of Sierra Leone immigrants should be limited at most to only a few ports, perhaps Port Morant in the East, Savanna-la-Mar in the west, and Port Maria in the central north. From these points the Africans could move to various parts of the island or join their friends or relatives as they wished. To equalize the supply of labor as much as possible without disturbing the successful working of the immigration measure, Barclay proposed to send immigrants from St. Helena and other places to ports which had no ties with Sierra Leone.[37] In reality, Barclay, along with many other Jamaicans, was refusing to recognize a significant change in the character of immigration: in 1841 only part of the volunteers were from the Africa yards; in 1842 they were almost entirely so, which made for only tenuous ties with Sierra Leone. When immigration was undertaken, pessimists had predicted that liberated Africans, if taken to Jamaica, would be the same "idle and useless creatures" they were in Sierra Leone. On the other hand, Jamaican planters who employed these voluntary African immigrants wanted more. Those who had not been able to secure the services of these immigrants clamored for the privilege of employing them. Further information was needed if any real evaluation was to be made of free African immigration.

John Ewart, as AGI, was expected to make a formal report for the year ending September 30, 1842. To that intent, and with the assembly scheduled to convene only a few weeks later, he queried employers for the information he needed about these African immigrants—whether they were satisfactory, and if the planters liked them. The replies were from the eastern part of the island, where most of the Sierra Leone immigrants were located. The first ones had arrived with Barclay, but others had come later; now, after sixteen months, no fewer than five hundred African immigrants were in St. Thomas-in-the-East, a much larger number than in any other

37. Barclay to Ewart, Sept. 21, 1842, in Ewart, Report, Sept. 30, 1842, ibid., pp.77-78.

parish. Managers reported that upon arrival these immigrants went to work, learned easily, and did as well as the natives; they performed various types of field work, cleaned and cut canes, and on several estates did much of the work about the sugar factories. They had also done well for themselves. Originally they had worked for one shilling per day, with free lodging and medical attendance, and rations of one quart of rice and a half pound of codfish per week. Later they undertook taskwork, and got the rate of wages raised to 1*s*. 6*d*. per day, retaining lodging and other perquisites. Their labor was not considered to be cheap, but other workers could not be secured. The few Krumen who had come were equally satisfactory. Although they were not agriculturalists in Africa, they had been adaptable. Quite notable was the construction of a lighthouse, the first in the island, almost exclusively with their labor.[38] From the Annotto Bay area came similar reports. There land was so abundant and cheap that old laborers had left the estates to settle on their own freeholds. It was the Africans, sober, orderly, industrious, who had by their labor saved the estates.[39]

It seemed important to know also whether the Africans were happy, for their attitude might provide a basis for predicting the ultimate fate of African immigration. Their actions, which provided the best basis for assessing their mood, would seem to indicate that they were satisfied. Of the first sixteen Krumen brought to Sierra Leone and guaranteed a return passage at the close of twelve months, not one had applied to be sent home. The other Africans, who were free to leave their original employer at the end of their twelve-month contract, rarely did so. Some who had prospered wanted to prove it to those still in Africa, and as concrete evidence sent back small sums of money. Many of these immigrants had had some formal education and could read; some could write. In general, they were eager to have friends and relatives join them, and, most encouraging from the planter's point of view, wrote to their friends in Sierra Leone to tell them so.[40] On this somewhat limited basis the planting interests in Jamaica could conclude that African immigration might become successful.

What Jamaica wanted, however, was a "stream" of immigrants which would enable her to compete successfully with the slave colonies. She esti-

38. Ibid.
39. James Maxwell, subagent, to Ewart, AGI, Sept. 21, 1842, ibid., pp.79-82.
40. Barclay to Ewart, Sept. 21, 1842; Maxwell to Ewart, Sept. 21, 1842; ibid., pp.77-82.

mated the number needed as between 15,000 and 50,000, not merely the 1800 who came from various quarters in 1842. In reality, if Jamaica had taken a closer look at the circumstances under which the 404 liberated Africans left St. Helena, she might well have had less optimism for securing in Africa the labor force which was needed.

4

Official Approval of Emigration

HELP FROM OUTSIDE THE COLONY WAS ESSENTIAL IF Jamaica was to secure the flood of contract laborers which she believed she needed. This would have to be in a form more concrete than quasi-official approval for Jamaica to manage by herself. It seemed possible in 1842 that something better might be in the offing. Arguments that only recently had fallen upon deaf ears now were heard more attentively.

West India interests were able to gain parliamentary attention and secured the appointment in March of a select committee[1] to enquire into the state of the West Indian colonies. This was broadened to include an enquiry into such matters as relations between employers and laborers, rate of wages, supply of labor, system and expense of cultivation, and the general state of rural economy in the West Indies.[2] In other words, the scope was broad enough to permit the introduction of testimony favorable to the sugar interests. Most of those called before the committee were proprietors, managers of estates, or local officials long resident in Jamaica or other West

1. Douglas Hall, *Free Jamaica, 1833-1865* (New Haven, 1959), p.52.
2. *PP*, 1842, XIII:iii. There were fifteen members of the committee: Lord Stanley, Pakington, Howick, Dodson, Darley Wilmot, Charles Howard, Charles Douglas, Vernon Smith, Emerson Tennant, Grantley Berkeley, Hawes, Banks, Villiers Stuart, Barclay, and Viscount Chelsea. Ibid., p.ii.

Indian colonies; a few were dissenting ministers or stipendiary magistrates hostile to planter interests.

Former slaves, the committee was told, were doing well for themselves, while planters were unable to hire the labor they needed. The only solution to shortage of laborers was immigration. Most of the witnesses only pointed up conclusions already drawn in Jamaica but restated now before the committee for the express purpose of enlisting sympathy from members of Parliament and assistance from the Imperial government. In summary, the testimony of the majority indicated that African immigrants generally were prospering,[3] were of good conduct,[4] and were content in their new home; their introduction did not reduce the wages of resident Negroes,[5] yet on estates fortunate enough to have immigrants from Sierra Leone, it was their labor which enabled the mills to be kept in operation on Saturday.[6] On the other hand, in some parishes suffering from an acute shortage of labor, cultivation had been curtailed by about fifty percent. In fact, there was the possibility of cessation of exports, withdrawal of planter interests, and "regression" of civilization.[7] Such testimony would appeal to humanitarians interested in the welfare of both Africans and West Indian Negroes.

Although witnesses were in agreement as to the necessity of immigration with financial assistance provided by the imperial government, they were of varied opinions as to the form which the assistance should take. Some suggested a loan, to be repaid over a ten-year period; others, outright contribution by Great Britain; one proposal called for the colony to pay one-fourth, Great Britain one-fourth, and the immigrant one-half the cost of transportation, this to be deducted gradually from his wages.[8] A few, utilizing the opportunity to display exasperation with British colonial policy, blamed exhaustion of the island treasury upon imperial directives for construction of prisons and penitentiaries; others, alarmed by the sugar duties bills, which would deprive the West Indies of some of their advantages in the British market, warned that reduction of sugar prices in England would cause abandonment of estates in Jamaica and hard times for laborers.[9]

3. Ibid., p.386.
4. Ibid., p.349.
5. Ibid., pp.401-402.
6. Ibid., p.343.
7. Ibid., pp.408-409.
8. Ibid., p.482.
9. For the copious minutes of evidence taken before the Select Committee on the West Indian Colonies, see *PP,* 1842, XIII.

Politically, the most prominent of those who testified was former Governor Sir Charles Metcalfe, recently arrived from Jamaica, who tended to support the planters' interpretation of cause and remedy. He, too, believed immigration was needed, but tactfully stressed the good wages and comfortable lives available to those who were brought from Sierra Leone. Metcalfe's testimony carried weight with all, including those whose motive was humanitarian rather than economic; yet unlike the proprietors, the former governor believed Jamaica was itself financially able to support immigration despite currently heavy taxation.[10]

It was Burge, however, who was undoubtedly the star witness for Jamaica. His purpose was to show that immigration was needed, that immigration was right, and that direction of immigration should not be the responsibility of the colony. His testimony was a restatement of assertions often made: the evil hanging over Jamaica was shortage of labor, for which the only remedy was large-scale immigration from a tropical zone, notably Africa; as neither individual planters nor colonial government had been able to bring about a mass movement from Africa, it should be taken up by the imperial government, which could raise the necessary funds and provide the organization and direction needed for every phase of the undertaking. Although he accepted the theory of partial financial responsibility on the part of the colony, when he suggested a tax on estates as a means of raising Jamaica's share of the cost, he did not elaborate as to type or rate of the levy. Protection of immigrants was no problem, he asserted, for the island had already adopted legislation which was exemplary for such purpose. Aware of the testimony of some stipendiary magistrates who had asserted there was no need for immigrant labor, Burge suggested they might possibly know a small area or town, but certainly not the island as a whole.[11]

As the committee worked to put the report into final form, it considered carefully each paragraph of the draft submitted by Pakington,[12] a draft which seemed to offer sympathy and perhaps hope for efforts to revive West Indian economy. The committee overwhelmingly refused one proposal[13] which would have deleted everything except praise for emancipation. In a few instances, after lengthy debate, resolutions were adopted by

10. Ibid., pp.512-516.
11. Ibid., pp.332-337.
12. John-Somerset Russell Pakington, later Sir John-Somerset Pakington, Secretary of State for the Colonies, March-December, 1852.
13. By Hawes.

only a narrow margin. On one occasion, when trying to assign cause for shortage of labor, the committee rejected a clause whereby the custom of alloting almost unlimited provision grounds was cited as proof of excessive remuneration. Howick[14] pointed out that because abundance of land would soon cause the new immigrants to withdraw from the labor market, the price of land should be raised artificially to ensure the immigrant's working for wages for a while. Nevertheless, the proposal was not accepted. The committee considered, but refused, recommendation for the government and legislature of the mother country to assist and encourage "in every possible way" the introduction of Africans into the West Indian colonies.

Planter interests had scored some success in their testimony. In laying the report before the House of Commons, the committee described the distress of the West Indies as not hopeless, yet great enough to require immediate attention. On evidence presented by the parade of witnesses and with full knowledge that a second committee (on West Coast Africa) might have specific recommendations, the Committee on the West Indian Colonies offered generalizations which might provide gradual but not immediate remedy.[15] In brief, it resolved that: (1) The Great Act of Emancipation had brought most satisfactory results to the Negro population, but staple production had fallen low enough to cause serious and in some cases ruinous injury to the proprietors, especially in Jamaica, British Guiana, and Trinidad. Because of the great loss, many estates were abandoned. (2) The principal cause of distress was difficulty in obtaining steady and continuous labor despite the high rate of wages. This resulted from an abundance of land and the ease with which former slaves entered other occupations, or lived comfortably without working more than three or four days per week. (3) The great distress of the West Indian colonies demanded immediate attention although there was no cause for despair. (4) The obvious remedy was promotion of African immigration on a huge scale in order to create competition for employment and thereby reduce wages to a modest standard. (5) Immigration should be conducted under the authority, inspection, and control of responsible public officers.[16]

The report was of great significance to Jamaica and the other West India colonies. For four long years, when they complained of scarcity of

14. Henry (Grey), Viscount Howick, later Earl Grey.
15. Report of the Select Committee on the State of the West Indian Colonies, *PP*, 1842, XIII:i-v.
16. Ibid.

labor they had been denounced as having brought it on themselves by reason of their poor treatment of the laborers. The report indicated acceptance in Britain now of their plea for more laborers. Still unsettled, however, was the question of the specific area from which the laborers might come.

Meanwhile, in April, 1842, a select committee was appointed to enquire into the state of British possessions on the West Coast of Africa.[17] This body, unlike the one relative to the West Indies, could not summon many witnesses with personal knowledge of the Negroes under investigation. Because the area was notoriously unhealthy for Europeans, anyone who had lived there for a few months, even if long ago, was considered as a possible source of information. They, along with men of current mercantile interests in West Africa, were invited to testify; official correspondence pertaining to Africa was examined; but above all, the report of Dr. Richard Robert Madden was studied by the committee. Madden, a former stipendiary magistrate in the West Indies, had been sent by Russell to investigate many aspects of affairs in Africa, including: (1) conditions in West Coast Africa, (2) rumors of African slavers trading on the Gold Coast, and (3) the prospect of emigration from Sierra Leone to the West Indies.[18] He covered a vast area in a relatively short time, with his work interrupted by illness, and his information sometimes gained from third parties; yet as he had acted in an official capacity, and his report was recent, it commanded respectful consideration.

Various witnesses who appeared before the committee were all too aware that Her Majesty's ships on station along the west coast of Africa were objects of suspicion to the European powers. They warned of probable opposition by those powers unless emigration was restricted to only those territories under British jurisdiction. In reality, with the exception of Sierra Leone, there were few such places from which emigration was feasible. The Gold Coast did not have sufficient population for emigration, while elsewhere, many of the chiefs, especially along the Kru coast, would not permit their people to leave unless they themselves received presents.[19]

By implication if not by actual statements, "emigration" was now thought of as being by liberated Africans rather than by ones who were

17. Originally it was a fifteen-member committee, including Stanley, Lord John Russell, Forster, and Buller; more members were added later.
18. Report of the Select Committee on West Coast Africa, *PP,* 1842, XI:ii.
19. Ibid., paragraphs 5607-5615.

tribal or settler. For many reasons Sierra Leone was considered the particular spot where emigration should be encouraged. Many slave ships, when seized by British ships on patrol, were brought to Sierra Leone for condemnation procedure, and liberation of the cargo threw a large number of "fresh savages" upon the colony.[20] It lacked sufficient resources to employ these people who not only hampered the progress there, but burdened the imperial government. Britain maintained a Liberated African Department at Sierra Leone, where Negroes released from slave ships were supported as long as six months at British expense, with the cost ranging from one to two pence per day per person. For all concerned, emigration was the logical solution, especially if the liberated African could be removed to the West Indies immediately upon emancipation. The colony to which he was sent would gladly pay his passage, thus sparing Britain the cost of his maintenance and transportation.[21] Moreover, Sierra Leone would be relieved of an unwanted increase in population; the West India sugar colonies would acquire needed laborers; and as an immigrant, the liberated African would gain the benefits of civilization which he might take back to Africa. At the same time, by encouraging this emigration, Great Britain could aid cultivation of sugar in her own colonies, where there was no slavery—thereby proving that free-grown sugar could compete advantageously with slave-grown sugar, and thus helping to discourage the slave trade.[22]

Jamaica Agent William Burge, who was also invited to appear before this select committee, made the most of his opportunity. While not permitting anyone to forget Jamaica's need of immigrant laborers, he wisely emphasized not the economic motive but rather the humanitarian aspect of what Jamaica had done and what Jamaica could do for the Africans. He pointed to the available religious and moral instruction (sure to have wide appeal), and to the prosperity of the laboring population, of which the African immigrants formed a part. Jamaica, he said, believed the conduct of immigration should be kept out of the hands of individuals and companies; in fact, the Legislature had already enacted measures designed to place it under the supervision of the executive and its responsible officers. Sure to appeal to humanitarians, abolitionists, and shipping interests was the assertion that Jamaica would like to see the imperial government prohibit any

20. Ibid., p.325.
21. Ibid., p.ii.
22. Ibid., p.359.

emigrant from leaving the coast of Africa without permission from some responsible officer of the government; only by such means could anyone be certain of totally voluntary emigration.[23]

All of the evidence was weighed by the committee. Although Sierra Leone had been mentioned as probably the only place from which African emigration could be anticipated, the committee noted one major but unanswered question—namely, that of the continuance of the Court of Mixed Commission at Sierra Leone. By international agreement, captured slave ships could be taken into Sierra Leone for adjudication before this court.[24] When slaving activity was centered 800 to 1,000 miles from Sierra Leone, the process of taking a prize to court became extraordinarily lengthy because of trade winds as well as distance. The mortality rate, always high, someimtes rose to fifty percent; survivors often were in a pitiable state when landed. Conscious of the need to protect the health of those to be rescued, there had been suggestion of moving the Court of Mixed Commission to a place nearer the center of slaving activity, perhaps to Ascencion. In such an eventuality, with few slave cargoes brought into Sierra Leone, the colony would cease to have a class likely to emigrate.

By 1842, however, the entire situation seemed to be changing. In the first place, the theatre of slaving activity again shifted, this time close to Sierra Leone. As the captured slaver now was taken only a short distance before adjudication, mortality of the cargo had decreased. In the second place, as modification in international agreement permitted seizure of ships merely on evidence of equipment, many slavers were taken without any cargo on board, which meant that even though slavers continued to be captured, there were fewer cargoes for release.[25]

On the basis of information provided by witnesses, the committee doubted that chiefs would permit many to leave from Cape Palmas, or that Krumen would migrate except for temporary employment. The Gambia was ruled out as a source for emigrants because, again, the people went only for temporary work. Sierra Leone unquestionably offered the greatest potential for emigration. The population included an estimated 40,000 to 50,000 descendents of the Negroes sent there since the early days of that colony; some Krumen, perhaps 1,000 to 5,000 in number; probably, also, some who

23. Ibid., p.465.
24. By British Law, slavers guilty of violating an act of Parliament could also be taken for trial before a Vice-Admiralty court.
25. Ibid., p.ix.

had been released from slave ships, or who might come into the colony if permitted, solely for the purpose of emigration.[26]

Granting there might be material for emigration, the committee had to decide whether the social climate—the "temporal, moral, and religious advantages"—in the West Indies outweighed those in Africa. Official reports, especially those by Metcalfe, provided information. In November, 1841, he had written to Stanley in glowing terms of Jamaica: the peasants flocked to Divine services; each had a Bible; many wore good clothes; some were sufficiently prosperous to ride horseback; the laborers sent their children to school, for which they paid a small sum; they built churches and chapels, and the Baptists supported a minister, as well. All over the island there were schools and religious instruction, with the colonial government giving financial support to the Church of England and to the schools. In short, no where in the world, wrote Metcalfe, could the laboring population be better provided with the necessities of life or be more free from oppression.[27] Such evidence might well serve to convince any doubting missionaries or antislavery forces of the wisdom of permitting emigration from Africa to a better life in the West Indies.

By contrast, the committee noted a rather desolate condition in Sierra Leone; there was little industry, not much trade, almost nothing for export except arrowroot and ginger; wages were only four to seven pence per day. There was neither a model farm nor provision for instruction in agriculture; the government in Sierra Leone did not contribute to educational or religious instruction. The committee had much praise, however, for the educational work of the Church Missionary Society and of the Wesleyans, whose efforts had brought nearly twenty percent of the population into schools; nonetheless, there was no doubt that better advantages could be found for the Africans in the West Indies. Furthermore, the newly liberated African who was unable to find employment in Sierra Leone, would be self-supporting in the West Indies, and would add to the prosperity of the empire. If he returned to Africa, he would take with him wealth, civilization, and a knowledge of religion with which to enrich his home continent.[28]

Emigration need not lead to accusations of slave trading, concluded

26. Ibid., p.16-17.
27. Ibid., p.18-19.
28. Ibid., p.20-21.

the committee, if proper regulations were adopted. For instance, authorities in Sierra Leone should guard against use of fraud or force; and free return passage to Sierra Leone might be provided after a certain period such as three or four years. Yet the committee also proposed a no-nonsense policy applicable to newly liberated Africans who had no means of support: after adjudication, they should be given the choice of settling at once in the West Indies or of leaving Sierra Leone without any specific destination. If the African opted for the West Indies, his transportation costs would be defrayed by the colony to which he was going. As slave trading still flourished, despite intervention by the Royal Navy, African emigration could be secure against abuse, warned the committee, only if it was under the supervision of Great Britain. In no other way could confidence in emigration be given to the African himself, to the British public, or to the civilized world.

The advantages of emigration were numerous: if emigration should become extensive from among the settled population of Sierra Leone, it might become possible for Britain to cut down on the establishment which she maintained there to watch over the interests of the liberated Africans; if the liberated Africans, on adjudication, were immediately located as immigrants in the West Indies, Britain would be freed from the expense of maintaining them for six months and from the task of supervising and protecting them. In summary, said the committee, advantages of emigration were many for all people, while disadvantages were few. Not only would the imperial government be relieved of a financial burden, but the African would be placed in a position where he would be most likely to raise himself in the moral and social scale; the free colonies would benefit economically, and their prosperity would discourage the slave trade.[29] "Your committee can not but strongly urge upon Parliament not only not to prohibit the emigration of free blacks from our African settlements to our West Indian colonies, but to encourage and promote it by the authority of Government, under the sanctions and regulations above suggested . . ."[30]

After years of nothing but opprobrium from Great Britain, Jamaica might now find some hope for understanding. Reports from the select committees, both on West Coast Africa and on the West Indies, had already been presented to parliament when in early November (1842) a deputation of West Indian merchants succeeded in gaining an interview with Stanley.

29. Ibid., p.22-23.
30. Ibid., p.22.

Having found him sufficiently sympathetic to request detailed proposals for Negro emigration under government supervision, they lost no time. Their suggestions, whether practical or impractical, reflected the feeling of desperate need and in some instances approached advocacy of pressure. They wanted government directives which would require managers of liberated Africans to encourage their charges to emigrate, and the governor to urge the general population to do so. Furthermore, when slaves were captured by Her Majesty's cruisers and brought to Sierra Leone under international treaty, the deputation would have the government agent distribute them at once among the different West Indian colonies qualified to receive them. This last step supposedly would reduce expenses for the government-financed Africa department at Sierra Leone.[31]

The West India Committee[32] would like to see constant and rapid transportation between Africa and the West Indies. It proposed using one steamer and two transports (sail), all three ships to be sent immediately to Sierra Leone in order to begin transatlantic crossings early in the next year. The government steamer, as proposed by the West India interests, would need to be of sufficient power to make good headway against the trade winds. The two government transports, in constant communication between Sierra Leone and the West Indies, should be large enough to carry four hundred emigrants each. One vessel at a time should take on emigrants at Sierra Leone but should not remain there more than fifteen days.[33] The committee also proposed the establishment of a line of steam packets which would operate between West Coast Africa and the West Indies. Among the many advantages claimed for the packets was "the transmission of European civilization from the West Indies to Africa"—an argument calculated to gain support from influential humanitarians and missionaries.[34]

The spokesmen for the West India interests asked for changes in some existing regulations that were obstacles to emigration. No one in debt was permitted to leave Sierra Leone, even if his indebtedness was small. Many

31. In A. Colville to Stanley, Nov. 15, 1842, enc. no.1 in no.2, Papers Relative to Emigration from the West Coast of Africa to the West Indies, *Votes,* 1843-1844, Ap.3, pp.89-91. These papers may be found also in *PP,* 1843, XXIV.

32. Perhaps the best brief description of this body would be "an organization of West India interests." For a history of the West India Committee, see Lillian M. Penson, *The Colonial Agent of the British West Indies* (London, 1924), pp.194-214.

33. In Colville to Stanley, Nov. 15, 1842, enc. no.1 in no.2, Papers Relative to Emigration from the West Coast of Africa to the West Indies, *Votes,* 1843-1844, Ap.3, p.99.

34. Ibid., p.91.

would-be emigrants who owed no more than six pounds sterling were unable to depart. The committee suggested that a sort of loan might be used to enable the emigrant to free himself of debt in Sierra Leone; he might then give bond to repay the receiver-general or treasurer of the colony making the advance, and to do so within a stipulated time.[35] The Colonial Secretary was unfavorably impressed with the proposal and refused to permit withdrawal of the regulation.[36]

The committee questioned whether the requirement of a six-weeks residence in Sierra Leone prior to embarkation should not be discontinued. Emigrants who came from neighboring areas would not have the resources to maintain themselves for so long a period. The regulation had been established to guard against any attempt at slave trading from Sierra Leone. Now, with emigration supervised by officers of the British government, there was no greater security that could be provided. Stanley concluded that under these new conditions the six-weeks residence might no longer be necessary, but he preferred to have further information from the governor of Sierra Leone before making a final decision.[37] Colonial emigration agents were not above trying to enroll each other's recruits. To forestall this practice, it was decided that the names and descriptions of all who agreed to go to a particular colony were to be recorded in a separate book for each colony. If an emigrant agreed to go to one colony and then changed his mind, the government emigration agent in Sierra Leone should refuse him a pass unless consent was given by the first agent and a fee was paid for the transfer.[38]

Stanley rejected the proposed steam vessel and packets as too expensive. He was agreeable, however, to the general plan of immigration by vessels hired by the imperial government, but insisted they must have a surgeon and a lieutenant of the navy on board.[39] The Colonial Secretary was all too aware that emigrants carried by only three ships could not possibly be so numerous as to alleviate the labor shortage in the West Indies; yet this very limited participation could have a psychological value out of all proportion to the three ships. It presumably could dispell in Africa any faint

35. "Statement, embodying Suggestions made by a Deputation of Gentlemen, with respect to the future Emigration from the West Coast of Africa to the West Indies, and Lord Stanley's Decision upon them," ibid., p.106.

36. Ibid.

37. Ibid., p.107.

38. In Colville to Stanley, Nov. 15, 1842, enc.1 in no.2, Papers Relative to Emigration . . . , ibid., pp.94-95.

39. Hope to Burge, Dec. 13, 1842, ibid., p.98.

suspicion of a renewal of the slave trade, and by giving the Africans confidence in emigration, might be the stimulus for a larger movement. At the same time, it would be a token of imperial interest in both Africa and the sugar colonies. It could serve as something of a pilot project to develop satisfactory methods of collecting and transporting immigrants; if successful, it could be enlarged to meet the needs of the importing colony.[40]

Everyone with West India interests was eager to get the project started, but until an official decision was made known, the colonies could do virtually nothing. Detailed plans were developed slowly, and were still incomplete when Stanley gave semiofficial approval in mid-December. Then he merely announced his readiness to approve the colonial agents' recommendation that emigration from West Coast Africa to the West Indies should be carried on in vessels hired by Her Majesty's government. But the entire expense was to be borne by the colonies to which the Africans might emigrate. The plan could not be put into operation for any colony, he emphasized, until it guaranteed Her Majesty's government against any loss.[41]

A fortnight later Stanley gave a more detailed reply to the proposals which had been presented by the colonial agents. He would instruct the governor of Sierra Leone to announce that the British Government intended to undertake both general management of emigration and protection of the individuals. He had no objection to the proposal that captured slaves brought into Sierra Leone for liberation should be sent on immediately for distribution among the colonies qualified to receive them, but stressed the possibility of discontinuance of the Court of Mixed Commission at Sierra Leone, a development which would make success of the plan highly improbable. Again he referred to financing. If Britain assumed general supervision of emigration from West Coast Africa, the West Indian colonies would have to give unquestionable assurance of repayment for any and all expenses incurred by Her Majesty's government in the course of that supervision.[42] Her Majesty's government had no intention of paying the bill for this project, and the Colonial Secretary missed no opportunity to emphasize that fact.

Jamaica, British Guiana, and Trinidad had for some time been at-

40. Stanley to Macdonald, Feb. 6, 1843, no.1 (87), ibid., pp.51-53.
41. Hope to Burge, Dec. 13, 1842, ibid., pp.98-99.
42. "Statement, embodying Suggestions . . . and Lord Stanley's Decision," ibid., p.101.

tempting actively to do something about the labor problem, and to that purpose had earlier set aside a sum of money and passed laws to encourage immigration. The Colonial Office was aware that as a considerable portion of this money was still unspent and unencumbered, the three colonies were currently in a position to assure reimbursement of Great Britain; no other colony had the funds to guarantee repayment. Consequently, to get the project under way with a minimum of delay, only Jamaica, British Guiana, and Trinidad would receive African emigrants in the initial stages of the effort.[43] Presumably all three colonies either had enacted or would enact legislation requiring correct procedure in collecting the emigrants in Africa, their reception in the colony, and their free return passage if they wanted it, at the end of five years from the time of their landing.[44]

Not until February, 1843, however, was the Secretary of State for the colonies able to send detailed information to Governor Macdonald of Sierra Leone. At the same time he pointed out that the select committee, whose members included several of the most active friends of the Africans, had supported emigration as beneficial not only to the West Indies but also to Africa and the Africans. Emigration might also free the Sierra Leone government from trying to find employment for the liberated Africans in the area.[45] At a time when a colony was expected to pay its own way, the proposal was expected to meet with ready support by the administration of Sierra Leone.

The new emigration plan so reduced responsibility of the colonial collecting agents as to suggest the feasibility of combining their remaining duties in the person of one agent serving all three colonies. Greater responsibility, however, was placed upon the governor and other imperial appointees. Because it was imperative for government ships to sail with a full load, thenceforth all emigration from West Coast Africa must be in vessels either chartered or licensed by Her Majesty's government.[46] To that intent, Governor Macdonald was directed to utilize every lawful means to prevent any emigration that was not government supervised.[47] Should a government emigration vessel fail to secure a full load at Sierra Leone, the governor

43. Ibid., pp.101-103.
44. Stanley, Circular, Feb. 25, 1843, *Votes,* 1843-1844, Ap.3, p.49.
45. Stanley to Macdonald, Feb. 6, 1843, no.1 (87), Papers Relative to Emigration . . . , ibid., p.51.
46. Stanley, Circular, ibid., p.49.
47. Stanley to Macdonald, Feb. 6, 1843, no.1 (87), Papers Relative to Emigration . . . , ibid., p.52.

could send it to Boavista or Loanda (where there were then Courts of Mixed Commission), if liberated Africans there were "at the disposal of Her Majesty's commissioners."[48] The governor was assigned such additional tasks as reducing fees for passports (of which Barclay had complained in 1841), and general supervision over both the government emigration agent and emigration in general from Sierra Leone. Moreover, in accordance with the 1842 Passengers Act, he must now make the final decision as to the seaworthiness of an emigrant ship.[49] As Stanley had already decided to abandon the requirement of six-weeks residence in Sierra Leone, Governor Macdonald was directed to persuade his council to modify it on the basis that it was no longer needed.[50]

The emigration agent for Sierra Leone, appointed by the imperial government but paid a salary by the colonies to which emigrants were sent, was to supervise the collecting agents of the various colonies. He was instructed to keep separate books and registers of emigrants for each colony; to provide a depot where emigrants might stay for as long as fifteen days while awaiting the sailing of their ship; to interview personally each emigrant to make certain he went voluntarily. In addition, he must issue clothing and certificates of acceptance for emigration; make certain there was at least one emigrant who could serve as interpreter, and accept adult emigrants at the ratio of one female to every two males. Kru and liberated Africans were excepted from this provision.[51] Eager as were both planters and government to promote emigration, they believed certain types of persons would be misfits. Consequently the agent was prohibited from certifying persons known to be addicted to "scandalous vices" or intoxication, or persons infirm, aged (above forty-five) or deserting dependents. Unaccompanied children were not acceptable unless some local authority certified permission. As before, couples of about thirty years of age were preferred.[52]

The government, in taking over direction of the project, seemingly had attempted to foresee every pitfall. In reality, this was among the responsibilities of the Colonial Land and Emigration Commission. When the 1835

48. Ibid., p.55.
49. Passengers Act, 1842, in *Votes,* 1843-1844, Ap.3, p.169.
50. Stanley to Macdonald, Feb. 6, 1843, no.2 (88), ibid., p.86.
51. Heads of Instructions for the Government Emigration Agent for Sierra Leone, ibid., pp.124-126.
52. Ibid., pp.126-127.

Passengers Act proved inadequate for protecting emigrants from Europe, the CL&EC consulted various emigration officials and shipping interests before suggesting amendments which were made effective in the Passengers Act of 1842. Although the act was designed primarily for European emigrants, with African emigration seemingly a reality it was extended to regulate transportation of passengers from the British possessions on the West Coast of Africa.[53]

Regulations were drafted in minute detail. Standardized forms were adopted for tenders, contracts, and reports. Tender of a ship to convey passengers between West Coast Africa and the West Indies must include information concerning equipment for the voyage, length and breadth of lower deck of the ship, where and when built, and date when it would be ready for inspection in dry dock. No ship could be accepted if it stood below the red diphthong at Lloyd's, had less than six feet between decks (instead of the old five and one-half feet), or did not have a poop and topgallant forecastle.[54]

With the CL&EC acting for Her Majesty's government, contract with the shipping firm was to be in effect for one year. Counting of time would begin at noon on the day the ship was reported by the government emigration agent as at the port of London and ready to sail. The navy officer and surgeon, as government officials, would have final word on matters pertaining to emigration.

For every one hundred tons burden there should be a crew of not less than five men, one boy, and a qualified male cook. The ship had to be armed with not less than four cannonade guns, with sufficient ammunition for each gun; and the crew must be supplied with small arms. Among the regulations pertaining to health and sanitation were maintenance of separate hospitals for males and females; and availability at all times of scrapers, brooms, swabs, sand and stones for dry-rubbing the deck, swing stoves, along with whatever else the CL&EC or their agents thought necessary for the cleanliness of the ship. After debarkation of the passengers, when the turnaround was being made, the boards of the berths must be lifted and washed and the deck cleaned and whitewashed with unslaked lime.[55]

53. Paragraph XLII, Passengers Act, 1842, in *Votes,* 1843-1844, Ap.3, p.102.
54. Tender of a ship to convey passengers . . . , enc. in no.2, ibid., p.111-112. The red "AE" stood third of five principal classifications of wooden ships. Henry B. Wheatley, *London Past and Present,* 3 vols. (London, 1891), 2:412.
55. Tender of a ship to convey passengers . . . , ibid., p.121.

Rations of food which the ship must carry were about the same as those established in 1841. The water allowable was increased to one gallon per day for each person instead of the old five gallons per week.[56] The ship must be supplied at all times with sufficient coals, wood, and coke, and—for the exclusive use of the passengers—such cooking equipment as might be approved by the CL&EC or their agents. These should include coffee mills and coffee roasters, scales, pewter, wooden and tin measures; tin drinking mugs, spoons, knives, forks. In addition there should be a new mat to serve as a bed for each person accepted on board the vessel.[57] Children above ten, instead of the old style fourteen, now must be paid for and rationed as adults; children one to ten years of age were to receive half rations, and three times per week were to be issued four ounces of rice or three ounces of sago in place of the salt meat provided for adults.[58] Children less than one year would not be paid for nor given rations. "Medical comforts" per one hundred persons included two hundred pints of lemon juice in one-gallon stone bottles, one hundred pounds of sago, one-half hundredweight of oatmeal, twenty-eight pounds of West Indian arrowroot, twelve bottles of port wine, twelve bottles of sherry, ten gallons of brandy, ten of rum, and ten of vinegar.[59]

All expenses of emigration were chargeable to the colony to which the emigrant was sent. Statements for expenses of passengers, foodstuffs, and the like had to be compiled quarterly, presented, and paid in London within fifteen days after presentation of the following documents: a signed statement of amount claimed for the tonnage of the vessel and for "victualling"; a certificate, signed by the naval agent, giving names and ages of all passengers; a certificate, signed by both the surgeon and naval officer, stating good treatment of the passengers during the voyage, condition of health of those arriving and the names of those who had died during the voyage.[60]

The ship was to fly a transport pennant; but as had been the situation in 1841, so it was now: a ship carrying Negro passengers might be suspect as a slave ship. Therefore, the officer in charge of the ship was provided papers to ensure against seizure by ships of the Royal Navy on patrol against the

56. The daily ration per person was only slightly different from the ration listed above, chap.3, n.31. Charter Party, ibid., p.115.
57. Ibid., p.116.
58. Ibid., p.115.
59. Ibid.
60. Ibid., p.117.

slave trade. At the same time he was directed not to oppose visitation or inspection, if that was requested. As further guarantee of status as a passenger ship, officers were absolutely forbidden to do any trading according to Instructions to Lieutenants in charge of Transports conveying Passengers between the Coast of Africa and the West Indies.[61]

If West Indian colonies wished to participate in the new plan for acquiring African laborers, they must do more than merely provide for paying whatever expenses might be involved; it was imperative for them also to adopt laws bringing their immigration regulations into agreement with those of Her Majesty's government. To avoid discrepancies, the Colonial Office provided a "Draft of Proposed Acts or Ordinances for the Encouragement of Immigration into [name of colony to be filled in]." The somewhat lengthy document, intended as the model for legislation by West Indian colonies, required the AGI of the receiving colony to provide the debarking immigrant with a statement of his right to a free return passage after a residence of at least five years and compliance with certain other requirements, including arrival on a government hired or licensed ship operating under the terms of this act.[62] It restricted conveyance of Africans (those from St. Helena excepted) to ships licensed or hired by Her Majesty's government, yet permitted use of the bounty system for introduction of immigrants from areas other than Africa.[63] But once an immigrant arrived in the colony and took the oath of allegiance, he immediately became a fully naturalized citizen.[64]

There had been careful preparation for an undertaking which might benefit more than one area of the empire. Free settler immigration, although wanted, was somewhat uncertain. But so long as the slave trade continued, and efforts were made to stop it, the by-product of liberated Africans might provide immigrants for Jamaica and the other sugar colonies of the West Indies. Under supervision by Great Britain, emigration from Africa, it was hoped, would become extensive. For their own reasons, each of the areas involved had concluded it was worth an effort.

61. Enc.3 in no.2, *Votes,* 1843-1844, Ap.3, p.119.
62. Paragraph 29, "Draft . . . ," ibid., p.147.
63. Paragraphs 5, 7, "Draft . . . ," ibid., pp.138-139.
64. Paragraph 33, "Draft . . . ," ibid., p.147.

5

Immigration by Imperial Supervision

JAMAICA SPENT SOME ANXIOUS MOMENTS WHILE THE select committees in London were carrying on their investigations and the Colonial Office was slowly moving toward a decision about emigration from Africa. What would be the effect upon Jamaica? The immigration policy currently used was a failure. Would there be a change? Would Jamaica get the assistance she needed? Official information seemed unduly slow in arriving.

Burge, as the colony's agent in London, had utilized every possible opportunity to remind British officials of Jamaica's plight. He had also constantly assessed the mood of the imperial government, gathered information as to what would be required of the colony, and above all, kept the island abreast of developments. With the advice of Burge, Jamaica was able to tailor a new immigration measure to anticipate requirements of the Colonial Office.[1]

Planting interests in Jamaica, desperate in the face of probable ruin, had become willing to grant concessions which they normally would have rejected summarily. The Legislature, reflecting their attitude, was deter-

1. Stanley to Elgin, May 31, 1843, no.113, and Burge to Stanley, Mar. 9, 1843, enc. in no.113, Papers Relative to Emigration, CO 137/273.

mined to place the colony in a position to acquire immigrant laborers the instant the new plan was officially announced. Members of the assembly were normally jealous of their own powers and restrictive of those of the governor; in this instance, however, in order to comply with all possible requirements under the new scheme, they took the extraordinary step of increasing the powers of the governor. By "An Act to Make Provision for the Introduction of Emigrants into this Island,"[2] the assembly placed at the disposal of the governor the sum of £30,000 for immigration purposes. Prior to January 1843 it was the AGI under whose authority immigration expenses were paid.[3] This same act also empowered the governor to appoint the island's immigration personnel and to continue one or both of the island ships in operation between Jamaica and Africa. In addition, it permitted him to send Africans back to visit their homeland. The planters expected the immigrants to become so convinced of the advantages of Jamaica that on their visit they would persuade their friends to accompany them on their return to Jamaica.[4] Jamaica's new immigration act became law on December 31, 1842, subject to possible disallowance by the imperial government. As in the preceding immigration measures, contracts beteeen employers and employees were limited to twelve months, and the Passengers Act was declared in force. The members of the assembly anticipated that details of actual recruiting and conveyance of immigrants would be assigned to the Colonial Land and Emigration Commission, so did not develop legislation in that area. There was a reversal of policy, however, with regard to European immigration. It had been found that Europeans, when they could be persuaded to come, brought with them certain skills which could contribute much to the welfare of Jamaica. To encourage the introduction of Europeans, the Act provided for a six-pound bounty for each European artificer or tradesman when he had remained for twelve months in the employment of the person who had borne the cost of his importation.[5]

Burge had been notified on December 31 of the Colonial Office decision and was expected to relay the information to Jamaica.[6] Not until

2. No.3531, enc. no.4 in Elgin to Stanley, Jan. 29, 1843, no.80, ibid.

3. Report of the AGI, Oct. 24, 1843, *Votes,* 1843-1844, Ap. 4, p.178.

4. Elgin to Stanley, Jan. 29, 1843, no.80, Papers Relative to Emigration, CO 137/273.

5. Act for the Introduction of Emigrants, no.3531, enc. no.4 in Elgin to Stanley, Jan. 29, 1843, no.80, ibid.

6. Hope to Burge, Dec. 31, 1842, Papers Relative to Emigration from the West

mid-February, however, was Governor Elgin told officially by Stanley that the imperial government was assuming supervision and control of emigration from West Coast Africa to the West Indies. The CL&EC had already been instructed to charter a ship each for Jamaica, British Guiana, and Trinidad.[7] A short time later, Elgin was sent a collection of documents on the subject of emigration from Africa. It included copies of Colonial Office correspondence with the West India spokesmen in London and with the governor of Sierra Leone, as well as a despatch from Stanley giving detailed instructions to the governor.[8] Certain responsibilities on the part of the colony were made quite clear. In order to ensure prompt payment by Jamaica and to avoid haggling, funds solely for African emigration must be set aside by the legislature; must be adequate, payable on demand, and by the governor of the colony by his own warrant, without requiring concurrence of the council, assembly, or commissioners of accounts. Requisite, too, was prohibition of emigration from West Coast Africa except under the direction of the imperial government.[9]

Jamaica's new immigration act had been passed by the Legislature, signed by the governor, and forwarded to London for approval before Stanley's instruction arrived in Jamaica. At the Colonial Office there was delay in disposing of the measure. The life of the bill, scheduled to expire December 31, would be about half over by the time Stanley's despatch giving his decision arrived in Spanish Town. Since in most respects the act met the requirements of Her Majesty's government, the Colonial Office concluded that it should be permitted to stand. There may have been some thought also of mollifying Jamaica. It was understood that a few objectionable provisions would be modified by the Legislature. For instance, the secretary objected to: (1) the clause authorizing the governor to use island ships to keep up communication between Jamaica and Africa; (2) the omission of a clause requiring intervention of the AGI in contracts between immigrant laborers and employers; and (3) failure to require the signing in Jamaica of all contracts between immigrant laborers and employers. On the assumption that those matters would be adjusted to meet imperial policy,

Coast of Africa to the West Indies, *Votes,* 1843-1844, Ap. 3, p.110.
    7. Stanley to Elgin, Feb. 15, 1843, Jamaica no.84, ibid., pp.46-47.
    8. Stanley to Elgin, Separate, Feb. 25, 1843, no.2, Papers Relative to Emigration, CO 137/273; Stanley, Circular, Feb. 25, 1843, *Votes,* 1843-1844, Ap. 3, pp.48-50.
    9. Stanley to Elgin, no.87, Feb. 28, 1843, Papers Relative to Emigration, CO 137/273; Stanley, Circular, Feb. 25, 1843, *Votes,* 1843-1844, Ap. 3, pp.48-50.

the act, which was to expire at the end of the calendar year, was not disallowed.[10]

At the beginning of the year 1843, Charles A. Darling succeeded John Ewart as AGI. Under Darling's direction, immigration records now followed the standardized and more detailed form newly required by the CL&EC. His first report, dated October 24, 1843, indicated that since September 30, 1842 (when Ewart made his last report), a total of 434 immigrants had entered Jamaica. Presumably all were Negro—110 from Canada, 23 from Baltimore, and 301 from Africa. All of those from Africa had arrived after January 1, most of them after mid-May.[11]

Before Jamaica received notice of imperial supervision of immigration, she had sent the two island brigs (the *Herald* and the *Treasurer*) to Africa for immigrants. The results were negligible. Cathcart, the Jamaica agent at Sierra Leone, had considerable difficulty in getting even sixty-two recruits for the *Herald,* which was the first to arrive. Lack of success he attributed to a variety of factors: complaints by Kingston Maroons about difficulty in obtaining a return passage to Sierra Leone; higher wages paid in Trinidad; liberal allowances given to delegates for Trinidad, which increased their zeal in persuading their friends to go there; change of allegiance by many of the recent Jamaica delegates, who recruited for Trinidad rather than Jamaica. Shipboard troubles of the *Herald* en route from Jamaica had added to the difficulty. The captain had taken with him a woman of low character, who — abused the returning Africans; they, in turn, retaliated, and conveyed to their fellow Africans an unfavorable impression of Jamaican women.[12] At the time of the *Herald's* sailing from Africa, Cathcart was reluctant to admit failure. Africans who wanted to go to Jamaica, he reported, were merely avoiding the *Herald,* delaying departure until the sailing of the next ship.

The results of recruiting for the brig *Treasurer* were even more dismal. Accompanied by several delegates, Cathcart used a boat belonging to the brig in order to go about the colony to enlist laborers. A large number reportedly would emigrate if the ship returned in April, but the people were agriculturalists who would not leave before they had harvested their crops and sold them. As the Sierra Leone population would not emigrate, Cath-

10. Stanley to Elgin, May 31, 1843, no.113, *Votes,* 1843-1844, Ap. 3, pp.38-39.
    11. Report by Charles A. Darling, AGI, Oct. 24, 1843, and Ap. F, *Votes,* 1843-1844, Ap. 4, pp.178, 192.
    12. Cathcart to Ewart, Dec. 26, 1842, ibid., p.196.

cart, with permission of the governor, next tried to get recruits from a group of young Africans liberated from a slaver. They, too, were reluctant to leave.[13]

The Jamaica agent offered further explanations for his failure. Merchants and river traders, he said, had increased wages in order to retain a supply of labor. Missionaries had raised their voices in opposition to emigration. The Wesleyans, in particular, by means of the publication, *The Watchman,* were propagandizing against emigration. The Jamaica agent pointed out that as prizes now brought into Sierra Leone were taken without slaves on board, liberated Africans, who had become the major source for recruits, were less numerous. Moreover, the recent Jamaica delegates were of no help in enlisting emigrants. In fact, they had been a distinct hindrance; they were disloyal, and either spoke unfavorably of the island or recruited their friends for Trinidad. It was small comfort to Cathcart that the ships for Trinidad sailed with little more than fifty percent of the maximum load of passengers, despite the large fees to delegates and a huge feast.[14] He himself had even less success.

The *Treasurer* was detained three months while efforts were made to secure a full cargo of emigrants; but the people simply would not go. Cathcart wrote resignedly that as it was clearly impossible to get emigrants during the growing season, ships might be sent during the rains (April-November), when it was more difficult for the people to procure the necessities of life. If under those conditions, with shortages and high cost of food stuffs, the people still refused to leave, it would be folly, warned the agent, to continue efforts to procure laborers from that part of Africa.[15] For some reason, perhaps because it was so damning to the project, the warning was not among the Cathcart despatches published in the sessional papers of Jamaica itself. In reality, the agent could not even half fill the brig. When it finally sailed, it carried only eight emigrants, each of whom had been advanced five dollars. The *Treasurer* arrived at Kingston on March 9, 1843. This was the last voyage of a Jamaica emigrant vessel under the old plan; it presented indisputable evidence of the plan's failure.[16]

13. Ibid.
14. Cathcart to Ewart, Feb. 4, 1843, enc.2 in Elgin to Stanley, no.118, May 1, 1843, CO 137/274.
15. Ibid.
16. David Smith & Co. to the Governor's Secretary, Kingston, Mar. 9, 1843, *Votes,* 1843-1844, Ap. 4, p.196.

About the time the *Treasurer* sailed from Sierra Leone (February 4) the Colonial Office was preparing to assume the task of supervising emigration from West Coast Africa. Had Cathcart's attitude been known then in England, the government might have had second thoughts about the entire scheme. But Jamaica hoped the new plan would produce a flood of immigrants sufficient to end the labor problem, and Stanley was willing to go along with the proposal although he believed the sugar islands overestimated the number who would leave Africa. To him the significance would lie in convincing West Indian laborers that proprietors were not dependent exclusively upon the home supply of labor, and could not be forced to pay wages beyond their means.[17]

Cathcart's report on conditions in Sierra Leone was still unknown when, under Stanley's instructions, the 420-ton *Glen Huntley* was chartered for Jamaica by the CL&EC. Rental on the ship was £3759 for one year. If it made three voyages per year, carrying 223 passengers each trip, total charge for the year would be £5279—an expense for which Her Majesty's government expected reimbursement without delay.[18] In accordance with the new procedure, the transport was inspected by a government agent in England in order to ensure compliance with all regulations for emigrant ships in the South Atlantic. When it sailed from England on February 9, 1843, it was bound directly for Sierra Leone with instructions to take on board Africans who were willing to go to Jamaica. The lieutenant (a government representative) was instructed to supervise personally all embarkation and to limit the passengers to the number for which the ship was certified.[19]

When the transport arrived in Sierra Leone early in March, it brought directives pertaining to the new emigration system. Accordingly, the governor by proclamation informed the people that emigration to the West Indies was being placed under the special care and protection of the Queen's government.[20] One ship, he stated, was then in harbor and ready to take to Jamaica all persons who wanted to go. Two other vessels, he promised, would soon arrive, one for Trinidad, the other for British Guiana. The governor was trying to encourage emigration, but it is doubtful if parts of the proclamation had much meaning to the people. For instance, they were

17. Hope to Neil Malcolm, Sept. 4, 1843, no.4, *Votes*, 1843-1844, Ap. 28, p.302.
18. Stanley to Elgin, Feb. 15, 1843, no.84, *Votes*, 1843-1844, Ap. 3, p.46-47.
19. Instructions to lieutenants in charge of Transports, ibid., p.120.
20. Cathcart to Ewart, Apr. 11, 1843, *Votes*, 1843-1844, Ap. 4, p.198.

told that emigration would be beneficial to them because "the state of civilization in the West Indies was more advanced" than in Sierra Leone; they could return to Africa and bring back with them "the improved habits and principles" which they would have the opportunity to acquire in Jamaica. Probably most absurd of all, since the African knew nothing about parliamentary government, was the assurance that "as soon as the necessary legislative provisions" could be made, return passage would be granted.[21]

Two days later, John R. Jeremie, who had been appointed government (imperial) emigration agent at Sierra Leone, issued a notice to the inhabitants of the colony. He assured them that immigrants in the British West Indies would be as free as in Sierra Leone; no such thing as slavery existed there; by taking over direction of emigration to the West Indies, Her Majesty's government (a leading opponent of slavery) had proved it. He offered various inducements, including "much higher wages," with religious establishments and schools available as in Sierra Leone. As proof of the good care which emigrants could expect during the passage, everyone was invited to board the *Glen Huntley* to view the list of daily rations provided for the voyage and inspect accomodations. All who wished to emigrate, he stated, should apply to Mr. Cathcart, the Jamaica emigration agent.[22] Although his terms were more intelligible to the people of Sierra Leone than were those of the governor, Jeremie could not give any specific statement relative to such matters as wages, because he himself had not been informed. In essence, recruiting of labor under the new plan was being attempted without getting down to terms which would appeal to people of non-European civilization.

Jamaica's agent complained that some of the old hindrances to emigration remained in effect: small loans still could not be paid out of future wages; and one third of the emigrants had to be females. If such regulations were continued, he warned, emigration would probably cease. Many men had small debts which must be paid before the debtor was eligible to leave the colony; yet by law the debtor could not be given an advance on his wages if he planned to emigrate. Krumen, who were fairly numerous among the recruits, went only to work for a time and then return home, hence left their wives in Africa. It was virtually impossible to secure enough women to

21. Proclamation by the Governor, Freetown, Mar. 17, 1843, ibid., pp.199-200.
22. Notice by John R. Jeremie, Government Emigration Agent, Sierra Leone, Mar. 19, 1843, ibid., pp.198-199.

make up one-third of any cargo of laborers, for women were less inclined to migrate than were men.[23]

The *Glen Huntley* waited in the harbor for about a month, but there was no rush of applicants. The governor of Sierra Leone, in compliance with instructions from the Colonial Office, ordered the managers of liberated African villages to encourage their people to emigrate. There was no response from that quarter either. No adults volunteered, and the only recruits were boys from the government school who wanted to work for themselves for money.[24] All were under fourteen years of age, and their total number was only eighty-five, or approximately forty percent of the number that the *Glen Huntley* was certified to carry. Cathcart still hoped for more recruits when the rains came, provided the agents were permitted to advance sums of money; but even if the restriction was removed, he warned, there would be difficulty in getting recruits except during the rainy season.[25]

There is little information available concerning the actual embarkation and first voyage of the *Glen Huntley* to Jamaica. Immunization against smallpox was required for all passengers who had not had the disease, but the Africans regarded vaccination as a mystery which could have a deleterious effect upon them. Therefore, to avoid creating a wrong impression in Sierra Leone and to comply with the request of the governor and government agent at the port, the process was postponed until after embarkation. There was not enough lymph for everyone, but vaccination was notably lacking in success.[26] There was only one other development of consequence. Passengers ordinarily prepared the food for themselves, but the young passengers in this instance seemingly were ignorant of the art of cooking. It became necessary for an adult to cook their food and to supervise its distribution. Otherwise the passage was uneventful.[27]

In Jamaica there were great excitement and expectation from the prospect of the arrival of an immigrant ship under Imperial supervision.

23. Cathcart to Ewart, Apr. 11, 1843, ibid., p.198.
24. Jeremie to the Government Emigration Agent at Jamaica, Apr. 11, 1843, ibid., p.197.
25. Cathcart to Ewart, Apr. 11, 1843, ibid., p.198.
26. Report by Sterling, Surgeon of the *Glen Huntley,* Embarkation of Laborers from West Coast Africa to the West Indies, *PP,* 1844, XXXV:50.
27. James Gordon to Darling, May 16, 1843, Papers Relative to Emigration from West Coast Africa to the West Indies, no.3, pp.23-24, CO 137/274 (hereinafter cited as Papers Relative to Emigration).

Hopefully, it would mark the beginning of a flood of immigrants who would augment the labor force. The planters filed their applications stating the number and type of laborers needed, and by the time the ship reached Montego Bay on March 16, requests had mounted to a total of 750 in that one locale.[28] Had the transport carried its legal limit of passengers, less than one-third of the requests could have been met. With only eighty-five passengers, some of whom would be sent back as delegates, there was the twofold problem of doing what was best for the immigrants and placating the maximum number of planters.

It seemed very important for these immigrants to be satisfied, for their treatment might be regarded as indicative of what others could expect, and presumably this would influence further emigration from West Coast Africa.[29] The immaturity of the boys presented a special problem, for in the absence of both natural guardian and parent, it was necessary for some official to act *in loco parentis*. The task was assigned to the stipendiary magistrate at Montego Bay, Henry Laidlaw. Upon him and the subagent James Gordon (subagent at Montego Bay) fell the task of selecting the boys' employers. This meant, in other words, deciding which planters would receive laborers and which would not. Insofar as possible, companions were not separated. Major emphasis was placed on such considerations as the general way of life of the prospective employer, his ability to promote the "moral and intellectual improvement" of the children, and the availability of schools and places of public worship, either on the estate or in the neighborhood.[30]

As finally arranged, all of the boys were sent to the interior where labor was scarce and there would be no danger of kidnapping. The group was divided into five lots of fifteen each, and one lot of six. Four were to return as delegates. Most of the receiving estates were in the parish of Hanover, and in sufficient proximity for the boys to meet frequently at church.[31] The contract, modified to suit the needs of minors, required the

28. Darling to Jeremie, May 25, 1843, *Votes,* 1843-1844, Ap. 4, pp.201-202.
29. George Macdonald to Elgin, Sierra Leone, Apr. 8, 1843, Papers Relative to Emigration, *PP,* 1844, XXXV:325.
30. Darling to Gordon, May 12, 1843, enc. no.2 in no.11, Papers Relative to Emigration, p.23, CO 137/274.
31. The assignments were as follows: to Lethe Estate (J. L. Walcott, Atty), 15 boys; to Copse Estate (L. Jackson, Atty), 15 boys; to Content Estate (Henry Brockett, Atty), 15 boys; to Chester Castle Estate (Wm. H. Cook, Proprietor), 15 boys; to Argyle

employer to feed and clothe the boys for one year, see that they kept themselves clean, and, at his own expense, send them to a regular school at least two days per week, four and one-half hours per day. In addition, the employer promised to permit government enquiry from time to time as to the condition of the boys.[32]

The first voyage of the *Glen Huntley* as an immigrant ship under imperial supervision had fallen far short of expectations, but better results were anticipated from the next trip. Because agents in Sierra Leone insisted upon having delegates to aid in recruiting, when the transport sailed on the return trip it took along twenty. A few of the men who had been specifically requested by Cathcart were unwilling to leave the island. Four of the delegates, who were from among the most recent arrivals, could give little in the way of an eyewitness account of the island, but could tell of the voyage. Above all, however, their mere presence in Sierra Leone again should inspire confidence in the project. Most of the other delegates had accompanied Barclay or had been in Jamaica for some time and could give an account based on personal experience. One of them, who was to receive £10 per month, was to remain in Africa for a few months to recruit emigrants in Sierra Leone and possibly in Liberia. Most of the others were to be paid £2 per month, but were expected to return when the emigrant ship made its second crossing. In some instances the money was paid directly to the delegates; in others, it was entrusted to the lieutenant who was with the ship.[33] There were a few Negroes who traveled merely as passengers returning to Africa; if they also served as recruiters and did well, they might be considered as delegates and paid for their work.

When the ship arrived in Sierra Leone in July, it brought not only delegates but more specific suggestions of advantages to be found in Jamaica. There was no difficulty in finding employment, it was stated. Greatest demand for labor was on sugar or coffee plantations. The work on the former entailed preparing the land for the cane, planting, weeding, moulding, trashing, and cutting and manufacturing the cane into sugar. On coffee plantations, described generally as requiring lighter work than on the

---

Estate (Daniel Sinclair, Atty), 15 boys; to Plum Pen (George Cragg, Proprietor), 6 boys.

32. Gordon to Darling, May 28, 1843, no.4 and enc.; Laidlaw to R. Bruce, May 23, 1843, enc.2; Papers Relative to Emigration, pp.24-26, CO 137/274.

33. Darling to Cathcart, May 29, 1843, no.24 and enc., *Votes*, 1843-1844, Ap. 4, pp.202-204.

cane estates, labor was needed for planting, pruning, and weeding the coffee trees, gathering in the coffee berries, and spreading them to dry.[34]

The emigration agents also could now give more definite information about wages: A laborer, whether man or woman, could easily earn 1s. 6d. One who worked nine hours between sunrise and sunset could earn 2s. and even 2s. 6d. for work requiring more skill than ordinary field work. Children below sixteen might earn 6d. to 1s. per day. There were additional advantages, such as a house and attached garden, medicine and medical attendance—all free of charge during the first year. After the first year the immigrant would pay rent, but probably no more than 1s. per week for house and garden. House rent was charged only to the head of the family, not to each member. Or, if the immigrant preferred, he could even buy land, which varied in price from £1 to £100, according to quality of the soil, distance from the coast, and various other factors. The laborer who did not buy land, yet preferred to work for himself by growing export products (such as sugar, coffee, ginger, arrowroot), could do so either by paying money rent for the land or by sharecropping, with probably one-half or one-third of the produce going to the proprietor.[35]

To give further allure to working in Jamaica, a list of average prices of necessities was provided for circulation in Sierra Leone. This information might be helpful if the African contemplating emigration knew English weights, measures, coinage, and some mathematics. It would then enable him to calculate buying power and on that basis decide there might be a good life awaiting him in Jamaica. For instance, with house and garden free for the first year, he could expect to raise his provisions and have no monetary outlay for shelter or for most of his food. If he earned 1s. 6d. per day, from that one day's wage alone he could buy one pound of bread (3d.), one pound of salt fish (3d.), or of fresh beef (4d.-6d.), and have money left for purchasing yams, cocos, sugar, and so forth. Or if it was clothing he wished to acquire, three days' wages would enable him to buy an oznaburgh shirt and drawers (3s. 10d.), with enough left to purchase some herrings or a pound of beef.[36]

34. Statement of wages and other advantages offered to African laborers in the Island of Jamaica, C. H. Darling, May 18, 1843, ibid., pp.204-206.
35. Ibid.
36. Ibid. Common prices of provisions and clothing in ordinary use were as follows: yams, 5-6s. per cwt.; cocos, 4-5s. per cwt.; plantains, 4-5s. per cwt.; salt fish, 3d. per lb.; salt pork, 9d.-1s. per lb.; sugar, 4½d. per lb.; herrings, 3d. per 4; fresh beef, 4-6d. per lb.; bread, 3d. per lb.; an oznaburgh shirt and drawers, such as for a Negro

Recruiting efforts were begun in Sierra Leone immediately after the emigrant ship arrived. The Jamaica agent sent the delegates into various villages to proclaim the advantages of life in Jamaica. A few were relatively successful, but most of them were ineffectual. Only one could be termed a "traitor to the cause"; he not only talked against Jamaica, but tried to recruit for a rival colony. As delegates were paid wages in addition to their expense-free trip, they merely added to the cost of Jamaica's efforts to secure laborers.[37] The agent thought it was the weather that was the principal deterrent to recruitment of a full complement of emigrants. A torrential rain had overflowed the ravines and interfered with people traveling overland.[38] Although the transport lay in harbor six weeks, almost no one wanted to leave Africa. It was far short of a capacity load when it finally sailed with emigrants for Jamaica. There were 163 passengers. Seventy-nine were adult emigrants (57 males, 22 females); 17 were delegates, five of them boys under fourteen years of age.[39]

The *Glen Huntley* was thirty-eight days en route. When it arrived in Jamaica it was directed to Old Harbor, on the south side of the island.[40] A few of the immigrants were described as cook, washer, or servant; most of them were classified as laborers. Geographically, they were assigned rather widely over the middle and eastern part of the island, with the largest number having first employment in parishes within relatively easy access to Old Harbor. Some went with friends (who were delegates) to estates where immigrants from earlier voyages were employed.[41] All told, 75 were assigned in the parish of Clarendon, 43 in St. Dorothy, 11 in St. George, 8 in St. Thomas-in-the-East, one in St. Ann's. The Reverend Dr. Stewart of Chapelton, Clarendon, received one; with that exception, all of the immigrants received in Clarendon were assigned to the Honorable E. Thompson, a member of the Assembly. The remainder of the immigrants were divided among fifteen other "first employers."[42]

---

man's working dress, 3s. 10d.; a working hat, 1s. 6d.; a working cap, 1s.; a blue cloth jacket, £2; a woman's working dress about the same as the man's; a woman's holiday dress about the same as a man's; ibid. pp.205-206.

37. Cathcart to Darling, Sept. 4, 1843, ibid., pp.206-208.

38. Ibid., p.207.

39. Register of African Immigrants, Jamaica, *Votes*, 1845, E of Ap. 5, pp.109-114.

40. Enc. in Elgin to Stanley, Jan. 26, 1844, no.25, CO 137/278.

41. Report, Darling, Oct. 24, 1843, *Votes*, 1843-1844, Ap. 4, p.181.

42. Register of African Immigrants, Jamaica, *Votes*, 1845, E of Ap. 5, pp.109-114.

There was no further importation of laborers by the government transport in 1843. The planters were disappointed by the number of Africans brought by the *Glen Huntley* although they were fairly well satisfied with the quality. The employers' early reports were unanimous in praising their good behavior and their value as laborers. These Negroes, they said, were useful in planting and cleaning young canes, worked well, and did a fair amount of work; in general, they respected property, were better workers and more obedient than the creole Negroes. Moreover, they made a splendid impression when they attended church—an account well calculated to appeal to humanitarians, missionaries, and their followers. Only one employer had reservations; he found them indolent unless closely supervised.[43]

Even with emigration from West Coast Africa under imperial supervision, Jamaica's agent at Sierra Leone continued to warn the island of doom for the project unless certain policies were changed.[44] Perhaps Jamaicans were moved by the small number of immigrants aboard the *Glen Huntley* on its first voyage; certainly within a few days after its arrival, and while disappointment was high, island officials took a good look at the situation and went into action. One of their targets was the old practice of preventing would-be emigrants from leaving Sierra Leone merely because of petty debts. Darling, as AGI and with the approval of Elgin, instructed the Jamaica emigration agent at Sierra Leone to pay small debts of would-be emigrants if he could not otherwise secure a full complement for the transport. There were of course, some restrictions, for the agent must have permission from the governor of Sierra Leone; must make certain it was a bona fide debt; and should not pay the creditor until the emigrant actually departed. The creditor, in turn, must agree to forgo his right of detention. Moreover, in order to prevent development of a system of fraudulent claims, there should be no publicity as to the amount which Jamaica would pay. In reality, £3 was the maximum debt payable for any one emigrant, while £100 was the total amount that could be used to relieve petty debt for any one voyage.[45] The debtor was in no way liable for repayment either in

43. Gordon to Darling, Oct. 24, 1843; Brocket to Gordon, Oct. 17, 1843; Sinclair to Gordon, Oct. 19, 1843; Jackson to Gordon, Oct. 23, 1843; Papers Relative to Emigration, pp.17-18, CO 137/274.
44. Cathcart to Ewart, Apr. 11, 1843, Papers Relative to Emigration, p.22, CO 137/274. See *Votes,* 1843-1844, Ap. 4 for Report of the AGI.
45. Darling to the JEA, Sierra Leone, May 29, 1843, no.24 in Papers Relative to Emigration, p.30, CO 137/274.

money or in services of any kind. This condition, stressed by Elgin when he reported the change to the Colonial Office, was almost mandatory, if charges of slave trading were to be avoided.[46]

Initiative in altering the policy with regard to petty debts had come from the colonial government, not the imperial. Only after they had sent instructions to their agent in Sierra Leone did Jamaica officials inform the Colonial Office. By the time approval was received from that department, Jamaica's alteration in policy had been in effect for several weeks. It was late in October when Stanley officially concurred as to the necessity of removing "every impediment" to emigration. No poor person anywhere, he wrote, could be expected to set out on a long voyage without some pecuniary assistance.[47] Unfortunately, he was so impressed with the plan that he proposed its adoption by Trinidad and British Guiana. This was a bitter blow to Jamaica, who was thereby deprived of what might have been an important advantage over the newer sugar colonies.

There was momentary encouragement for Jamaica when Captain Terry was made government (imperial) emigration agent for Sierra Leone. Because he formerly had been guardian of captured Africans, he was expected to have a powerful influence in overcoming their reluctance to leave their refuge.[48] Nonetheless, this optimism was short lived. Soon after the *Glen Huntley* had sailed on its second voyage, a large prize was brought into Sierra Leone with about five hundred Africans on board. They were sent to the Africa yard, where they were fed and required to do only such "light work" as weeding the street. The work was not heavy enough to cause them to want to leave, and while still in the yard, these liberated Africans were visited by people unfriendly to Jamaica and to emigration. As long as the Africans remained in the "yard" leading a life of indolence, complained the Jamaica agent, there was little likelihood of their deciding to emigrate. Captain Terry was not able to persuade them to depart. Furthermore, when they were removed to villages, it was asserted, their minds were poisoned against emigration by false reports spread by a few persons who had been misfits in the West Indies.[49]

46. Elgin to Stanley, July 29, 1843, no.18, ibid.
47. Stanley to Elgin, Oct. 22, 1843, no.158, CO 137/247; *Votes*, 1843-1844, Ap. 28, pp.226-227.
48. Cathcart to Darling, Sept. 4, 1843, *Votes*, 1843-1844, Ap. 4, p.208.
49. Cathcart to Darling, Nov. 21, 1843, enc. no.2 in Elgin to Stanley, Jan. 26, 1844, no.25, CO 137/278.

The results of the two voyages by the *Glen Huntley* in 1843, which were far below expectations, made it obvious that mere superintendence by the imperial government was not sufficient stimulus to produce large-scale emigration. Officials at the Colonial Office and in Jamaica wanted to get rid of any deterrents to emigration, but it was necessary first to determine what they were. To this intent, there was a review of policies which in the past had been subjects for complaint by the colonial officials.

Although it was generally recognized and reported by agents in Sierra Leone that African women, for various reasons, seldom emigrated, there had been no less proportion than one female for every three males. Jamaica had complained about this long and bitterly, but in vain. Now, the Secretary of State for the Colonies asked Elgin if there was any objection from the moral point of view to relaxation of the restriction; if not, he requested the governor to recommend some modification of it.[50] The governor saw no objection. In fact, he believed it would provide a positive advantage toward assimilation. Under the existing arrangement and despite similarity to island laborers, new settlers tended to form separate communities. With the proposed modification, men who came from Africa would far outnumber the women, and would probably marry creole women—a development which Elgin believed would facilitate their integration into the island society.[51] Stanley postponed a decision until he could determine the attitude of the governors of British Guiana, Trinidad, and Sierra Leone. Then, with the concurrence of all, the requirement of a fixed proportion of females was abolished.[52]

The policy of requiring six weeks' residence in Sierra Leone prior to emigration had also been a subject for severe criticism by those associated with the mechanics of emigration.[53] A nonresident did not have the means to maintain himself for six weeks, yet when the regulation was enforced, it prevented Africans who were not permanent residents of Sierra Leone from migrating. As the governor of Sierra Leone was the official in the best position to have first-hand information on the subject, he was asked for an opinion. There had not been "any semblance of kidnapping" in the colony, he reported, and the rule seemed utterly unnecessary. It, too, was with-

50. Stanley to Elgin, Dec. 13, 1843, no.175, ibid.
51. Elgin to Stanley, Jan. 31, 1844, no.24, CO 137/276.
52. Fifth General Report of the CL&EC, 1845, "Immigration into the West Indies," *PP,* 1845, XXVII:18.
53. The policy was not applied to Africans liberated from captured vessels.

drawn.[54] Because there were many complaints about the life of ease led by liberated Africans in the Africa yard, the practice of providing indefinite maintenance was ended.[55]

Suggestions for increasing emigration included reference to the need for more careful selection of delegates—that is, those immigrants who were provided a salary and free round-trip fare from Jamaica to Sierra Leone for the purpose of recruiting emigrants. The Jamaica agent in Sierra Leone believed that certain villages or tribes were more responsive than others to explanations of advantages awaiting laborers who moved to Jamaica. If the delegates included men who had lived and were known in these specific villages or tribes, their recruiting efforts should be successful. Agent Cathcart sent a list of those tribes and villages to Jamaica.

When the transport *Glen Huntley* returned to Sierra Leone after its second voyage of 1843, it took along six regular delegates to aid in recruiting for the third voyage. Each delegate was to be paid £2 per month in addition to an advance payment of £3. This time, Darling, as AGI, had tried to choose as delegates immigrants who would be returning to the areas mentioned by Jamaica's agent in Sierra Leone. The AGI was able to send a Sherbro man, but no Timmonese was available. Several nondelegates, who were given return passage at the expense of Jamaica, were promised compensation if they became successful recruiters. Again, it was hoped that the large number returning to Africa might well prove to the population of Sierra Leone and of neighboring tribes that transportation to return from Jamaica was easily obtainable and that Jamaica had no wish to restrain any who wanted to leave. Some in Jamaica even proposed to send a planter with a few of his African employees to impress upon the people in Sierra Leone the wisdom of migrating to Jamaica. Needless to add, the suggestion was promptly dropped.[56] Once more, however, in an effort to convince Africans that greater advantages were available in Jamaica, Cathcart was asked to print and circulate, if the Sierra Leone government did not object, information pertaining to advantages in Jamaica.[57]

In 1844 the transport again made only two voyages with immigrants

54. Extract, Macdonald to Stanley, Feb. 19, 1844, Fifth General Report of the CL&EC, "Immigration into the West Indies," Ap. 12, *PP,* 1845, XXVII.
55. Stanley to Macdonald, Feb. 10, 1844; Proclamation by the Lt. Gov. Ferguson, Sierra Leone, June 12, 1844, in Papers Relative to Sierra Leone, *PP,* 1845, XXXI:1-2.
56. Darling to Cathcart, Nov. 11, 1843, *Votes,* 1844-1845, Ap. 3, pp.148-149.
57. Ibid.

instead of the anticipated three. Despite the use of delegates and various promotional activities, results were disappointing. One delegate who had attempted to recruit in Liberia met with both indifference and active opposition.[58] It would be interesting to know why and by whom (settler, missionary, or natives) the opposition was promoted, but no further information was offered or requested. It was impossible to secure a full load for the ship, which finally sailed on its third voyage with only 119 emigrants. Presumably the crossing was uneventful; certainly nothing concerning the voyage was recorded. The immigrants were landed at Annotto Bay on March 8, 1844. Of the 89 who were above fourteen years of age, 66 were males, 23 females; of the 30 who were under fourteen, 23 were males, 7 females. Except for three infants, all were classified as laborers; 84 were employed in the parish of Metcalfe, 35 in St. George. Again the employers included men who were of political as well as economic prominence, for they were among those actively involved in seeking a solution to the labor shortage.[59]

As usual, on its return voyage the transport carried several delegates as well as passengers. Agent Cathcart reported passengers and crew in good health upon arrival, but of little help in recruiting. Immediately after landing, delegates and passengers went to their friends in the villages, and for the most part remained there. The Mandingo delegates brought in a few would-be emigrants who were too advanced in years to be acceptable. Three of the delegates tried to be useful, but despite their efforts, few Africans could be persuaded to leave. A total of only 102 agreed to emigrate from the colony to Jamaica. Unless others could be induced to join them, the ship again would be far below a capacity load.

It was at this juncture that a Spanish prize, with 346 Congolese on board, was brought into the harbor. After adjudication, Cathcart was able to enlist 128 of them—78 males and 50 females between the ages of eleven and twenty-five. This success he attributed in part to having given six of the Congolese an inspection tour of the ship to impress them with the arrangements which had been made for their comfort. When these six returned to the Africa yard, they persuaded many of their associates to join with them in the journey to Jamaica. Efforts of both agent and Congolese would have

58. Extract, Cathcart to Darling, Feb. 7, 1844, *Votes,* 1844-1845, Ap. 3, pp.152-153.
59. The employers included the Hon. J. Maxwell, MD, John Thornburn, Henry Westmoreland, and William Hosack. Register of African Immigrants, *Votes,* 1845, E of Ap. 5, pp.121-125.

been useless, however, had not the lieutenant-governor intervened. Aware that horror tales were a device which the Sierra Leoneans were using to prevent emigration, he ordered strict watch over those most recently liberated in order to prevent the inhabitants from getting to them. As a result, the Jamaica agent was somewhat more hopeful of success in recruiting *if,* he emphasized, there was continuance of the system of excluding outsiders from the Africa yard for a certain period after the slaves were emancipated.[60] Cathcart hoped the *Glen Huntley* would be returned promptly in order to be in advance of transports from the other West Indian colonies.[61] His persuasive efforts continued to be successful, and according to his report, 232 emigrants sailed on the fourth voyage of the transport.[62]

Five days after the *Glen Huntley* sailed, it was struck by disaster. For the first time since emigration from Africa was begun, smallpox appeared among the liberated Congolese. Although several days before departure of the ship efforts were made to secure lymph, only a very limited supply was obtained, and in no case was the vaccination successful. The disease spread, and when the transport arrived (August 8) at Lucea, on the northwest of the island, thirty of the passengers were ill. Seemingly three had died en route and two while still on board ship in the Lucea harbor. The vessel was placed in quarantine, medical services were obtained, and a lazaretto was set up at the back of Lucea. Both the unaffected and the convalescent were sent to the lazaretto where they were vaccinated and detained for a time. Nonetheless, the disease appeared there also, and not until mid-October did health and immigration authorities consider that danger of an epidemic had passed. All told, there were fourteen deaths on board and in quarantine. One child died from pleurisy, three persons at the lazaretto from diarrhea, ten from smallpox.[63] With the exception of four domestics, all of the surviving immigrants were classified as laborers. More than fifty percent (114) were under fourteen years of age; of these 90 were boys and 24 were girls. When quarantine was lifted, the survivors were all employed in the parish of Hanover, most of them by various attorneys.[64]

The *Glen Huntley* now presented a problem. Many faults had devel-

60. Cathcart to Darling, July 4, 1844, *Votes,* 1844-1845, Ap. 3, pp.157-158.
61. Ibid., p.159.
62. Ibid., pp.157-158.
63. Darling to Elgin, Oct. 15, 1844, *Votes,* 1844-1845, pp.40-41.
64. Register of African Immigrants, *Votes,* 1845, E of Ap. 5, pp.126-133. Among the nonattorneys, H. E. Walcott employed twelve; Alexander Grant, five; George B. Vidal, seven; and W. B. Mowatt, six.

oped in the structure, some of them such as to make any passengers quite uncomfortable. While the ship was in harbor after the fourth voyage, the works were caulked all around. Many defects, however, could not be remedied so easily, and were in fact so serious as to cause the navy lieutenant (a government appointee with the transport) to question the advisability of using the ship for further voyages. He noted, in reporting to Jamaica authorities, that the copper was becoming defective; the vessel made about ten inches of water in twenty-four hours; and whenever there was heavy or rainy weather, the upper deck leaked, despite repeated repairs. With the next voyage the ship would complete two full years of tropical service. The lieutenant recommended either terminating the contract or sending the vessel to England for overhaul.[65]

The lieutenant's report was a blow to Jamaica. Despite the outbreak of smallpox, with the most recent voyage the long-anticipated flow of emigrants from Africa appeared at last to be developing. Either course proposed by the lieutenant would be disruptive. If the vessel should be sent to drydock, Jamaica would be left for a time without transportation for African emigrants; if it should be discharged there would be delay while another transport was sent out and the Africans learned to identify the new ship with Jamaica. Both the governor and the AGI were anxious not to disturb that emigration. As the *Glen Huntley* was merely uncomfortable, not unseaworthy, they decided to continue its use for one more trip and gave instructions to proceed with its fifth voyage. At the same time they directed the ship's officers to use "every possible means" to prevent the passengers from being "inconvenienced" by the leaky deck.[66]

Several months prior to the incident, Stanley had asked if Jamaica wished to continue employment of the *Glen Huntley*.[67] When this despatch arrived in Jamaica, it was directed to the AGI, who did not put his views into writing until after the *Glen Huntley* had been sent on its way to Africa for another voyage with emigrants. Only then, when it was too late to stop a fifth voyage, did he support the recommendation to send the ship to England for repairs, and in the interim engage another ship which should be sent out at once to Sierra Leone. There would be no delegates with the substitute ship, but as immigrants were mainly Africans recently liberated

65. G. A. Leary to Darling, Oct. 20, 1844, *Votes,* 1845, G of Ap. 5, p.160.
66. Darling to Leary, no.84, Oct. 26, 1844, *Votes,* 1845, Ap. 5, pp.160-161.
67. Stanley to Elgin, no.270, Aug. 26, 1844, in no.204 Jamaica, CO 137/283.

from captured slavers and not residents of Sierra Leone, lack of delegates was thought not to be important.[68] Something more than four months elapsed, however, between the date of Stanley's query and the governor's reply.

The fifth and last voyage of the *Glen Huntley* shattered any illusion of success for emigration under imperial supervision. On March 12, 1845, the transport arrived at Savanna-la-Mar with 42 passengers—approximately twenty percent of its complement—nineteen of them under fourteen years of age. Almost the entire group was classified as laborers, and all were employed in the parish of Westmoreland.[69] It seemed useless to continue the effort. As the imperial government had already modified the arrangement under which the transport was contracted, Elgin, as governor of Jamaica, had authority to decide what course should be followed.[70] By order of the governor, employment of the *Glen Huntley* was terminated, thereby bringing to a close the attempt to promote immigration by imperial supervision.[71]

The undertaking from which Jamaica had hoped for so much, unquestionably had been a complete failure. The island must now decide where to turn for a solution to its labor problem.

68. Memorandum by Darling, enc. in Elgin to Stanley, no.3, Jan. 6, 1845, in no.204 Jamaica, CO 137/285.
69. Register of African Immigrants, *Votes*, 1845, E of Ap. 5, pp.136-138.
70. Darling to Elgin, Oct. 15, 1844, *Votes*, 1844-1845, pp.41-42.
71. Darling to Watt, Mar. 20, 1844 [*sic*, 1845], *Votes*, 1845, Ap. 5, p.16.

6

Review and Reorganization
of the Program

THE BEGINNING OF VOLUNTARY AND LARGE-SCALE
emigration from Africa had appeared to Jamaicans as a certainty on two
occasions. Each time it had proved to be only an illusion. The most recent
undertaking had been with the prestigious supervision of the British government, long famous as a bitter foe of slavery. This crown backing, which
Jamaica had wanted for so long a time, had not made the venture any more
successful than the efforts made by the colony alone. Seemingly every care
had been taken to ensure success: provisions of the Passengers Act were
enforced; license was refused to ships which fell short of standards such as
minimum space between decks; and presumably there had been careful
attention to the welfare of the emigrants, and adherence to all regulations.[1]
Nonetheless, Jamaica, as well as British Guiana and Trinidad, had failed in
the objective. What, actually, had happened?

Recruitment had been centered in Sierra Leone, where delegates had
been expected to give valuable assistance. Some of the delegates who returned in the *Glen Huntley* had been educated in Sierra Leone schools, and
presumably could give an unbiased account of life as an immigrant. Both the
general public and the liberated Africans had been invited by means of a
government notice, to talk with these delegates in order to learn what

1. W. C. Terry, JEA [to Darling], Sierra Leone, no.3, Dec. 30, 1845 [*sic*,
1844], Jan. 7, 1845, in no.733 Jamaica, CO 137/283.

benefits and comforts could be obtained by ordinary industry in the West Indies. In compliance with a directive from Britain, the people were told of the arrival of each emigrant ship.[2] When the Sierra Leone settlers continued to be disinterested, attention was then shifted toward the Africa yard where Negroes rescued from slave ships were being cared for "temporarily." To persuade them to emigrate to the West Indies, they were told (by government proclamation) that clothing and maintenance would be supplied only until there was an opportunity to emigrate to the West Indies, but no longer.[3] However, the notice produced no appreciable results. Cathcart eventually reported that not one of the captured Negroes who had been receiving government allowances for several months was willing to emigrate. They were finally moved out of the yard and located in the villages.[4]

There remained the question of why there had been no increased emigration under imperial supervision. Did the cause lie in factors over which the West Indies had no control? As it became important for Jamaica to know the answer, reports of emigration authorities were studied by officials in Jamaica. These revealed some astonishing information.

For some time the settler population of Sierra Leone had seemed indifferent to emigration; by 1844, they appeared to have become definitely hostile toward it, and expressed their hostility by violence. Delegates were set upon in the streets; emigrants awaiting their transport were robbed by companions who absconded; Sierra Leone magistrates refused to take action against the attackers. The Jamaica agent believed the settler population had suddenly realized the extent to which emigration might deprive them of very cheap labor, and that merchants and shippers of timber feared a loss by reason of increases in the wage rates and demands for payment in cash, not goods. In fact, it was reported that all the local population which lived from exploitation of cheap labor had become opposed to emigration. Moreover, Church and Wesleyan missionaries who were particularly influential with those who had received some education, opposed emigration because they believed it would lessen their own effectiveness and prestige.[5]

2. Government Notice, by command of the Lt. Gov., Freetown, June 12, 1844, in Report of C. H. Darling, AGI, Oct. 15, 1844, *Votes,* 1844-1845, Ap. 3, p.159.
3. Proclamation by William Ferguson, Lt. Gov., Sierra Leone, June 12, 1844, ibid., p.158-159.
4. Cathcart to Darling, Freetown, July 4, 1844, *Votes,* 1844-1845, Ap. 3, pp.157-158.
5. Terry to Darling, Feb. 12, 1845, no.6 in no.733 Jamaica, CO 137/283; Terry [to Darling], no.3, Dec. 30, 1845 [*sic* 1844], CO 137/283.

Jamaica, wanting to know more about conditions than had been provided from accounts by emigration authorities, did not send out its own investigating commission, but was fortunate to receive copies of reports by special agents from other colonies. The governors of Trinidad and British Guiana, in an effort to find an explanation for refusal of Africans to emigrate, appointed two commissioners, R. G. Butts and Robert Guppy, to conduct investigations in Sierra Leone itself. While these agents found the lieutenant governor of Sierra Leone cooperative and public officials in favor of emigration, they came up with accounts of conditions which in some instances were already known but lightly regarded. Their reports were communicated to the Colonial Land and Emigration Commission and were eventually presented to Parliament. Extracts were made available and studied in Jamaica. The Butts-Guppy investigation, although to a large degree a confirmation of conditions already noted by the Jamaica emigration agent, afforded a more detailed explanation for the failure of the West Indies to secure African emigrants, even under the aegis of Great Britain. They cited a general aversion to manual labor, especially field labor, and a preference for hucunstering, even if profits were less than might be obtained from other types of work. In fact, throughout Sierra Leone the people sought a life of ease and tranquility. They were not interested in expending energy to acquire commodities considered as necessities in the West Indies. "Comforts" in Sierra Leone were simple to the extreme. Most houses were wattled, plastered with mud or cow dung and covered with grass. There was a hammock from which the head of the household could issue orders without interrupting his day of lounging. Furniture consisted of a mat or two, a few gourds, a water jug, and an iron pot. Dress, too, was simple. Even in Freetown, the capital, young people of twelve and fourteen went entirely naked; most of the adults, however, wore a large waistcloth, but nothing more. Education and religious instruction were simple. Church and Wesleyan missionaries provided instruction for the general population; government schools supplied it for the newly liberated Africans. Creole children were not taught in the same schools with the newly liberated Africans and did not associate with them as equals.

Manual labor was performed by newly liberated Africans, whose position, despite official classification as apprentice or free laborers, was in reality little different from that of a slave. The old-settlers and headmen had less fortunate people, including apprentices, hanging about and working for subsistence—shelter, a bit of food, and perhaps a waistcloth. Hiring of labor, except by merchants, strangers, or officials, was unknown; wages were seldom paid in money.

Headmen, too, were not inclined to encourage emigration because it might deprive them of their source of cheap labor and decrease the value of their property. When in 1844 the apprenticeship system in Sierra Leone was briefly suspended, the chiefs and headmen became vehement in their opposition to emigration.[6] At the time the commissioner's report was written, a three- to seven-year apprenticeship had been revived with the consent of the governor of Sierra Leone; but there was no means for supervision of the apprentices, who became virtually unprotected slaves of their master.[7] In short, neither settler nor native population of Sierra Leone had any disposition to seek a "more advanced civilization" in the West Indies, nor to want anyone else to do so. They were content with their life in Sierra Leone, where they could live well enough and do so without manual labor.

Liberated Africans, who were so very low on the economic and social scale, did not volunteer to emigrate. One factor in this situation was not surprising to Jamaican officials, for their agent had already alluded to it, namely, revival of the custom of celebrating marriages between entire strangers. Slaves who had been recently liberated from a slave ship were sent to the Africa yard; a man who needed a wife went to the yard, selected a newly liberated female, and took her to the church, where a clergyman married the two. There were very few females left in the yard, and although the practice was regarded as making a travesty of a rite of the church, seemingly no effort was made to prevent it.[8]

Apprentices and "drudges," it was found, were afraid to quit the service of their master, who provided security of a sort. Furthermore, having spent some time on a slave ship, and in some instances having spent even more time on the same ship while it was being taken to a prize court, the Negro en route to liberation sometimes died from the additional rigors of the lengthened voyage. His companions who survived had suffered a traumatic experience and did not forget the terrors of the voyage. In many instances the African had never seen a white man until he was aboard the slave ship; neither the man who helped get him aboard nor the white man

6. Copy of a Report from R. G. Butts to the Governor of British Guiana, March 13, 1845, pp.21-24, in *PP,* 1847-1848, XLIV.
    7. Ibid., p.27.
    8. Ibid., p.23.

on the ship could speak his language; as a result, he was terrified of both a white man and a sea voyage. No tale of horror was beyond his credulity. One story, particularly effective as a deterrent to emigration, recounted that liberated Africans were well fed and cared for on the voyage to the West Indian colonies in order to make their blood rich; when the ship arrived at its destination in the West Indies, the immigrants were taken to a large house where they were hung up by the heels and their throats cut. The blood was used in coloring the soldiers' coats to make them brave warriors and ensure victory. The heads were cut off and boiled to provide medicine which would make "high white men" clever.[9] With such rumors spread about, it was not to be wondered that some Africans refused to board a transport, even to inspect accommodations and provisions.

Certain other factors, which may well have been deterrents, were overlooked by those Jamaicans who attempted to improve recruiting. Seemingly it did not occur to anyone that delegates might report to their friends in Sierra Leone as to the faults of the leaky ship from which they had just debarked. The language barrier, too, was almost ignored. In some instances officials dealing with liberated Africans were unable even to determine the tribe to which the individuals belonged. Assuming the availability of an interpreter, British officials had no way of knowing whether he followed instructions or talked against the colony and emigration.

Neither Butts nor Guppy anticipated a very extensive or long-continued supply of people from Sierra Leone. They did not, however, ascribe failure of recruitment solely to conditions and attitudes among the people themselves. Rather, they found the agents far from blameless, for they had made no effort to develop any systematic procedure. During the months when the transport was on voyage, agents made no effort to interest the people in emigrating. Not until the ship had actually arrived in port to take on passengers was recruiting begun. There was no organized recruiting staff, only an uncertain number of delegates, who frequently were not dependable. Except for inviting the people to talk with those who had just returned, no effort was made to gather an audience for the delegates to work upon.[10] While the program for emigration to the West Indies was

9. Extract of Butts's Report to Gov. Light, Aug. 7, 1844, Ap. 13 in Fifth General Report of the CL&EC, p.39, in *PP*, 1845, XXVII.
10. Copy of a Report by R. G. Butts and Robert Guppy, as Commissioners of Enquiry into the Subject of Emigration from Sierra Leone to the West Indies, July 7-23, 1844, in *PP*, 1847-1848, XLV.

hampered to some degree by factors beyond the control of Jamaica or any of the West Indian colonies, it was not entirely so, and reorganization of the recruiting program was obviously needed.

In England, also, there had been some skepticism about the program even while it appeared to be gaining momentum. When it met with so little acceptance in Africa, the Colonial Office undertook its own review in an effort to find ways for improvement. It arrived at recommendations quite different from those of the two West Indian investigators. Emigration officials, it noted, seemed numerous in proportion to the number of emigrants, and cost per emigrant was high; there needed to be changes in the agency for collecting emigrants and in the manner of conveying them to the West Indies. One move in that direction was made when the CL&EC closed the Government Emigration Agency at Sierra Leone as a separate office, and assigned its duties to the Collector of Customs. To compensate the latter for the additional work, £150 was added to his salary, with the amount apportioned among the three colonies receiving immigrants, Jamaica, British Guiana, and Trinidad.[11] As a further move toward economy, when the use of government transports was abandoned, the West India colonies gave up their separate collecting agents and agreed to a single agent at Sierra Leone to serve all three colonies. To the governor of Sierra Leone was assigned the unpleasant task of notifying the colonial agents of termination of their services. The new official, to be known as the West Indian Agent for Emigration, would be paid a salary of £300 per annum (to be borne equally by the three West Indian colonies) with an additional sum of $1.00 per head for each emigrant received in the colony. He was not to receive any further remuneration but was expected to have assistance from some subordinates.[12] For protection of the emigrants, however, the office of government emigration agent was soon revived, and the governor of Sierra Leone was assigned the task of general and overall supervision.[13] The costly system of delegates, which had been inaugurated in anticipation of a large emigration by settler population and tribesmen, and used for some four years, was now recognized as useless and was abandoned.

11. Fourth General Report of the CL&EC, "Immigration from Africa to the West Indies," p.14, in *PP,* 1844, XXXI.
12. Elgin to Stanley, June 12, 1845, no.53, CO 137/284; Stanley to Elgin, Aug. 15, 1845, no.356 (copy), *Votes,* 1845, pp.28-29; Stanley to Elgin, Aug. 15, 1845, no.357, CO 137/283.
13. Sixth General Report of the CL&EC, Apr. 30, 1846, in *PP,* 1846, XXIV.

Shipping expenses, too, were scrutinized in an effort to find areas for further reduction of cost, perhaps in personnel. When the decision was made to require both a navy lieutenant and a surgeon for each emigrant ship, large numbers of passengers had been anticipated. In reality, emigrant loads were small. If African passengers were placed under the sole charge of the surgeon, as was the custom on convict vessels, there would be the additional saving of one salary. General approval of the proposal brought an end to the requirement of a navy lieutenant, in addition to a surgeon, on every transport carrying emigrants.[14]

Small economies, however, were not enough. When success for the program of government supervision appeared so doubtful during the first year of the experiment, authorities in England deemed it inadvisable to continue contracting for vessels on a twelve-month basis. Rather, the West Indian governor, on the scene and immediately informed of the results of a voyage, was the official best qualified to determine whether or not it was wise to continue the transport in service and send it on another trip to Africa. Consequently, in the second year of the experiment, it was agreed by all concerned to replace the policy of contract for a year with a "contract terminable at once on notice by the governor."[15]

Although African emigrants were too few to justify maintaining the transports, some provision was necessary for enabling the West Indian colonies to obtain emigrants from Sierra Leone whenever they were available. Delay and expense would be too great if ships, sent only from Britain, were not ordered until there was a load ready and waiting. The best solution, it was decided, was to add to the duties of the West Indies emigration agent and leave it to him to hire a suitable British ship (foreign ships were not permitted) on the spot at Sierra Leone whenever there was a sufficient number of emigrants to justify such action. When he had made certain of the seaworthiness of the vessel and of its compliance with provisions of the Passengers' Act, he should apply to the governor of Sierra Leone for a license. These emigrant ships were to be despatched in rotation to Jamaica, British Guiana, and Trinidad, in that order; but payment would be by

14. Fifth General Report of the CL&EC, Mar. 20, 1845, "Immigration into the West Indies," p.18, in *PP*, 1845, XXVII: Memorandum by Darling, enc. in Elgin to Stanley, no.3, Jan. 6, 1845, in no.204 Jamaica, CO 137/283.

15. See chap. 5 above. Darling to Wall, Mar. 20, 1845; G. A. Leary to Darling, Oct. 20, 1844, *Votes*, 1845, Ap. 5, pp.160-161; Fourth General Report of the CL&EC, p.14, in *PP*, 1844, XXI.

bounty. In the case of Jamaica, it was set at seven pounds sterling per adult landed alive, and half that sum for each child, provided conditions of the Passengers' Act were met. The arrangement was a distinct advantage to Jamaica, which thus would pay only for what it actually received.[16] Transportation of emigrants was limited to ships licensed for that purpose by the governor of Sierra Leone. Two objectives might be attained by such restriction: a full load would be assured to the designated ships, and any foreigner who might wish to engage in the slave trade would be excluded. As a further move to forestall any possibility of illegal trade by interlopers, Elgin, as governor of the receiving colony, was instructed not to pay bounty for an emigrant sent by any other means.[17]

Reappraisal of the program of Negro immigration necessitated a review also of results from areas other than Sierra Leone. For instance, there was St. Helena, which had been and continued to be uncertain as a source of labor. Briefly, in 1842, this branch of African emigration had given promise of becoming an important collateral in the general scheme, but within a matter of months few liberated Africans remained there. It seemed logical when a Court of Mixed Commission was established at the Cape of Good Hope (early in 1843) for captured Africans to be taken there for adjudication rather than to St. Helena. Despite this, by mid-year the number of captured Africans reportedly had increased at St. Helena. Jamaica officials, alert to any possible opportunity for securing additional laborers, were hampered by lack of personal acquaintance in St. Helena and looked for advice in London. There the investigation was handled by Commissioner Burge, who first verified through the Colonial Office the accuracy of the report. His next move was to contact John Ranken, a merchant who knew something of Africa and whose mercantile firm had been connected with the Africa trade. Ranken was willing to give assistance, and with Burge chartered the 422-ton *Salsette* to take emigrants from St. Helena to Jamaica. Terms of the contract stipulated that the *Salsette* would comply with all provisions of the Passengers' Act and of government regulations pertaining to clothing and medical attendance. Proper supplies were either scarce or

16. C. H. Darling, Report upon Immigration into Jamaica, Oct. 28, 1845, *Votes,* 1845, p.84. The victualling scale for ships carrying African emigrants had been revised: *per day*—rice, 1½ lb.; beef and pork or salt fish, ¼ lb.; lime juice, ½ oz.; sugar, 2 oz.; water, 1 gal.; *per week*—vinegar, ½ pt.; palm oil, 1½ gil; salt, 2 oz.; African pepper, 2 oz. Stanley to Elgin, Aug. 15, 1845, no.356 (copy), ibid., p.31.

17. Ibid., pp.28-31.

completely unobtainable in St. Helena so the ship would have to be equipped and provisioned in England. Both vessel and provisions were to be inspected in London by the government agent there. Duration of the voyage was fixed at eight weeks, which meant the *Salsetts* must carry 58 days' provisions per person—56 days for the voyage, with forty-eight additional hours in harbor at Jamaica. Costs of transportation were to be paid by Jamaica from the island immigration fund. The owner of the ship, which was certified to carry 206 adult passengers, was to be paid at the rate of £7 per adult landed in Jamaica, but guaranteed £600 for expenses if no emigrants were secured. If there were any emigrants at all, however, the master could charge for half the maximum number which the vessel was licensed to carry. Additional ships could either be sent out from England or hired by the agent on the spot in St. Helena.[18]

Jamaica had wanted its own agent for collecting emigrants at St. Helena because it feared a common agent would give preference and unfair advantage to other colonies, but Stanley and the CL&EC ruled against it on the ground of needless expense and competition. One agent, they had decided, should serve Jamaica, as well as British Guiana and Trinidad. Governor Elgin tactfully concurred, but reflected the concern of Jamaica when he stressed the importance of impartiality and official control of such an agent. Elgin also pledged to pay Jamaica's share of the official's salary if the legislature continued to leave to the governor the expenditure of immigration funds.[19]

The *Salsette* remained at St. Helena for the full twenty-one days permitted by contract for taking on passengers. It secured 200 persons, but by computation, only 177 statutory adults; in other words, it lacked 29 adults of having the full load of 206 for which it was certified. The captain wanted to extend his stay in port in order to have time for recruiting additional passengers. However, St. Helena officials, determined to protect the health of those Africans already on board, were adamant in their refusal to concede any extension of time in port. In compliance with their orders, the captain put to sea without further delay.[20]

Although accounts of the voyage itself are not available, there was no loss of life; in fact, two infants, born during the crossing, were alive when

18. Fourth General Report of the CL&EC, pp.16-17, in *PP*, 1844, XXXI.
19. Elgin to Stanley, Nov. 2, 1843, no.2269, CO 137/275.
20. William Hyleak to Capt. Ronan, Dec. 28, 1843, in no.566, Jamaica, CO 137/278.

the ship arrived in Jamaica. As directed by Jamaica officials, the ship proceeded to Savanna-la-Mar to land its passengers, February 6, 1844. They were described as a "fine lot," with approximately twenty-five percent under fourteen years of age.[21] All of them were promptly employed in the parish of Westmoreland, more than half by one man, the Honorable T. McNeal of Caledonia estate.[22]

It seemed doubtful, however, whether there would be many more immigrants from St. Helena. In February, Stanley had directed a large number of liberated African children to be sent to Jamaica; yet none arrived because they had been sent elsewhere before the instructions reached officials in St. Helena.[23] The mistake could not be remedied by sending the next group to Jamaica, for the Admiralty had instructed their officers not to take captured Negroes to St. Helena under any circumstances. This seemed to mean an end to the policy of liberating Africans in that small island, and the emigration agency at St. Helena was discontinued.[24]

Africa was not the only continent from which Negro emigration seemed possible. In the western hemisphere, Canada had a Negro population reputedly skilled and accustomed to handling agricultural tools, hence it might be particularly useful should Jamaica change its methods of cultivation. The island maintained a salaried agent in Canada for a time, and repeatedly received optimistic reports of Negroes who were interested in Jamaica and would emigrate in the near future. Few of them, however, ever left Canada. Jamaica was told on one occasion of 400 people ready to embark; it was five months later when they arrived, and instead of 400, there were 35, some of whom were delegates. Under these conditions it seemed futile to continue the expense of a salaried agent; but in the event that any of the Negroes in Canada should decide to emigrate, some official was needed to direct them to the Island. It was agreed that Jamaica's representative should continue to have authority to recruit emigrants, but would no longer be salaried. His compensation thereafter would be only in proportion to the benefit Jamaica received, that is, his remuneration would be on the basis of the actual number of immigrants who arrived in Jamaica.[25]

21. H. A. Whitelock, subagent, to Darling, Savanna-la-Mar, Feb. 6, 1844, ibid.
22. Register of African Emigrants, Oct. 28, 1845, *Votes,* 1845, Ap. 5, pp.114-121.
23. Stanley to Elgin, Mar. 12, 1845, no.324, CO 138/66.
24. Elgin to Stanley, Feb. 22, 1844, no.28, in no.566, Jamaica, CO 137/278; Darling to Elgin, Report, Oct. 15, 1844, *Votes,* 1844-1845, p.42.
25. Report of Darling, AGI, Oct. 28, 1845, *Votes,* 1845, p.85. Darling to

Cuba became a better source of immigrants than Canada. To the Court of Mixed Commission at Havana, prizes could be taken. Jamaica officials seemed either ignorant of its existence or indifferent, until one of the Jamaica newspapers carried a notice suggesting the possibility of obtaining the services of Africans liberated by this court. The notice caught the attention of Governor Elgin, who directed the AGI to enquire as to their availability for Jamaica. The Colonial Office, it was soon learned, had named the government of Jamaica as one which would defray transportation costs of these Africans, and was therefore entitled to preference, along with Trinidad and British Guiana. With that information, Jamaica officials requested the superintendent of liberated Africans at Havana either to engage vessels there or to utilize occasional space in ships bound for Jamaica. Jamaica was so eager to secure the services of these people that the AGI authorized their shipment without first securing an estimate of the cost per head. He suggested Montego Bay as the port most accessible from Havana, but hoped it would be possible to use Kingston or some other southside port occasionally. Just as it did for ships bringing immigrants from Africa, Jamaica reserved the right to require the master to keep his passengers on board and maintain them for forty-eight hours after the vessel anchored in a Jamaica port. And in order to permit the subagent adequate time to prepare for them, the AGI requested advance notice of both departure and destination of the vessel.[26] Prospects that many immigrants would come from Havana were slim, however, for there seemingly were no prizes taken into Cuba during 1844, and admittedly the number decreased as Britain proceeded with the policy of extinguishing the slave trade at its source.[27]

When the captain-general of Cuba placed *emancipados,* too, at the disposal of the superintendent of liberated Africans at Havana, it was decided that steam packets, making the monthly trip from Havana to Jamaica, were the most practical for their transportation. The number per trip varied from a low of 4 to a high of 48, but the total per year did not exceed 200. They were located in the parishes of St. Mary, St. Andrew, Port Royal, and

Dunscomb, Jan. 27, 1845; Dunscomb to Darling, June 28, 1844; *Votes,* 1845, Ap. 5, p.168-171.

26. Darling to Lt. Robert McClure, RN, Supt. Liberated Africans, Havana, Apr. 1, 1844; McClure to Darling, Apr. [n.d.], 1844; Darling to McClure, May 27, 1844; all in Elgin to Stanley, June 4, 1844, no.74, CO 137/279.

27. Report of C. H. Darling, AGI, Oct. 15, 1844, *Votes,* 1844-1845, Ap. 3, pp.142-143.

St. Thomas-in-the-Vale—only part of them convenient to entry through the Kingston area.[28]

Darling's official report for the year ending September 30, 1845 was submitted to the assembly soon after that body convened in October. Immigration for the year had been costly, he emphasized—531 immigrants with the average expenditure of seventeen pounds sterling per immigrant, not including the *emancipados* from Cuba.[29] Part of the expense was attributable to the *Glen Huntley,* which had cost Jamaica no less than £2500 in its last six months of service, yet had brought only forty-two immigrants.[30] Darling questioned the real advantages or prestige of having a ship identified as the Jamaica transport when immigrants on its last voyage were so few.[31]

Not everyone in Jamaica agreed that immigrant labor was needed; a few definitely objected to it. Some of labor's friends opposed not only immigration but also field work, which was vital to the economy of the colony and the particular phase of sugar cultivation for which immigrants were sought. These humanitarians regarded field work as degrading because of its earlier association with slavery.[32] When efforts were made to introduce agricultural education as a means of furthering the island's economy, one group, through the *Baptist Herald,* even depicted it as something designed merely to keep agricultural laborers in a lowly state.[33] Two petitions against importation of laborers were presented to the House of Assembly. One was from "certain inhabitants" of the parish of Hanover, the other from "certain persons united in the Association of the Baptist Western Union." Both opposed any plan of immigration which would be supported by general taxation or loan; they asserted no additional laborers were needed, and they objected to importation of coolies.[34] Unfortunately, names were not recorded for these or many other petitions, regardless of the views which they expressed.

28. Report of the AGI, Oct. 23, 1845, *Votes,* 1845, pp.84-85; Return of Immigrants into the Island of Jamaica, Oct. 16, 1844-Oct. 27, 1845, *Votes,* 1845, B of Ap. 5, p.103. On a very limited scale, importation of Europeans under the bounty system was resumed in 1845. Public Notice, Feb. 27, 1845, *Votes,* 1845, I of Ap. 5, p.185.

29. Darling, Third Annual Report upon Immigration into Jamaica, Oct. 28, 1845, *Votes,* 1845, pp.81-82.

30. Ibid., p.83.

31. Ibid., p.84.

32. Elgin to Stanley, Confidential, Aug. 5, 1845, CS 102/12, Series 1845.

33. Ibid.

34. *Votes,* 1845, pp.139, 326-327.

Meanwhile, in keeping with his duties as governor, Elgin had sent confidential reports to London. Despite some improvement in the economy, he was doubtful of prospects for Jamaica's recovery. Crops were still far short of those produced during slavery. Financial embarassment and ruin had spread to an extraordinary extent, with the list of bankruptcies unusually long.[35] Elgin did not oppose immigration, but neither would he rely upon it alone to solve the labor problem. His proposals were of too long range to be immediately helpful to the colony, for he wished to create among laborers a desire for goods obtainable only by money, for which they would need to hire themselves out; and to remove the stigma attached to field work by developing pride in the skills requisite for modernized methods of cultivation. Planters were introducing use of fertilizers and of such tools as the plough. To encourage adoption of these innovations, they sponsored lectures, ploughing contests, and the like, and organized agricultural societies.[36] Moreover, because of this interest in new methods of cultivation, Elgin believed that employers no longer had faith in immigration as the panacea for the island.[37]

Planter interests, on the other hand, were hopeful of economic recovery, and found some basis for that hope. The sugar crop was better than in the preceding year, and over most of the island prospects for the next year were encouraging. When Elgin delivered his speech at the opening of the 1845 session of the Legislature, he was careful not to dispell their optimism. He struck a correctly cheerful tone, and in no way suggested the skepticism that his confidential reports had reflected. After referring to improvement in the crops, he noted that many people still believed immigration was indispensable to the development of Jamaica's resources.[38] He cited as evidence petitions from "proprietors and others" from many parts of the colony, including the parishes of Hanover, St. Elizabeth, and St. Mary, wanting immigrant laborers as the only means of bringing prosperity back to Jamaica.[39] Because African immigration was inadequate for Jamaica's needs, interest had already been directed toward other possible sources of labor, and the recent petitions asked for coolie laborers as well as African immigrants.

35. Elgin to Stanley, Sept. 23, 1845, Confidential, CS 102/12, Series 1845.
36. Elgin to Stanley, Aug. 5, 1845, ibid.
37. Ibid., CS 102/12, Series 1845.
38. Address by the Governor, Oct. 21, 1845, *Votes,* 1845, pp.6-7.
39. Ibid., pp.127-129, 225-227.

Immigration from India had been reopened, and the West India interests in England had placed with the Colonial Office an order for 5,000 coolies for the first shipping season. The Jamaica assembly was more cautious: it provided funds for transportation of the 5,000, but by resolution made known its opinion that the experiment should be on a much smaller scale, with a maximum of 2,000. It requested countermanding of the larger order, if possible. Only a few of the coolies had arrived when the AGI wrote his report for the year.[40] The coolies did not "blend into the Jamaica scene" as did the Africans, but the island was in need of any and all laborers.[41] Planters, anticipating further economic improvement, filed with the AGI offers for employment of nearly 8,000 coolies, including those already engaged.[42] The Legislature passed the measures necessary to continue the immigration program for another year, and in addition authorized raising a loan of £45,000 for the same purpose.[43] There was a spirit of optimism prevailing when the session closed in late December, 1845; it was destined, however, to be dispelled quite abruptly within a matter of months.

40. Darling, Report of the AGI, Oct. 28, 1845, ibid., p.86.
41. Ibid., p.87.
42. Ibid., p.84.
43. Ibid., p.534.

7

Free Trade, the Sugar Producers, and a Change in Immigration Policies

JAMAICA CONTINUED TO PREFER AFRICAN LABOR although it had become clear that she could not depend upon it alone. During the year ending September 30, 1846, Negro immigration virtually ceased. No immigrants came from Sierra Leone; 126 Africans, all of whom had been liberated from slave ships captured by British cruisers, were brought from St. Helena; 163 *emancipados* arrived from Cuba, where the British member of the Court of Mixed Commission at Havana now served as superintendent of liberated Africans, and from Jamaica funds was paid 5 shillings for every immigrant for Jamaica.[1] Thirty-nine of the St. Helena immigrants were assigned in Westmoreland to the Honorable Thomas McNeel, of Caledonia. Presumably they were the 39 Africans landed at Lucea in February by the *Mandarin,* which had called at St. Helena en route from India with a cargo of coolies. Only one other load of Africans was brought from St. Helena during the year. Eighty-seven were taken to Port Maria by the *Nelson,* which carried only Africans. All, in lots ranging from one to 21, were employed in the parish of St. Mary in the north of the Island.[2] Throughout the year, royal mail steamers coming from Havana

1. Darling to Lt. Gov. Berkeley, Dec. 16, 1846, in *Votes,* 1846-1847, p.178.
2. "A Return of Immigrants into the Island of Jamaica, Oct. 1, 1845–Sept. 30, 1846," in *Votes,* 1846-1847, Ap. 14, p.151; "A List of African Immigrants from St. Helena," ibid., p.157.

brought *emancipados* in numbers ranging from a low of 13 to a high of 20. All were landed in Kingston, and over half of them were employed by W. M. Anderson of Preston, in the parish of St. Mary.[3] The basis for selecting employers is not clear. The high percentage of *emancipados* assigned to Anderson and of liberated Africans to McNeel would indicate that, at least in those instances, proximity to port of entry was not a determining factor. Only a small portion of Jamaica's expenditures for immigration purposes was for these Africans from St. Helena—£841 out of £30,100.[4] Records of expenditures for *emancipados* are not available. With additional African laborers virtually unobtainable, Jamaica turned more definitely to the use of coolies from India. Almost 2,000 arrived during the year.[5]

It is necessary now, however, to give some attention to events in London; for just as the Jamaica legislature was concluding its session in December, 1845, there began a series of British political developments which were to have lasting effects on Jamaica. Sir Robert Peel and his ministry were faced with the necessity of providing relief measures for Ireland, where failure of the potato crop had caused a severe famine. They were not in agreement as to how this relief should be accomplished. Ultimately, Peel and his ministry continued in office, but Stanley was lost. He was succeeded at the Colonial Office by William E. Gladstone.[6]

The Tories had long supported the principle of high import duties in order to protect domestic products from foreign competition. In January, 1846, however, Prime Minister Peel explained in parliament that his views had undergone a great change and he no longer would support the principle of protection. He proposed to relax the protective duties, and to do so without partiality to any group. It would require sacrifice, he warned, from all interests—manufacturing, commercial, and agricultural.[7] The West India sugar interests realized that they were among those from whom great "sacrifice" would be required.

Planting interests had long been unhappy with the results derived from recruiting free laborers in Africa. Now, while the tariff controversy

---

3. "A Return of Immigrants into the Island of Jamaica . . . ," ibid., p.151; "A List of Employers of Emancipado Immigrants," ibid., p.156.

4. Ibid., p.152.

5. Ibid. Nine Europeans were brought in for a bounty of £90.

6. William E. Gladstone was Secretary of State for the Colonies, Dec., 1845-July, 1846.

7. Great Britain, Parliament, *Hansard's Parliamentary Debates,* 3d ser., vol.83 (1846), cc.239-285 (hereinafter cited as *Hansard*).

rocked parliament and the country, the West India Committee and the Colonial Land and Emigration Commission studied the problems of emigration from Africa to the West Indies. If they could find the flaws in the existing policies and regulations, and then bring about the needed corrections, large-scale emigration from Africa might become a reality. The West India Committee wanted changes in many of the current practices. For example, there was no central contracting agency. Ships might be chartered in the West Indies, in Africa, or in Britain. Consequently, too many ships arrived at an African port in proportion to the number of emigrants, and the colonies were unhappy with the distribution of the laborers. To alleviate the situation, the CL&EC proposed that emigrant ships for Africa should be chartered only in England and by a single agency, the CL&EC. Emigrants from Sierra Leone would be restricted to these ships, which would be sent to Jamaica, British Guiana, and Trinidad in rotation. If this policy was to become effective, the CL&EC needed active cooperation from the West India Committee. To that body would be assigned such responsibilities as finding and recommending ships for license, recommending suitable intervals between the calls at Sierra Leone; and sending the ships in proper rotation to the three colonies.[8] In short, success of the new proposals for African emigration was predicated upon assistance by the West India Committee.

But would that body cooperate? In an attempt to resolve the question the Colonial Office notified it of the proposed changes and of Gladstone's willingness to approve them. It also asked the committee for definite assurance that it would perform whatever tasks were assigned to it.[9]

The West India Committee was in no hurry to give a firm reply. Its immediate objective was a modification of restrictions on contracts-for-service made outside the West Indian colonies. Furthermore, the committee was exceedingly sensitive to anything which might be in the nature of adverse criticism of West Indian policy. When in the course of the correspondence it seemed to be accused of trying to revive a form of slave trade, it was enraged by the implication. It then became sharply critical of Britain's policy toward her West Indian colonies and professed astonishment at any attempt to "vindicate the restrictions" to which Britain adhered.

8. T. Frank Elliot and C. Alexander, CL&EC, to James Stephen, Mar. 31, 1846, *Votes,* 1846-1847, Ap. 2, p.82.
9. Lyttleton to Macgregor, Apr. 27, 1846, ibid.

They were utterly indefensible, charged the committee: as suffering parties the members could not "acquiesce in ascribing any humane character" to laws which produced an artificial scarcity of labor, grievous injury to the landowners, even irretrievable ruin to some. The committee angrily proclaimed its inability to understand how importation of hired servants could possibly be confused with importation of slaves.[10] The members soon were somewhat mollified by assurance that they had misinterpreted the communication.[11]

Weeks passed, however, without a direct reply from the West India Committee regarding the particular question of cooperation. It wanted more than the CL&EC was offering. What the West India Committee now wanted was removal of prohibition against recruitment of Africans in territories beyond the boundaries of British Africa. Using the longstanding argument of "benefit to Africa as well as to the West Indian Colonies and to the cause of abolition," the committee contended that Her Majesty's government should afford the British West Indies "every facility for obtaining additional labor," rather than imposing restraints. As further support for its proposal to extend the recruiting area, the West India Committee asserted," . . . as there never could be any doubt with regard to the effect which the successful cultivation of the British colonies in a state of freedom would have upon slavery and the slave trade, the committee have always felt the utmost surprise that the desire to procure additional labour, without which it can not be accomplished should in any way be discouraged."[12] Africa was the most logical source for this labor, it contended, and immigrants from there were more likely than others to become permanent settlers.[13]

The committee was fully aware that many in Britain would object to the proposal and might even equate it with revival of the slave trade. To anticipate such a charge and rob it of any effectiveness, the committee set up a series of premises which it then demolished, at least to its own satisfaction, with refutations:

> *Premise:* As slavery was general throughout Africa, there would be no emigrants unless they were purchased. *Refutation:* Freedom prevailed in extensive districts in Africa; it was impossible for slavery to exist in any British territory.

10. Macgregor to Gladstone, Apr. 9, 1846, ibid., pp.77-80.
11. Lyttleton to Macgregor, Apr. 22, 1846, ibid., pp.80-81.
12. Macgregor to Gladstone, June 17, 1846, *Votes,* 1846-1847, Ap. 2, p.90.
13. Ibid.

Premise: Emigration would of necessity assume the character of a disguised slave trade. *Refutation:* Slave trading was impossible if the emigrant embarked from a British settlement; no emigrant ship could clear from a British settlement except in conformity with the Passengers' Act.

Premise: Introduction of large numbers of barbarous people, recently freed by prize courts, would lower the moral condition of the West Indian laboring population. *Refutation:* West Indian negroes were Christianized; past experience had proved that liberated Africans were absorbed into the West Indian population.

Premise: Foreign powers would be jealous and might claim the fight to carry emigrants to their possessions. *Refutation:* These powers could not justly claim an equal right to convey emigrants to their possessions until they conferred equal freedom on their inhabitants.[14]

The West India Committee went so far as to hint that by earlier restrictions on emigration from Sierra Leone, Her Majesty's government had implied distrust of those conducting emigration and thereby hampered it. Perhaps, suggested the committee, the greatest cause for disinterest in emigration was the low condition of the people in Africa and absence of any wish to improve it; perhaps what was needed was more definite assurance of good employment in the West Indies. This could be provided, they said, in the form of contracts made in Africa. Such a device, which might also serve as a spur to those who were recruiting emigrants, was one which the British government had adamantly opposed on the basis that it would offer an opportunity for virtual slave trading. As a matter of fact, the West India Committee offered a startling four-point program:

1. Contracts for service in the West Indies should be valid if made in any British settlement or in the Kru country, on the west coast of Africa, under the same conditions as contracts made in countries other than Africa or India.

2. Free emigration should be permitted directly from these places to the West Indian colonies, with remuneration for conveyance at the same rate as for emigration from Sierra Leone.

3. Emigration agents should be appointed at each of the

14. A. Macgregor to W. E. Gladstone, June 17, 1846, ibid., pp.89-92.

recruiting stations and paid at the per capita rate, except at Sierra Leone and in the Kru country.

4. Official instructions should be given to remove to the West Indies all Africans who might be liberated at Sierra Leone.[15]

Following this proposal, the tone of the correspondence became quite sharp. Gladstone accused the West India Committee not only of evading the original question, but of poor reasoning. How, he asked, would contracts stimulate emigration if, as the committee alleged, the people had no desire to improve their condition?[16] The West India Committee "respectfully" retorted it could not ascribe the limited amount of emigration exclusively to the low condition of the people, and charged that more important were the restrictions imposed by Her Majesty's government. It wanted the governor of Sierra Leone to issue a proclamation explaining to the people the advantages of emigration as presented in the 1842 select committee report. Only in this way, it asserted, could any seeming mistrust by Her Majesty's government be dispelled. Furthermore, maintained the West India Committee, misunderstanding would be impossible under the conditions which it proposed: contracts, made in Africa before a representative of Her Majesty's government; option for the emigrant to change employment; and payment at the current rate of wages in the colony if that should be higher than the one specified in his contract.[17]

The committee still ignored the query as to whether it concurred with the proposal to send ships only from England to convey Sierra Leone emigrants. More than two months had passed without a direct answer. Gladstone grew impatient and, in the absence of a direct no, informed the committee he would assume its concurrence in the proposals. He also reminded the members that authorities in Sierra Leone were already aware of the government's desire to publicize advantages offered to emigrants in the West Indies. Nonetheless, the governor of Sierra Leone would be advised to use every means of information and "legitimate persuasion" to encourage the people to emigrate.[18] But the secretary remained skeptical of any appreciable increase in emigration and rejected the committee's proposals for

15. Ibid.
16. Lyttleton to Macgregor, June 27, 1846, ibid., p.92.
17. Macgregor to Gladstone, June 29, 1846, ibid., pp.93-94.
18. Lyttleton to Macgregor, July 4, 1846, ibid., p.94.

contracts.[19] These exchanges between the West India Committee on the one hand, and the CL&EC and the Colonial Office on the other, occurred while Parliament and political parties were beset by the tariff issue. And more and more, tariff was becoming of vital concern to the British West Indies.

It was not the sugar duties but the corn laws that were the immediate target of Peel and his ministry. For fifty years they had been the linchpin for the whole system of protective tariffs, which now could be expected to collapse. The sugar duties (vital to the Jamaica economy because they gave West Indian sugar preference in the British market) had not been dealt with when the Peel cabinet resigned as the result of defeat on an Irish measure.

The new Prime Minister was Lord John Russell, who had for some years been advocating equalization of the sugar duties. As the Anti-Corn Law League (a well-financed and well-organized pressure group whose views Russell shared) had just staged a great victory in obtaining the abolition of the corn laws, a bill relaxing the high tariff on foreign sugar was expected to follow immediately. On assuming office, Russell announced adherence to a policy of general benefit to all interests of the country; but it was late in the session (July 20) when the ministry's sugar duties bill was introduced. Although the high rate of protection for British colonial sugar had been reduced in 1844, (63s. per hundredweight on foreign, free-grown sugar; reduced in 1844 to 34s. per hundredweight; 24s. per hundredweight on British colonial sugar) slave-grown sugar presumably was excluded from the British market. Now, alleging a domestic consumer demand too great for the British colonies alone to meet, and asserting the right of people to buy in the cheapest markets without reference to the manner of production, Russell proposed what he said would be a permanent settlement for all interests, whether consumer, producer, or financial. He advocated ending all protection of British sugar. To cushion the blow for the colonies, he would decrease the differential annually so that after July 1, 1851, the duty would be the same for colonial and all foreign sugar, including slave-grown.[20] In other words, Russell's measure not only would remove any preference for British sugar as opposed to foreign, but would also throw it into unrestricted competition with any that was slave-grown. Hitherto such a policy had been considered contrary to general principles in Great Britain, where it

19. Gladstone to Macdonald, July 4, 1846, ibid., p.98.
20. *Hansard,* 3d ser., vol.87 (1846), cc.1304-1313.

was believed that slave-grown sugar could be produced more cheaply than free-labor sugar, hence should be barred from the British market.

As compensation for withdrawal of protection, Russell announced, the government proposed to facilitate the introduction of free labor into the West Indies by permitting one-year contracts-for-service to be made with Negroes in Sierra Leone or other British settlements in Africa. The government had refused, said Russell, to permit similar agreements in African areas which were not under British jurisdiction.[21] Permitting contracts-for-service to be signed in Africa was an extraordinary change in policy. Hitherto the British government had been adamant in its requirement that any contract with an African for service in a West Indian colony must be signed only within the colony.

Debate in Parliament became acrimonious. Opponents of the Sugar Duties Bill charged it would be a stimulus to the slave trade and tartly suggested that, if the government would give confidence to the British planters and security to investment of capital in the sugar plantations, the British colonies could produce ample supplies of sugar for consumption in the United Kingdom. All that was needed to accomplish this was an adequate supply of labor.[22] Peel, now in opposition, hoped the government might find it possible to give some advantages to West Indian proprietors to enable them to compete with proprietors who had slave labor at their command. He did not oppose importation of foreign free-labor sugar, but he did not approve of this measure, particularly the admission of slave-grown sugar. Those views notwithstanding, he voted for the measure rather than have a government again tipped from office.[23] Before the close of August, the Sugar Duties Bill had been hurried through both houses of Parliament and had received the royal assent. It was another blow to the economy of Jamaica, for it would have the effect within a few years of depriving that colony's sugar of any preference in the British market.

In the meantime, when the Russell ministry came into office, Earl Grey had succeeded Gladstone at the Colonial Office (July, 1846). The West India Committee continued to insist upon changes in the rules and regulations pertinent to recruitment of free laborers in Africa. It repeated its demand for the Colonial Office to permit agents in Africa to conclude there

21. Ibid., c.1314.
22. Ibid., vol.88 (1846), cc.32-53.
23. Ibid., cc.93-103.

contracts-for-service in the West Indies. Contracts made in any of the British settlements in Africa, or in the parts of West Coast Africa not under British jurisdiction, should be valid, they argued, if made under the same conditions which were approved for contracts made in other countries.[24] Their proposals, however, exceeded those to which Russell as Prime Minister had said he could agree.

Grey, for his part, was reassuring up to a point. He asserted that he realized the importance of providing every lawful and proper means for the West Indian planters to obtain an adequate supply of free labor; and he professed to believe the committee's proposal was in the interest of world-wide humanity, as well as of the planters. Nonetheless, he could not concur with most of their proposals. He restated the position indicated to Parliament by Russell on July 20. The government would have no objection to contracts for labor concluded in Africa if: they were for no more than one year, were under the superintendence of government agents, and were in compliance with regulations for similar contracts made elsewhere than in Africa. Having also said he would sanction those contracts primarily in deference to the wishes of the West India Committee, he then delivered the blow: he was convinced they would lead only to constant disputes between employers and employees, and to unwilling service. To support his position he cited difficulties with indentured laborers in New South Wales and with coolies in Mauritius.[25] On the other hand, Earl Grey was willing to encourage emigration from any British settlement in Africa, with remuneration at the same rate as from Sierra Leone. But payment must not be at a rate per head on emigrants. In the case of the Kru coast, where there were no British settlements, he would welcome any suggestions which the West India Committee might offer. Their proposals must, of course, include adequate securities against abuse. Recruiting could not be extended to any tribe where slavery existed, or to individuals lacking freedom of choice. Otherwise, although emigration might be beneficial to the individual, it would lead to revival of the barbarities and warfare associated with the slave trade.

Her Majesty's government believed emigration was advantageous for liberated Africans at Sierra Leone, but assumed no authority to compel them to leave. The governor of Sierra Leone had already been advised to do everything legally possible to further emigration. For the same reason, he

24. Macgregor to Earl Grey, Aug. 12, 1846, *Votes,* 1846-1847, Ap. 2, p.95.
25. B. Hawes to A. Macgregor, Aug. 29, 1846, ibid., pp.95-96.

was instructed to prevent extension of the boundaries of the colony, and to prevent squatting on lands outside the colony.[26] The legal question here, "By what right could the governor exercise authority beyond the boundaries of British Territory?" went unnoticed. These concessions were not as extensive as the West India Committee wanted, but approval of their program might well have caused Great Britain to be charged with attempting to revive the slave trade.[27]

West Indian interests continued to press for permission to recruit outside British settlements, and for changes in the method of conveying emigrants from Africa to the West Indies. There had been occasional proposals to transport African emigrants by steamship, thereby presumably improving communication, increasing confidence, and stimulating emigration. Invariably, in the past, a study of the advantages and disadvantages of using a steam transport for African immigration had disclosed a cost so high that it would be impractical. Now, however, it was not only a steam vessel which was wanted, but one belonging to the Royal Navy. Such conveyance would be a definite innovation.

The government, perhaps motivated by conscience, perhaps by political acumen, was sympathetic. In the course of the interdepartmental correspondence pertaining to the steamship, Grey explained that because of changes in commercial policy of Great Britain, it seemed only just to make some concessions to the West Indian proprietors, who needed a supply of free labor in order to compete with foreign sugar producers. Coolie immigrants from India had been too expensive; cost for transportation of laborers from West Coast Africa was not so great, but few would leave the British settlement. As the West India body repeatedly asserted the availability of a large supply of labor on the Kru Coast, where the slave trade did not exist, support of their proposal seemed advisable.[28]

Meanwhile, Grey had consulted the Admiralty to determine if one of its steamers might be used for a one-year experiment in transporting emigrants from Africa to the West Indies. If so, he needed to know capacity and cost per year of the ship. Grey wanted also, if possible, a smaller vessel with a screw propeller for maintenance of communication between the Kru Coast and British possessions on the coast of Africa. Having this attempt to pro-

26. Ibid., pp.95-97.
27. Hawes to W. F. Barnley, Aug. 22, 1846, ibid., pp.97-98.
28. James Stephen to C. E. Trevelyan, Jan. 27, 1847, in "Papers Relative to . . . Emigration from Africa to the West Indies," *PP,* 1847, XXXIX:3.

cure emigrants from the Kru Coast under the immediate supervision of officers in Her Majesty's service should ensure against any suspicion or hint of slave trading.[29]

Two months after the Colonial Office made the enquiry, the Admiralty replied. A steamer of 1059 tons (the *Growler*) was available for an annual sum of £14,217, which included cost of repairs, wages, victualling of crew, and coal allowance for full steam on 122 days. Alterations, which included the addition of a poop deck, would require four or five weeks, but would enable the ship to carry 400 or 500 passengers per voyage, with six round trips during the year. There was one warning note, however: the Admiralty hoped recruiting agencies in Africa would be well organized, for it was imperative for reasons of health not to detain European crews in the rivers or harbors of Africa.[30]

The program was to be one of government assistance, not gift, with financial arrangements somewhat different from those for the earlier project from Sierra Leone (when full cost had been borne by the receiving colony). It was now proposed to charge the receiving colony £10 per emigrant, with the governor making the payment from a special fund set aside by the colony for that purpose. Even should the vessel never carry more than two-thirds its maximum number of passengers, at £10 per emigrant the colonies would pay £18,000—a sum considerably in excess of the £14,217 estimated as operational cost of the *Growler* for the year. But total cost of equipment, including hulls, masts, rigging and machinery was put at an estimated £30,000. It was asked who would bear the difference. All expense of the vessel, it was decided, was to be treated as a charge on the Naval Estimates submitted to Parliament. As rapidly as the £10 per head payment was received, it would be used for reimbursement.[31] Thus, little if any of the cost would rest permanently upon Her Majesty's government.

Following the customary procedure for emigration projects, details were left to the CL&EC, who applied to the *Growler* many of the regulations previously devised for earlier experiments. They agreed upon a supervising agent at Sierra Leone, who should be paid a salary, as well as a fee of one dollar per head for each emigrant sent to the West Indies. This agent was to send a few subordinate agents to the Kru Coast; these, too, would be

29. James Stephen to H. G. Ward, Sec'y. Admiralty, Nov. 3, 1846, ibid., pp.1-2.
30. H. G. Ward to B. Hawes, Admiralty, Jan. 18, 1847, ibid., p.2.
31. Stephen to Trevelyan, Jan. 27, 1847, ibid.

paid both salary and fee (half a dollar for each recruit). Fees so low, it was asserted, could not possibly invite revival of slave trading or kidnapping, yet might be an incentive for securing emigrants. Moreover, to make doubly certain against charges of involuntary emigration, the agents were forbidden to go beyond the Kru Coast or into any place where there had been slave trading.[32] Expenses of the collecting agents would be apportioned among the receiving colonies, which presumably would include Jamaica.

This project of emigration by use of a steamship belonging to the Royal Navy had been sponsored and demanded by the West India Committee in London, not by the Jamaica government or its agents as such. But in order for Jamaica to be fully informed of developments, copies of correspondence between the Colonial Office, the Admiralty, the Treasury, and the Colonial Land and Emigration Commission were sent by Earl Grey to the governor of Jamaica. Grey promised to supply further details as arrangements were matured.[33] In the long run, however, Jamaica was not included among the participants.

The year 1846 was a bitter one for Jamaica. Ordinarily the legislative session, beginning in October or November, extended well into the new year. In the 1845-1846 session it had concluded its business in December, 1845, and was not convened again until the following November. Therefore, planting interests in Jamaica were not together in a body or within convenient communication range of each other from January until mid-November of 1846. During this ten-month interval, repeal of the corn laws had been passed through Parliament, and work on the Sugar Duties Bill rushed to completion. In fact, proceedings dealing with the latter were too hurried for the news to reach Jamaica and evoke any semblance of organized protest before action by Parliament had been completed and the Sugar Duties Bill was a reality. Jamaica learned she would soon be deprived of the one advantage she had retained after 1834, namely, preferential treatment for West Indian sugar marketed in Great Britain. As previously stated, Jamaica sugar interests believed their production costs far exceeded those of foreign growers using slave labor. Now, confronted with the prospect of unrestricted competition, they foresaw nothing but ruin. Financial losses suffered by planters soon would be reflected in the public revenue, since much

---

32. T. F. Elliot, C. A. Wood, F. Rogers, CL&EC, to James Stephen, Mar. 8, 1847, and encs., ibid., pp.5-8.
33. Earl Grey to Gov. Grey, Feb. 1, 1846, ibid., p.5.

of it was derived from taxes upon land and various phases of sugar production.[34]

Early in September, Darling, the AGI, issued a public notice intimating that arrangements had been made to transport 5,000 coolies to Jamaica during the 1846-1847 season and invited applications for their services. There was no rush to offer employment. Six weeks after the notice was given, application had been made for only about 1,200. Darling issued a second notice, and implied that no applications would be accepted after November 5. This resulted in few additional applications. Unlike the preceding year, planters now were reluctant to undertake any additional financial responsibility. In order to prevent the island from being confronted with the arrival of more coolies than it could absorb, Darling (who was both a proprietor and member of the assembly) suggested that emigration agents in India be advised immediately of the limited demand for coolies. If the ships could not be diverted elsewhere, it would be wiser for Jamaica to pay a forfeit than to have the immigrants arriving under such uncertain conditions. Soon after the assembly met in November it embraced Darling's proposal and asked for stoppage of embarkation of coolies.[35]

This reluctance to employ coolie laborers in 1846 was in marked contrast to the interest shown in previous years when thousands of applications were made offering employment. Change in the views of planters was attributed, in a very limited degree, to such minor causes as illness among the arrivals and a tax levied upon employers of coolies. Towering above everything else was a serious apprehension of the effect of the new sugar duties arrangements.[36] Colonists in Jamaica were now in a fury over what they regarded as rank injustice on the part of the mother country. An American journalist who visited the island reported that planters insisted the imperial government had recognized their right to full compensation for their slave property, but had paid less than fifty percent of the appraised value. They said in lieu of any further monetary payment they were promised a prohibitory duty on sugar, which was now being swept away.[37]

At this critical time in Jamaica's history, there was an acting governor but no governor. Elgin had returned to England even before the intro-

34. For an excellent account of Jamaica and the Sugar Duties Act, see Hall, *Free Jamaica*, ch. 3, pp.81-120.
35. *Votes*, 1846-1847, p.27.
36. Darling to Berkeley, Oct. 22, 1846, ibid., pp.97-98.
37. John Bigelow, *Jamaica in 1850* (New York, 1851), p.72.

duction of the Sugar Duties Bill in Parliament. Major General Berkeley, acting as governor only until Sir Charles Grey should arrive, postponed calling the Legislature.[38] But as time passed and Sir Charles did not arrive, Berkeley decided to summon it in mid-November in order to secure renewal of annual grants. In his brief address November 17, he referred to the "truly beneficial change in the weather," which was an aid to sugar production.[39] There was little else which he could mention as a cause for cheer. While the Peel government was still in office, the Colonial Office had rejected Jamaica's request for a loan to be used for immigration purposes, and this news was now formally conveyed to the assembly.[40]

If there had been any faint doubt as to the mood of the island, it was soon dispelled by the actions of the House of Assembly. For months the lieutenant-governor had ignored the legislators' demands that they be summoned. These men were angry, and, at last, were formally meeting together. Petitions calling for protest against the recent action of Parliament were presented almost at once; within forty-eight hours after it convened, the assembly went into a committee of the whole house to consider the state of the island.[41] Frustration, conviction of the certainty of economic ruin, utter despair, as well as the feeling of betrayal by the mother country were all reflected in a series of resolutions to which the members quickly agreed. They accused the imperial government of applying to the West Indian colonies a policy detrimental to the interests and prosperity of those colonies. The Sugar Duties Act of 1846 would complete their financial ruin by subjecting them to an unequal struggle with slave-holding and slave-trafficking countries. It was a flagrant violation, they charged, of national faith and honor. The resolutions referred to the colonies' having been "cast off" by the imperial government, which, after emancipation, had forced them to increase public expenditures. Now, with little hope of returning prosperity, it was the painful duty of the House of Assembly, in justice to all (property owners, laborers, and creditors) to reduce the island commitments in accordance with the "diminished means of its impoverished inhabitants."[42] A

38. Sir Charles E. Grey, the Governor of Jamaica, was a cousin of Earl Grey, Secretary of State for the colonies. In any instance where they might be confused, the Secretary of State for the Colonies will be referred to by title or as Earl Grey.

39. *Votes,* 1846-1847, pp.6-7.

40. Gladstone to Elgin, Apr. 29, 1846, Jamaica no.23, ibid., pp.46-47.

41. *Votes,* 1846-1847, p.25.

42. Ibid., pp.25-26.

committee, which included Alexander Barclay, was named to draw up a petition to the Queen in terms of these resolutions.[43]

The result, presented as a memorial, first reviewed the difficulties of Jamaica since emancipation, then asked for: reductions of the duty on British colonial sugar to afford moderate and permanent protection and competition with slave-grown sugar; removal of all restrictions on free African immigration, but retention of regulation needed to prevent it from being made a cover for carrying the people into slavery; and authorization to conclude contracts-for-service for three years, not one. The memorial concluded:

> "If these our reasonable requests are withheld, if we are to be
> involved in a ruinous competition with slaveholding countries, if
> your Majesty's government are of the opinion that protection
> and assistance which alone can avert our ruin are incompatable
> with the national interest, it will only remain for us, in the face
> of the nation and of the world, to demand of Parliament that
> equitable compensation to which as British subjects we are
> clearly entitled.[44]

Jamaica planters anticipated a decline in both market and price commanded by their sugar. From all over the Island petitions from "merchants, bankers, traders, planters and other inhabitants" continued to pour into the assembly. Much alike in tone, they complained of serious depreciation in the value of property because of the unjust policy of the British government.[45] The assembly committee, to which the numerous petitions were referred, blamed reduction in the price of sugar as the reason for lack of profit and continued abandonment of estates. It recommended revision in taxation and in salaries, and proposed abandonment of Asiatic immigration as too expensive for competition with slave labor. It urged African emigration, but at the cost of Britain, as the cheapest and most direct means of putting an end to the slave trade by establishing free labor as cheaper than slave labor and the only means of saving the colony.[46] There was no effort to reconcile this assertion with the usual claim that free labor was the more expensive.

The assembly was concerned with retrenchment and in no hurry to

43. Ibid., p.27.
44. Ibid., p.217.
45. Ibid., p.55.
46. Ibid., pp.73-75.

renew annual appropriations. The immigration act, under which the island had assumed heavy financial liabilities, was among those acts which would expire at the close of December. If it was not renewed, Jamaica might find itself the recipient of immigrants for whom it could not provide. Legally, the executive could withdraw the balance of the immigration fund, if he did so before the end of the year, and then use it to pay immigration expenses. Such action by a governor would be extraordinary, and would result in very bad relations with the Legislature. By letting it be understood there would be no adjournment until arrangements were made to pay transportation and other costs of the immigrants who had been "ordered," Berkeley was able to prod the assembly into action—though it merely extended the immigration act until March 31, 1847. (It had also passed a retrenchment bill, which the Council refused.) Berkeley then agreed to a request for adjournment, for the new governor was expected to arrive at any moment. Before he met the legislature he would need to become familiar with the situation as it related to finances, immigration, and the temper of the assembly. Plans for securing emigrants from the Kru Coast were still in the formative stage, but in view of the assembly's action, after March 31 Jamaica might be left without machinery or funds for immigration purposes.

Not until mid-February, however, did Earl Grey, at the Colonial Office, reply to the memorials against the Sugar Duties Act. While acknowledging and rejecting them, he berated the colonists for having brought their troubles on themselves. At the same time he was anxious to appear solicitous of their welfare, and instructed the governor to direct attention of the memorialists to recent imperial proposals for increasing the supply of laborers to the West Indies.[47] Jamaica had already been informed, however, of his intention to restrict the experimental use of a naval steamship carrying African laborers to Trinidad and British Guiana, as they were the colonies nearest to Africa. One steamer from the Royal Navy would take immigrants alternately to each of the two colonies. Jamaica was not to be included in the initial stage. If the experiment was successful, it would be extended to such other colonies as would be prepared to provide the necessary funds.[48]

The Jamaica assembly was of no mind for the island to be counted out as a recipient of African laborers. By resolution they assured Her Majesty's government of willingness not only to pay the expense of coolies then

47. Earl Grey to C. E. Grey, Feb. 12, 1847, no.24, CO 138/66.
48. Ibid.

en route, but also to appropriate a sum specifically for defraying transportation costs of Africans. They agreed to provide a sum of £10,000 for transportation costs at £10 each, of such Africans as might be sent by government steamers during 1847. Negro laborers had always been considered the most satisfactory; planters now feared that if Jamaica should be omitted from the initial voyage, it would be overlooked by later immigrants. To guard against such an eventuality, the assembly (which reflected the attitude of planter interests throughout the island) not only petitioned for permission to send delegates to the Kru Coast, but sought assurance of a portion of the first immigrants. Jamaicans really wanted a further safeguard for their colony's interests: they wanted one steamer to bring immigrants exclusively to Jamaica. Thoroughly irritated by the latest in a series of Parliamentary enactments detrimental to the colony's economy, the assembly was in a truculent mood. Reduced circumstances, it asserted, gave it a strong claim on the parent government; in as much as the undertaking was scarcely less important to national than to colonial interests, the island was entitled to the gratuitous use of a steamer.[49]

The good intent of the assembly was demonstrated by a measure actually appropriating £30,000 to purposes of immigration. With the amount still unspent from the 1846 fund, it would be sufficient for any coolies already embarked and for 1,000 Africans at £10 per head. In the official report to his superiors, Governor Grey noted the probability of a much larger sum for the next year, and suggested the assembly and planters generally would be mollified if a steamer for conveying Africans should be assigned exclusively to Jamaica.[50] Nonetheless, the suggestion was completely ignored at the Colonial Office. When the memorial by the assembly was forwarded from it to the CL&EC, almost the entire covering message of the governor was deleted.

Jamaica's request for a share in the experiment was again rejected. Several reasons were given, such as too great distances for one steamer to serve three colonies, uncertainty of securing a complement for even one vessel, and the strictly experimental stage of the entire scheme. Should the plan prove successful, Jamaica was told, Her Majesty's government might extend its operation to that colony, if the Legislature so wished.[51] The real

49. House of Assembly Resolution, Mar. 25, 1847, in no.1223 Jamaica, CO 137/291; *Votes,* 1846-1847, pp.272-273.
50. C. E. Grey to Earl Grey, Apr. 6, 1847, in no.1224 Jamaica, CO 137/291.
51. Earl Grey to C. E. Grey, May 31, 1847, *Votes,*1847-1848, p.63.

reason for omitting Jamaica from the experiment is to be found in a draft version of the despatch not sent to the colony: at the time when it was decided to use the steamer to bring Africans from the Kru Coast, it was assumed in the Colonial Office that Jamaica would not be willing to incur any additional expense for immigration.[52] In the official despatch sent over Earl Grey's signature, there was no mention of mere assumption of disinterest on the part of Jamaica. Whatever the reasoning in the Colonial Office, Jamaica would have to wait until some future date for possible inclusion in the experiment.

52. Earl Grey to C. E. Grey, May 31, 1847, draft, in no.1224 Jamaica, CO 137/291.

8

Further Changes in Policy: Immigration with "Imperial Assistance"

CONFRONTED WITH UNCERTAINTIES RESULTING FROM the Sugar Duties Act forced upon them by Parliament, planter interests in Jamaica refused for many months to believe that the measure would not be rescinded. When efforts to restore some degree of protection resulted in nothing more than postponement of equalization, it seemed to portend the doom of cane production. Continued cultivation of estates would be futile: assumption of new financial risks appeared unwise. Economy in public expenditures became the general tendency; as a consequence, there was a sharp change in the approach to the whole problem of immigration.

The Immigration Report for the year ending September 30, 1847, was the first which covered a full year following passage of the Sugar Duties Bill. It indicated the number of Negro immigrants to Jamaica as only slightly larger than in the preceding year. *Emancipados* from Havana decreased to a total of only 79—due perhaps to the loss of a government steamer and delay in securing a replacement. Most of these 79 were employed in the southern part of the island.[1] No immigrants arrived from Sierra Leone. There were only 337 from St. Helena, all of them liberated Africans brought by the *Indus,* which docked at Morant Bay in November, 1846. The entire lot was

1. Report by Darling, AGI, Oct. 21, 1847, *Votes,* 1847-1848, D of Ap. 8, pp.20-21, 33.

employed in the parish of St. Thomas-in-the-East. For two reasons the *Indus*
immigrants should be noticed. In the first place, many of them were children below the age of ten; in accordance with the immigration law effective
in 1846, as minors who did not have a known parent in the island they were
apprenticed for five years.[2] In the second place, effective since January,
1846, was the requirement that first employers of immigrants from Africa
or islands adjacent thereto pay a tax of £2 for each of those eight years of
age or above, and £1 for those between three and eight years of age. Revenue from the tax should be applied to immigration expenses.[3] These laborers who came in the *Indus* were the first African immigrants for whom the
employers were taxed. When the agent general for immigration totalled the
expense of importing them and deducted the tax paid by their first employers, he reported the cost to the public treasury as averaging £5 11s. 3d. per
immigrant.[4] Moreover, as Darling reported having visited most of the estates
where the *Indus* immigrants were located, he could and did give an eyewitness report of their good appearance and of their almost always good
conduct and usefulness.[5] There is one point which should be observed:
arrangements for the immigrants via the *Indus* undoubtedly had been made
before reaction to the Sugar Duties Act had swept over Jamaica and then
back across the Atlantic. No other immigrants were transported from Africa
to Jamaica during the twelve months covered by Darling's report.

The 1847 report was the last written by Darling as AGI. Although a
planter in St. Thomas-in-the-East and a member of the assembly, he left
Jamaica only a few weeks later to become governor of St. Lucia. An acting
AGI (Richard Hill) was appointed, but with Jamaica wanting to end coolie
transportation and immigration from Africa uncertain, there was some question as to whether the office warranted a full-time agent. Ultimately David
Ewart, a stipendiary magistrate and son-in-law of Alexander Barclay, was
appointed AGI and permitted to continue holding the former office. It was
stipulated, however, that if the work of the AGI again became heavy, Ewart
should relinquish one of the two positions. He was chosen in an effort to
lessen distrust of the imperial government and its avowed intent to further
immigration. As Barclay had been so prominent in efforts to promote immi-

2. Ibid., pp.20, 22. There were 2,433 coolies brought from India; ibid., p.23.
3. *Jamaica Gazette,* Jan. 8, 1846, in no.451 Jamaica, CO 137/288.
4. Report by Darling, AGI, Oct. 21, 1847, *Votes,* 1847-1848, D of Ap. 8, p.22.
5. Ibid., pp.22-23.

gration, it was hoped to recover confidence of the planter interests by putting the agency into the hands of his son-in-law.[6]

Rumors had come with the *Indus* of a special St. Helena agent employed by Trinidad to charter vessels exclusively for it. Inasmuch as the St. Helena collector of customs, who served as government emigration agent, might well give preference to any colony with a ship chartered and ready for departure, a special agent for Trinidad gave that rival colony an undue advantage. Some in Jamaica suggested that it, too, should appoint a chartering agent, and do so with a minimum of delay;[7] but as the Colonial Office was not amenable to the suggestion, Jamaica could not proceed with the proposal.[8] There was no abatement of unrest stemming from the Sugar Duties Act. Throughout the colony various groups continued to express their grievances by means of memorials to Her Majesty's government. Invariably they included a plea for adoption of some method by which a greater supply of labor could be acquired from the coast of Africa.

As already noted, Charles Edward Grey, the new governor, had arrived in Jamaica on December 22, 1846—a time when tempers were inclined to grow short as a result of imperial policy. He undertook to reassure the people, and, in so far as possible, to explain the nature of the measures by which the imperial government was endeavoring to promote their welfare.[9] Although at times he found traveling difficult, he visited parts of the island, addressed meetings, and displayed dutiful concern for the colony. He received memorials in protest against the policies pursued by Britain, among them one by the Chamber of Commerce of Kingston. When he forwarded it to the Colonial Office, the governor observed that the memorialists had borrowed some of his own expressions, although their conclusions were not always his.[10]

Grey knew that, contrary to the hopes of some in Great Britain as well as in Jamaica, the government would not restore protection; but with the hope of soothing the assembly and the planters, he had previously advised the assignment of a steamer to convey African immigrants for

6. C. E. Grey to Earl Grey, Feb. 21, 1848, no.25, CS 102/13, series 1848.
7. Darling to Lt. Gov. Major-General Berkeley, Nov. 21, 1846, in no.2588 Jamaica, CO 137/284.
8. Earl Grey to Sir Charles Grey, Jan. 17, 1847, Jamaica no.14, CO 137/289.
9. C. E. Grey to Earl Grey, Apr. 24, 1847, no.47, *PP*, 1847-1848, XXIII, Part 1:753.
10. C. E. Grey to Earl Grey, June 7, 1847, no.1890 Jamaica, CO 137/292; and CS 102/113, series 1847.

Jamaica.[11] Now he undertook to warn Colonial Office officials of the temper of the colony. Nothing would content Jamaica, he emphasized, but supplies of African laborers. In fact, he suggested, planters believed immigration was a blessing to the Negro who came to Jamaica where he might exchange the "barbarities and oppressions" of Africa for the lot of a free laborer. The governor, who seemingly shared their views, made a proposal which he said should further the welfare of both planters and Africans. It was indeed startling: Her Majesty's government should establish places of refuge and safety to which Negroes might go from the interior of Africa; from there they could be conveyed to Jamaica. But the memorialists went a step further and proposed procuring prisoners of war as immigrants by the simple device of ransoming them from their captors. There the governor drew the line. He foresaw that someone might believe an outlay of public money gave planters or government a sort of property in the laborers. Furthermore, Grey felt it necessary to correct some misleading statements by the memorialists. Jamaica's expenditures for immigration were not as large as their figures implied. Although, as stated by them, £345,000 had been voted by Jamaica for immigration purposes since 1839, before those grants had been expended they often were superseded or stopped by successive grants. The AGI had noted £152,528 as the sum actually expended in the period January, 1840-May 1, 1847.[12]

Sir Charles continued to warn that mere expressions of interest in Jamaica's welfare would not suffice. Some definite action, such as the arrival of numerous African laborers, was essential to prove sincerity on the part of the imperial government. As the governor of Jamaica still had authority to transfer and pay sums from the immigration fund, Governor Grey used that power to deposit £2,000 for expenses of the agency on the coast of Africa. He hoped thereby to make Jamaica eligible for receiving African immigrants conveyed by the *Growler* experiment. Even after deduction of the £2,000, there still remained approximately £8,000 of the fund which had been appropriated for African immigration; from this it was possible to pay the £10 per immigrant which the imperial government required the colony to bear for actual conveyance. Grey stressed the importance of sending many Africans, and of having them arrive within the next three

11. C. E. Grey to Earl Grey, Apr. 6, 1847, no.1224 Jamaica, CO 137/291.
12. C. E. Grey to Earl Grey, June 7, 1847, in no.1890 Jamaica, CO 137/292.

months, before the next meeting of the Legislature.[13] Presumably he expected the arrival of these laborers to go far toward mitigating resentment throughout the island.

The commercial depression prevailing in Great Britain in 1847 was felt also in Jamaica. Failure of merchant houses and tightened credit made it difficult or impossible for planters to secure financing.[14] By autumn there was restlessness coupled with possible political maneuvering. A month before the assembly was summoned the governor advised the Colonial Office of an impending financial crisis in Jamaica. The low price of sugar on the London market, without any corresponding reduction of duty, seriously threatened many planters who had been struggling to "keep their head above water." Making a careful appraisal of the discontent, he detected a movement within the island to support, in the next session of the imperial parliament, whichever party adhered to the principal of protection. To that purpose, the planter party in the assembly might attempt to delay the annual revenue bills and other business until after Christmas.[15] The state of public feeling in Jamaica and the clamor arising throughout the West Indies convinced Governor Grey of the wisdom of calling the Legislature into an early session. Otherwise, the members might be pledged, by resolutions of parochial assemblies, to a course of obstructionist tactics incompatible with the discharge of their legislative function.[16] The governor had reminded his superiors earlier that most of the island's revenue was not secured by act of the imperial parliament, but was dependent upon the annual vote of the House of Assembly.[17] A recalcitrant assembly now might well embarass the imperial government by refusing to vote the funds necessary for administration of the colony.

When the assembly convened in October, the island was enveloped in gloom which nothing could dispel. An adequate supply of labor, as well as fair treatment on the London sugar market, seemed essential to the colony's well-being. It was receiving neither. Well aware of the usual cry of lack of labor, and the earlier rebuff by the Colonial Office when participation in the *Growler* experiment was sought, Governor Grey was sympathetic, but

13. Ibid.
14. *CHBE,* 2:705-707; Hall, *Free Jamaica,* p.92.
15. C. E. Grey to Earl Grey, Sept. 21, 1847, no.92, *PP,* 1847-1848, XXIII, Part 1:753.
16. C. E. Grey to Earl Grey, Nov. 6, 1847, no.106, ibid., p.758.
17. C. E. Grey to Earl Grey, Mar. 9, 1847, no.30, CS 102/113, series 1847.

dubious about relief. While he hoped for some African laborers before the close of the year, he advised the assembly they would be very few. Warning against expenditure of energy in futile efforts to reestablish protection, the governor emphasized his own conviction of Jamaica's right to claim relief by further reduction in the duties on sugar and rum imported into Britain. But that was purely a personal view, and of no help to those facing free trade in the immediate future.[18]

It is not the intent of this work to dwell upon the political tactics in which the Legislature, West India interests, and growing factions in Jamaica indulged. Suffice it to say, the governor's worst fears were realized. Soon after the assembly convened, there were occurrences which had great bearing upon Jamaica's inclusion in plans for African immigration and upon the future of the island. In October, the assembly resolved not to consider any new measure involving the expenditure of public money. The term "new measure" was not defined and seemingly remained inexact to assemblymen and governor alike. About a fortnight later, the assembly learned of the intention of Her Majesty's government to disallow an act of the previous session which provided for transfer of certain parochial charges to the general revenue. Planters, whose income was dwindling, had hoped to shift a part of their tax burden to revenues which were more generally derived. Now, with that denied them, their dissatisfaction was transformed into fury.[19]

Meanwhile, nonresidents with financial interests in Jamaica presented memorials to the imperial government. Their topics of complaint were much the same, and, like those of Jamaica residents, included references to both need for African laborers and requests for government assistance. When the Secretary of State for the Colonies sent one of these memorials, along with his own lengthy covering despatch, to the governor, the latter, adhering to instructions, had it placed before the assembly. The document set forth clearly the views of Her Majesty's government as to the introduction of free laborers from the coast of Africa and is illustrative of the failure to comprehend conditions or attitudes in Jamaica.

Earl Grey noted the frequency with which planters and merchants stressed want of an adequate supply of labor. Concurring in the belief that coolie immigration was too expensive for Jamaica, he turned to their greater

18. Speech by the Governor, Oct. 19, 1847, *Votes,* 1847-1848, pp.5-12.
19. C. E. Grey to Earl Grey, Nov. 8, 1847, no.106, *PP,* 1847-1848, XXIII, Part 1:758.

interest in African labor. His government did not intend, he emphasized, to purchase Africans in order to remove them from slavery to freedom—a scheme qualified to abet, not to end slavery. Focusing on the *Growler* experiment which then engaged the attention of Her Majesty's government, he pointed to the successful first voyage, when emigrants were taken from Sierra Leone. Earl Grey professedly expected the second voyage to be made from the Kru Coast, and to mark the beginning of a large migration from that area. The government was prepared to take steps immediately to convey these people to the West Indies as cheaply as possible by merchantship, but, he stressed, the colonies must be prepared to bear the cost. Moreover, Jamaica was told bluntly that the imperial government could not recommend either a loan or grant of money for immigration purposes. Earl Grey foresaw the possibility of Africans, introduced at the expense of the colony, refusing to hire themselves out, and he suggested levying a monthly tax on all immigrants to ensure against such an eventuality.[20]

In referring to the use of merchantmen for transporting emigrants, Earl Grey did not bother to explain that the steamer *Growler* had proved less than satisfactory as an emigrant ship for the South Atlantic crossing. The portholes, lower than on a frigate, had to be closed even in moderate weather. The clutter of bunks placed on the main deck to increase passenger load had further impeded circulation of air. Heat from the engine and dirt from coal necessitated constant cleaning. For the sake of economy, the ship relied primarily on sail. All steam vessels lay deep in the water, rolled much, and on sail provided much rougher passage than a sailing ship. The space required for engine and coal made it impossible to carry provisions sufficient for the complete round-trip. Three weeks were necessary for refitting when the ship returned to Sierra Leone, a place hazardous to the health of Europeans. There was a fairly high rate of mortality among the passengers and of illness in the crew. After the second voyage it was decided not to continue using the ship for immigration purposes. When the *Growler* arrived in Bermuda in December, the entire crew was ill with fever; the captain was among those who died.[21]

A nonsteamship, it was intimated, would be healthier for passengers

20. Earl Grey to C. E. Grey, Oct. 30, 1847, no.99, *Votes,* 1847-1848, Ap. 44, pp.180-185.
21. Testimony by Commodore William King Hall, the *Growler,* in "Minutes of Evidence Taken before the Select Committee on Sugar and Coffee Planting," *PP,* 1847-1848, XXIII, Part 1:124-125.

and crew and offered many advantages, such as: refitting in a matter of hours, not weeks; no heat and dirt from the engine or coal; and space for supplies sufficient for the entire round trip. Although a frigate could carry more passengers with greater health and comfort yet at less cost than a steamer, it was not the most economical type to operate. Distinction in the category of cheapness of operational costs fell to merchantmen. Their officers and crew were paid less; but above all, unlike ships of the royal navy, they could carry freight on the homeward trip, thereby cutting appreciably overall costs for passengers. It seemed time for a change in Britain's plans which related to immigration.[22]

It was soon decided, however, to give a further bit of imperial assistance to African emigration. Reports coming by way of the *Growler* indicated many Africans at Sierra Leone and on the Kru Coast might wish to emigrate. Shipowners were now willing to transport laborers from those areas to Jamaica at £10 per head passenger fare (or "bounty") if assured of reimbursement for their expenses in the event of failure to obtain passengers. Instead of applying to the House of Assembly for reimbursement, Earl Grey informed Sir Charles, henceforth Her Majesty's government would assume the responsibility, if it should be necessary. In addition, as health hazards made it impossible to station a regular officer in Sierra Leone to certify procedures, Britain would pay the cost of sending a naval officer along with the ship to supervise the service and guard against abuse.[23]

Just after the Legislature convened, the governor had assessed its mood and concluded it was so resentful of the Sugar Duties Act as to make unpredictable what measures, including financial, it would adopt. Under those circumstances he advised the home government not to direct more African laborers to Jamaica unless the assembly requested them. If any Africans should arrive before the end of the year, he would have funds to pay for them but was doubtful as to what the situation would be after that date. The governor's despatch was not received at the Colonial Office, however, until after Earl Grey's message had been sent to Jamaica.[24] A month later, the governor noted the unwillingness on the part of the assembly to

22. Ibid., pp.125-126.
23. Earl Grey to C. E. Grey, Nov. 16, 1847, no.105, *Votes*, 1847-1848, pp.349-350; "Eighth General Report" of the CL&EC, *PP*, 1847-1848, XXVI:21-22.
24. C. E. Grey to Earl Grey, Oct. 23, 1847, no.105, in Ap. "Third Report from the Select Committee on Sugar and Coffee Planting," *PP*, 1847-1848, XXIII, Part I:387.

incur any additional expense for immigration and repeated his advice to suspend conveyance of liberated Africans to Jamaica.[25] Eventually the Legislature provided for an agent general of immigration with a salary of £300 (instead of £500 as formerly) and an immigration fund of £15,000. It did not, however, authorize continuance of the office beyond the end of 1848.[26]

Perhaps Earl Grey's gesture of underwriting African emigration was designed solely for political effect in England, where there was considerable criticism of the Sugar Duties Act. It would not be the first time that Jamaica was tossed back and forth for political purposes. But the colony was not in a mood to be tossed about or to be gracious in return for futile gestures. In fact, it was on the verge of flouting imperial authority.[27] The House of Assembly had appointed a select committee to inquire into the depressed state of agriculture. The assignment was broad enough to include investigation of causes for abandonment of cultivation, and break-up of sugar and coffee plantations since passage of the emancipation act of 1833. The committee's report, which followed by only two days reception of the communication from Earl Grey, was soon embodied in a memorial from the assembly to the Queen.[28]

Essentially, the memorial by the assembly was a review of the decline in sugar and coffee production since 1834. Of 653 sugar estates in cultivation in that year, 140 had been abandoned by late 1847. The abandoned estates totaled 168,032 acres and had employed 22,553 laborers. During the same period 465 coffee plantations, consisting of 188,400 acres with 26,830 laborers, had been abandoned. Certain estates still in operation in 1847 had only 13,973 resident laborers instead of the 41,820 employed in 1834. Until 1847 (the first year following the Sugar Duties Act), funds had been available regularly to pay for labor, but most laborers who left the estates did so in order to become independent settlers.[29]

The memorial reaffirmed dissatisfaction with Asiatic laborers, but

25. C. E. Grey to Earl Grey, Nov. 22, 1847, no.115, ibid., p.409.

26. C. E. Grey to Earl Grey, Feb. 21, 1848, no.25, CS 102/13, series 1848.

27. C. E. Grey to Earl Grey, Dec. 21, 1847, no.123, CS 102/13, series 1847.

28. *Votes,* 1847-1848, pp.361-363. The committee report was believed to have been written by Barclay, who had presided over all of the committee proceedings. The governor advised Earl Grey that costs of production varied widely on different estates and in different parts of the island. C. E. Grey to Earl Grey, Feb. 7, 1848, CS 102/13, series 1848.

29. Memorial to the Queen, Dec. 24, 1847, *Votes,* 1847-1848, pp.421-424.

stressed the usefulness of Africans, as demonstrated in the parish of St. Thomas-in-the-East. Precariousness of cultivation in Jamaica it attributed to uncertainty of labor. It then pointed an accusing finger at Great Britain, and intimated that the British government was "annihilating" sugar and coffee cultivation in its own colonies, thereby giving foreigners a monopoly of those commodities in the British market. Only by protection, it asserted, would the tragedy be averted. Therefore, the assembly petitioned for: 1) abolition of duties on West Indian sugar in order to place growers of the area on equal terms with slave-holding foreigners; and 2) immediate as well as extensive immigration into Jamaica from Africa. Because the resources of Jamaica were exhausted, immigration should be conducted at the national expense. The memorial closed with an angry assertion that if measures then in progress had been undertaken earlier, they would have been beneficial; but they had been delayed until despair had paralyzed the colony, and would be of little value unless accompanied by other relief.[30] Earl Grey's proposal would leave with Jamaica the burden of passenger fare for immigrants as well as costs of reception and care for them in the island. The colony was in no mood to be grateful for such niggardly gestures.

Neither was Jamaica very favorably impressed with ramifications of the modified immigration program, which seemed to have many thorns. Nonetheless, about ten days prior to the assembly's approval of the December petition, the Colonial Office and its agencies began to implement the plans for conveying Africans to the West Indies in merchant ships.[31] With Great Britain assuming the responsibility for guarantee, several ships were to be sent to Jamaica; yet the contract was concluded immediately for only two, the *Amity Hall* and the *Morayshire*. Through agencies of the Colonial Office, inspection was made and license quickly obtained for procedure to the British possessions on West Coast Africa and to the Kru Coast; from the Admiralty, passes were provided to ensure against mistaken identity or seizure as slavers.[32] Passenger fare had been determined in part on the basis of maximum number of days en route, with forty-eight additional hours in port of destination. The shipowners, who wanted to make the passage as economically as possible, asked permission to call at a port nearer than Port Royal: for the *Morayshire*, they wanted Ocho Rios or Port Antonio as the

30. Ibid.
31. "Eighth General Report," CL&EC, *PP*, 1847-1848, XXVI:22.
32. Earl Grey to C. E. Grey, Dec. 16, 1847, no.120, CO 138/66.

port of debarkation; for the *Amity Hall,* they requested Port Morant. Earl Grey and the CL&EC acquiesced and instructed the governor to send the necessary information to some public official at those ports. From the local point of view this needlessly complicated the administrative tasks and invited fresh accusations of favoritism to the eastern part of the island.[33] The *Morayshire* passengers were landed at Port Maria, February 17, 1848; those of the *Amity Hall,* at Kingston on March 3.[34]

In past years, ships had often called at eastern ports for instructions. When the *Vanguard,* chartered for Jamaica by the governor of St. Helena, reached Jamaica with immigrants (April 15, 1848), the master put in to Morant Bay for orders as to port-of-debarkation—a course the St. Helena agent had instructed him to follow.[35] But the AGI had not been informed of the arrangement, and no instructions awaited the master.[36] In fact, the local official was not even within thirty miles of the port. A week elapsed while the master waited. He then wrote to the AGI in Spanish Town, received directions, and proceeded to Annotto Bay where he discharged passengers. The ship had a full load (198 immigrants, 106 of them under fourteen years of age) who had to be maintained during the additional days. The master presented Jamaica with a charge for demurrage along with a bill for £7 7s. per adult, rather than the £7 formerly in effect. As the emigration agent in St. Helena had agreed to the higher fare, Jamaica eventually paid both passage-money and demurrage, but not until after exchange of very tart words by both AGI and master.[37]

Immigrants from the *Vanguard* were distributed on estates in the parishes of Metcalfe and St. George. When the subagents undertook to collect the £2 or £1 tax from their employers, payment was refused on the ground that the law (sec. 10, 11 Vic. c.27) did not apply to immigrants from St. Helena because it was not considered adjacent to the coast of Africa.[38] It was a problem of status of the Africans from the *Vanguard:* Had they been residents of St. Helena or merely captured Africans liberated there? The question was referred to the Attorney General, who, without

33. Earl Grey to C. E. Grey, Dec. 16, 1847, no.121, CO 138/66.
34. Report of David Ewart, AGI, Nov. 1, 1848, "Return of Immigrants, Oct. 1, 1847-Sept. 30, 1848," *Votes,* 1848-1849, A in Ap. 1, p.10.
35. R. S. Norris to Ewart, May 24, 1848, *Votes,* 1849-1850, Ap. 26, pp.38-39.
36. D. Ewart to R. G. [*sic*] Norris, May 22, 1848, no.225, ibid., pp.37-38.
37. Ibid.
38. Petition of Henry Westmoreland to the House of Assembly, *Votes,* 1848-1849, p.182.

defining status, ruled that employers of African immigrants were not exempt from the tax. Therefore, subagents were to continue its collection.[39]

Ships which arrived with immigrants during 1848 usually carried a full load. There had been an increase in the slave trade, with a resultant increase in the number of slavers which were captured. These newcomers to Jamaica were liberated Africans who had agreed to migrate to the West Indies. David Ewart, making his report as AGI for the year closing September 30, listed six ships from Africa between February 17 and July 30, 1848. Four were from Sierra Leone with 905 immigrants; two from St. Helena with 480 immigrants. As no ship made a second voyage, most of them presumably were chartered on the spot. Although it was extraordinary to use any but British ships for transporting immigrants from Africa to the British West Indies, a Dutch barque was chartered for one of these voyages. Neither the AGI nor the CL&EC in their reports offered an explanation for using the foreign ship.[40] Quite possibly the Africa yard was full, and at a time when some of its occupants had agreed to go to the West Indies, no British ship was available. Haste was undoubtedly important—to relieve the crowded yard, and to get the people on the way before they changed their minds. Of the 1,305 who arrived in Jamaica, 921 were adults. The ports of debarkation were well chosen to minimize jealousy in Jamaica: Kingston received two ship loads; Port Maria, Annotto Bay, Montego Bay, and Savanna-la-Mar one each. These immigrants, together with the 56 *emancipados,* were assigned to employers fairly widely dispersed over the island.[41] Among the employers were Henry Westmoreland, Joseph Gordon, and William Hosack, men of political as well as economic importance.

The annual report of the CL&EC for 1848 covered the period January 1 through December 31 and showed a total of 1,887 immigrants from Africa during that period. By their records, three ships brought a total of 741 Africans from St. Helena, five ships brought 1,146 from Sierra Leone.[42] The vessels left Africa well filled with immigrants, as Jamaica had

39. Report of David Ewart, AGI, Nov. 1, 1848, *Votes,* 1848-1849, A in Ap. 1, pp.4-5.

40. Ibid., p.10.

41. Reports of David Ewart, Nov. 1, 1848, "Return of Employers of Emancipados"; "Return of Employers of Africans from St. Helena and Sierra Leone"; *Votes,* 1848-1849, Ap. D, Ap. E, pp.15-19.

42. Ninth General Report of the CL&EC, "Return of Ships Chartered by Her Majesty's CL&EC . . . ," *PP,* 1849, XXII:67.

wanted; but both the AGI and the CL&EC reports showed a mortality rate so high as to warrant attention. Of 859 Africans embarked at St. Helena, 118 died en route; for the five ships from Sierra Leone, the mortality was less (57 of 1203), but the *Amity Hall* with 277 immigrants had 37 deaths during the crossing.[43]

Immigrants who were seriously ill on arrival were removed to Public Hospital in Kingston. Of 44 sent there in March, 36 died, 2 remained at least two months, with only 6 recovering sufficiently to be discharged.[44] In other instances African immigrants became ill soon after arrival at the estate, and died there. Employers who had paid the £2 or £1 tax for presumably healthy laborers then filed petitions for refund of the tax.[45]

Cause for the large number of deaths on these voyages was not determined to the entire satisfaction of everyone. Regulations to be observed on board ships carrying liberated Africans to the West Indies were much as they had always been. There were rules pertaining to cleanliness of ship and of individual: Africans not in the hospital were to be washed every morning, and then rubbed with coconut or palm oil; they were to be mustered every morning at ten, with each African bringing his clothes and blankets with him; sick Africans were, of course, to remain in the hospital. The medical officer was to examine every African at the time of the muster, and report to the captain; he must visit the hospital at least twice each day, and give the captain a list of those who were ill; he should encourage any exercise not interfering with the ship. The lower deck, quarter deck, and all parts of the ship used by the Africans must be washed with water and sprinkled with chloride of lime every morning. Decks should be swept after every meal. Provisions were about the same as those customarily used, except for a slight increase in the per day ration of rice and biscuit (two pounds) and a decrease in water (three quarts), served out four times per day.[46] Apparently explanation for the increased mortality would be found in factors other than conditions on immigrant ships.

Officials at the public hospital attributed the high incidence of death to conditions in densely crowded holds of the slave ships, insufficient re-

43. Ibid., p.68.

44. J. Magrath and James Scott, Public Hospital, May 6, 1848, Ap. J of Report by Ewart, Nov. 1, 1848, *Votes,* 1848-1849, Ap. 1, p.23.

45. Extract, subagent Henry Walsh to D. Ewart, AGI, Mar. 13, 1848; Henry Walsh to Henry Westmoreland, June 8, 1848; *Votes,* 1848-1849, Ap. 34, pp.184-185.

46. Rules . . . ships carrying liberated Africans . . . ," no.7, B, *Votes,* 1849-1850, Ap. 26, pp.41-42.

covery time in the Africa yard prior to embarkation for Jamaica, and strange food on the immigrant ship.[47] Reports of ship's surgeons listed dysentery and scurvy as the most common disease on the voyages. Africans weakened and disease-ridden as a result of their incarceration on the slave ship, concluded the CL&EC, were in ill health when they boarded the ship for Jamaica. A diet adequate for healthy adults was not sufficient for passengers already suffering from undernourishment or for growing children, among whom the death rate was particularly high.[48]

Perhaps just as significant as official explanations of the high death rate were some casual remarks and a few implications. Africans, sick when taken from the slave ships, were sent to the Africa yards where at the time, if accounts were accurate, there was a death rate of about one in ten. From these Africa yards the immigrant ships acquired their passengers. Moreover, despite regulations and required keeping of records, agents sometimes either did not keep them or failed to send them. David Ewart, as AGI, complained of failure on the part of the St. Helena agent to list names and supposed ages of passengers. He noted the ease with which records could be falsified under such circumstances. Sometimes ships did not meet minimum standards; there was also occasional suspicion, but not positive proof, of overcrowding.[49] Illustrative of this was the notation, "Tembo, age 8," cause of death, someone "stepped on her chest during the night."[50] In at least one instance the government agents accompanying the ship might well have been charged with neglect of duty. Governor Grey, interested in knowing more than had been presented in the official reports of the surgeon and Admiralty agent who accompanied the *Amity Hall*, did not like what he learned. The Admiralty agent apparently had left the ship as soon as it arrived in port instead of remaining until all of the immigrants were landed and a concluding report had been written. Worse yet, one immigrant had died on board the vessel in port and her body was tossed into the harbor. Although an inquest attributed the death to "natural exhaustion," and the governor

47. J. Magrath and James Scott, May 6, 1848, Ap. J, *Votes*, 1848-1849, Ap. 1, p.233.

48. Thomas C. Murdock and Frederic Rogers to Herman Merivale, May 5, 1848, enc.4 in no.9, "Papers Relative to Emigration from Africa to the West Indies," *PP*, 1850, XI:15.

49. D. Ewart to C. E. Grey, May 18, 1848, in no.1523 Jamaica, CO 137/296.

50. Report by John Harrison, Morant Bay, Nov. 4, 1848, in Jamaica no.235, CO 137/298.

did not question the verdict, he regarded the conduct of the two men as worthy of censure.[51]

The CL&EC, however, concluded that the trouble lay with the condition of the people who were selected as immigrants. They therefore recommended an increase in the per day food allotment, and the addition of an interpreter to facilitate the surgeon's care of the ill, as well as a longer recovery period, such as three or four weeks, in the Africa yard before embarkation for the West Indies. A more careful selection of immigrants, they advised, would also be helpful by reason of preventing those already ill from undertaking the journey.[52]

A question which arose to plague Jamaica just at this time, as it would do periodically in the years to come, was one of return passage. The immigration acts of 1846 and 1847 were somewhat ambiguous as to whether immigrants brought in under colonial bounty were entitled to return passage.[53] According to the Jamaica immigration act in effect in 1848, every immigrant from the coast of Africa might claim a free return passage if: (1) no bounty had been paid for his passage; (2) the claim was filed not less than five nor more than seven years after his arrival; and (3) his application was made six months prior to notice of demand.[54] One party without legal claim to return passage had been returned to Africa by government transport; but they had been thoroughly unpleasant, disobedient, filthy, and in general troublesome on a government ship. In consequence, naval officers thereafter opposed having them aboard, and Jamaica could not rely upon this means of returning such persons to Africa.[55]

When one William Johnson asked return passage for himself and a party of five, he unwittingly raised some questions so technical as to require legal opinion. He had entered Jamaica in 1842, when there was no provision for return passage; he returned to Africa as a delegate, but came back to Jamaica in 1843, when provision for return passage applied only to immigrants from the Kru country. As the other five in the party had entered Jamaica in the year 1843, they and Johnson were in the same category and without legal claim to return at the expense of Jamaica. Nonetheless, be-

51. C. E. Grey to Earl Grey, Mar. 23, 1848, no.34, CS 102/13, series 1848.
52. Murdock and Rogers to Merivale, May 5, 1848, enc.4 in no.9, "Papers Relative to Emigration from Africa to the West Indies," *PP*, 1850, XI:15.
53. Earl Grey to C. E. Grey, Aug. 20, 1847, *Votes*, 1847-1848, p.119.
54. Report of David Ewart, AGI, Nov. 1, 1848, *Votes*, 1848-1849, Ap. 1, p.5.
55. Thomas Bennett, Commodore, *Imaum* at Port Royal, to T. F. Pilgrim, July 19, 1848, in no.2235 Jamaica, CO 137/297.

cause they were regarded as influential men whose good will was to be valued, the six eventually were returned to Africa by government transport. It was hoped they would encourage their fellows to migrate to Jamaica.[56]

But the Johnson party had caused the whole question of return passage to be brought up for judicial review. The first immigration act to provide return passage for African immigrants in general came into effect January 1, 1844 (7 Vic. c.29, sec. 8) and required five years residence as qualification for return passage. Of those Africans who had entered prior to January 1, 1844, only Krumen were entitled to claim return—and Krumen did not wish to leave Jamaica.[57] Those who had entered Jamaica since January 1, 1844, did not yet meet the five-year residence requirement. By the same token, *emancipados* from Cuba, who first arrived in Jamaica in 1845, also were ineligible to claim return to Africa at public expense. Had they been returned to their place of origin they quite possibly would have been sold again to slavers. To reiterate, under the existing law no Africans except Krumen were then pronounced eligible for return passage.[58] Under the earlier immigration law (7 Vic. c.29), which provided for the return of African immigrants generally, eighty-seven notices had been filed prior to November 1, 1848, all to become effective after January 1, 1849.[59] This was only the beginning of such demands upon Jamaica, and they came at a time when revenues were falling sharply.

Disaster struck Jamaica when, after the receiver-general died in January, 1848, serious deficiency was found in his records. Just as merchant ships were arriving with African immigrants (as previously noted), and Jamaica's dream of many African immigrants seemed a possibility, there was suddenly the very real problem of finding money to meet transportation and other expenses incidental to their reception. The new receiver-general, Alexander Barclay, was asked the extent to which island funds could cover these expenses. He replied only that it was impossible to give a satisfactory answer, for funds were exhausted. Actually he had tried, without success, to borrow money. Public funds were so low that he was then uncertain of the colony's ability to meet the expenses of the ships already en route. Under

56. Report by David Ewart, AGI, Nov. 1, 1848, *Votes,* 1848-1849, Ap. 1, p.5.
57. It was said that if a Kruman returned to Africa, his chief would confiscate his earnings and property.
58. D. Ewart to C. E. Grey, July 10, 1848; Ewart to T. F. Pilgrim, Governor's Secretary, Aug. 15, 1848; in no.2235 Jamaica, CO 137/297.
59. Report by David Ewart, AGI, Nov. 1, 1848, *Votes,* 1848-1849, Ap. 1, pp.5-6.

the circumstances, he could not advise sending out any more vessels from Africa to Jamaica. Although the Legislature had voted £15,000 for immigration purposes, the money was not in the treasury, and probably never would be.[60]

Such was the situation when Jamaica received a message which formerly would have been welcome: "Additional ships had been chartered by the CL&EC to transport liberated Africans to Jamaica." Treasurer, AGI, and governor of Jamaica were in agreement that Jamaica could not possibly meet those expenses. She must request a halt to emigration from Africa to the island. There was no alternative.[61]

The Russell ministry had been contemplating modifying the regulations for African emigration. By the time the governor's despatch (warning of the depletion of Jamaica's finances) arrived in London, the Russell government had already decided to pay from the British treasury the transportation costs of liberated Africans who volunteered to go as immigrants to the West Indies.[62] Consequently, the condition of Jamaica's treasury did not then seem to be a significant deterrent to her reception of immigrants.[63] Ships already chartered for Jamaica were allowed to proceed as planned. Entries in the annual report of the AGI indicate that Jamaica paid the transportation costs of ships which arrived prior to May, 1848; after that date the costs were borne by the British treasury.[64]

Explanation for the change in British policy was not to be found in Jamaica or any of the West Indian colonies, but in Africa, where Britain attempted to care for those Africans newly liberated from slave ships. Revival in the slave trade and an increase in the number of ships captured with slaves on board had resulted in a sudden and enormous increase in the number of liberated Africans. The Africa yards became full to the point of serious overcrowding. When the *Growler* called at Sierra Leone it had been a blessing in the guise of a ship. Sierra Leone authorities twice filled it with

60. A. Barclay, Receiver-General, to D. Ewart, May 22, 1848, in no.1553 Jamaica, CO 137/296.

61. C. E. Grey to Earl Grey, May 22, 1848, ibid.

62. Earl Grey to Russell, July 13, 1852, Grey, *Colonial Policy of Lord John Russell,* 2 vols. (London, 1853), 1:78.

63. Minutes by H[enry] T[aylor] and [Earl] G[rey], June 26, June 27, 1848, in C. E. Grey to Earl Grey, May 22, 1848, no.1553 Jamaica, CO 137/296.

64. Return of Immigrants into the Island of Jamaica; State of the Amount Drawn from the Public Treasury for Purposes of Immigration; Ap. A, Ap. B, in Report by D. Ewart, Nov. 1, 1848, *Votes,* 1848-1849, Ap. 1, pp.11-12.

liberated Africans rather than send it to the Kru coast, as had been planned in London. As more prizes were brought in for adjudication and their "cargos" were added to the yard, it became necessary to displace some of the occupants already there. In some instances adults were distributed over the colony of Sierra Leone. Those who wandered beyond its confines were beyond British jurisdiction, yet were considered by the natives as British subjects, therefore exempt from native law. Children who were sent from the yard to make room for newer arrivals were placed in government schools where, hopefully, they might learn a trade.

Within a period of approximately two months in 1848, six prizes were brought before the Vice-Admiralty Court in Sierra Leone and 2,400 Africans were emancipated there. Less than 1,000 of this number would emigrate to the West Indies.[65] A few months later, of the 1,080 Africans in the yard, only 150 could be persuaded to leave Africa.[66] Equally critical was the situation in St. Helena, where the area for possible expansion was sharply limited. It was useless to help any of the liberated Africans return home, for they probably would be resold into slavery. The only solution was to continue either the policy of locating them in the villages of Sierra Leone, where prospects for the future were indeed bleak, or of encouraging emigration to the West Indies where they might appreciably improve their economic as well as their social status. It was the old story, however; the longer they remained in the yard, the more firmly they were under the spell of the resident population, who did not want them to leave. Now, with West Indian colonies unable to pay transportation costs of those willing to emigrate, Great Britain would bear the charges herself in order to make way for temporary care of those who were recently liberated. Jamaica planting interests had been trying for almost eight years to persuade Britain to provide "imperial assistance" for African immigration—that is, assumption of both financial and managerial responsibility for transporting immigrants from Africa. Had it come too late to save the economy?

Because of its significance as background for the story of African immigration, it is necessary at this point again to allude briefly to the political situation. In the early part of 1848 Jamaica had not yet given up hope of parliamentary action which would restore preferential duties for

65. Acting-Governor Pine to Earl Grey, Sierra Leone, Sept. 2, 1848, no.76, "Papers Relative to Emigration from Africa to the West Indies," *PP,* 1850, XL:4.
66. Pine to Grey, Jan. 2, 1849, no.3, ibid., p.5.

West Indian sugar. During April and May, when the House of Commons Select Committee on West Indian Affairs was conducting investigations and hearings in London, Jamaicans undertook to lend support by holding public meetings in Kingston and over the entire island. Addresses, petitions, resolutions expressed the temper of the people. All were for the purpose of having the Legislature convened in order to exert pressure on the imperial government for modification of its free-trade policy and to ward off the "baneful effect of imperial legislation."[67]

In Parliament, as the debates on the sugar duties continued during June and July, Jamaica planting interests were castigated. When Jamaica received news of victory for Lord John Russell's government with its continuance of free trade, the island was put into an explosive mood. The Kingston Chamber of Commerce passed a resolution which contained three warning notes: it would be useless to expect any help from the government; the most powerful weapon was the purse; the colony should withhold supply until the government made reforms.[68] When the assembly was convened in August, 1848, Governor Grey was apprehensive, for he feared the influence of a party in England which, like the Kingston Chamber of Commerce, recommended stoppage of supply as a means, perhaps, of bringing down the government in Britain.[69] The imperial government (in September) offered the colony a guaranteed loan of approximately £100,000 to be used for any one of several purposes, including importation of immigrant laborers, construction of roads, railroads, drainage or irrigation facilities, or other public undertakings of similar character.[70] To people now without access to their customary credit, confronted with the probability of a continued fall in price for their produce, and faced with almost certain ruin, not even a proffered loan for immigration purposes was attractive. Their urgent need was credit, such as might be obtained from a bank; yet the guaranteed loan could not be used for establishing a bank and would have entailed a minimum annual repayment and a pledge of certain taxes fixed for 20 years.[71]

67. C. E. Grey to Earl Grey, Mar. 27, 1849, no.41, CO 137/302; Addresses from the inhabitants of Kingston, and other enclosures, in C. E. Grey to Earl Grey, June 19, 1848, no.59 in "Despatches from Charles Grey," in *PP,* 1847-1848, XLIV:1-5.
68. Enc. in C. E. Grey to Earl Grey, July 7, 1848, no.59, in "Despatches from Governor Grey," ibid., p.7.
69. C. E. Grey to Earl Grey, Nov. 4, 1848, no.96, CO 137/298.
70. 11, 12 Vic. c.13, *Votes,* 1848-1849, Ap. 1, p.1.
71. The proposed twenty-year loan, at four percent, would have been redeem-

The assembly, after noting the condition of the island revenue, again undertook to retrench, and to do so in part by a graduated but sharp reduction in salaries of public officials. After the governor and the council rejected this measure, the assembly resorted to the device of designating the specific purposes for which revenue measures could be spent. Salaries for governor, councillors, clergy, and many other public officials were not among those designated. The immigration act was extended only to mid-February, 1849.[72] By reason of the assembly's failure to take further action on the measure, Jamaica's legislative provision for immigration was permitted to lapse. It meant no funds for maintenance of immigrants upon their arrival, no money for paying salaries of officials whose duty was to care for them—in short, a complete rejection of the colony's responsibility for immigrants, who needed care and supervision after their arrival. For the welfare of both Jamaica and the liberated Africans, it was imperative to stop immigration at once.[73] Even with word of the situation sent to England by the next packet, the relayed message did not arrive in Africa until weeks later. During the interval, emigrants were embarked for Jamaica. By early March, 1849, Governor Grey was reporting great difficulty in meeting a charge of £200 for maintenance and medical attention to immigrants from only one ship: three more vessels were expected, yet there were no funds available to meet the expenses connected with debarkation, care, and placement of these liberated Africans.[74]

Additional complications arose as a result of an increase in the number of earlier arrivals who decided to ask for return to Africa. By April, 1849, 231 of them had completed a five-year residence and filed request for free return passage. Again the AGI classified the applicants according to their date of entry. The first and largest group had entered prior to January 1, 1843. As their claims continued to be based solely upon alleged promises of agents employed by the Jamaica government, the AGI again asserted there was no proper authorization for any Jamaica official to provide them with return passage; therefore, it would be necessary for these applicants to petition the House of Assembly. For the second class, introduced under

---

able only after termination of the period. Jamaica would have to make provision to pay annually at least £6,500 for twenty years and with the taxes pledged for repayment enacted for not less than the whole period. *Votes,* 1848-1849, pp.47, 49-52, 183.

72. C. E. Grey to Earl Grey, Mar. 27, 1849, no.41, CO 137/302.

73. C. E. Grey to Earl Grey, Mar. 10, 1849, no.36, *PP,* 1850, XI:140-141; CO 137/302.

74. Ibid.

imperial supervision in 1843, and with the distinct understanding that the Jamaica legislature would provide return passage, the AGI now pronounced Jamaica morally if not legally obligated, despite inadvertent omission on the part of the House of Assembly formally to accept the obligation. In the third category were those who came via the *Glen Huntley* after January 1, 1844, when the immigration act guaranteed them return passage. Those entitled to free passage to Africa in 1849, Ewart concluded, were immigrants of the year 1843; all those who had resided in Jamaica for five years since January 1, 1844; and all Krumen who had arrived in 1841, 1842, 1843.[75] Excepted from this generalization were those who came from St. Helena. On the basis of official commitments, it was decided that less than fifty percent of all applicants could be regarded as automatically entitled to a free return passage to Africa merely by filing a request with the AGI.[76] The subject of sending immigrants back to Africa soon became embarrassing. The House of Assembly in its last session had made only limited appropriations. Jamaica now had no money anywhere to pay the return fares of African immigrants who wished to go "home."[77] Although officials acknowledged the responsibility of Jamaica to provide return passage for some of the immigrants, they were unable to fulfill the obligation.

Meanwhile, there remained the question of what, if anything, could be done to provide funds to care for immigrants who were still arriving in Jamaica. Ewart, the AGI, proposed that he be given authority to hire them out. He believed there would be no difficulty in finding employers who would be willing to pay two pounds sterling per head. The resultant funds supposedly would be large enough to provide maintenance for arriving immigrants and salaries for immigration officials. The plan was not approved by either the governor or Colonial Office.[78]

Alexander Barclay was a resourceful man who applied himself assiduously to the duties of his office. Unable to secure a loan for Jamaica, he looked about for possible funds within the island itself. He found that many first employers of liberated Africans were in arrears on the payments of £2-£1 tax per immigrant for which they were liable. At a time when money

75. Ewart to Sir Charles Grey, Apr. 20, 1849, in no.4960 Jamaica, CO 137/302.
76. Ibid.
77. C. E. Grey to Earl Grey, May 8, 1849, in no.4970 Jamaica, CO 137/302.
78. C. E. Grey to Earl Grey, Mar. 10, 1849, no.36, in "Papers Relative to Emigration from Africa to the West Indies," *PP*, 1850, XL:140-141.

was tight, Barclay and the AGI succeeded in collecting enough of the delinquent tax to meet temporarily the reception costs of immigrants and the salaries of the immigration officials. Fortunately, as the planters were still eager for the services of African laborers, the immigrants were placed on estates without delay.[79]

Despite Barclay's work, there was no dependable revenue to be used for immigration purposes. Equally as grave as the lack of funds was the question of administration, for the governor no longer had authority to make contracts for immigrants or frame regulations for immigration officials. In short, with the lapse of the immigration act, there was no longer any legal basis for official assistance to immigration in Jamaica. Although in April the Colonial Office sent instructions to agents in Sierra Leone and St. Helena and directed them not to send any more African immigrants to Jamaica, it was July before the last immigrant ship reached Jamaica. During the months January through July, 1849, Jamaica received nearly one thousand liberated Africans; 713 came from St. Helena, 228 from Sierra Leone.[80] Apparently there would be no more.

It was an ironical situation. Britain at last would recruit and transport, without cost to Jamaica, African immigrant laborers whom the colony had long wanted for help in the production of sugar. Jamaica's only expense would be to care for them immediately after their arrival. But the island's economy was being seriously damaged by Britain's free-trade policy, and in the process of curtailing expenditures, the House of Assembly had placed the island in a position where she could not provide any assistance to arriving immigrants. As a consequence, Jamaica was not to receive any more African immigrant laborers, for whose recruitment and transportation Great Britain was bearing the cost.

79. C. E. Grey to Earl Grey, May 31, 1849, ibid., p.144.

80. Ibid.; "Return of Immigrants and Liberated Africans Introduced into the West Indian Colonies, 1847-1855 . . . ," Sixteenth General Report of the Emigration Commissioners, Ap. 2, *PP,* 1856, XXIV:408.

9

Renewed Efforts to Secure
African Immigrants

JAMAICA WAS SOON STRUCK FULL FORCE BY THE
consequences of its failure to pass an immigration act. Liberated Africans
willing to emigrate were still sent to the West Indian colonies but only to
those which provided for them properly. As Jamaica had not made such
provision, immigrants who might have agreed to go there were sent elsewhere. Many planters on the island now contemplated a new immigration
act. Because there had been widespread dissatisfaction with the old term of
indenture, mere reenactment of former measures was not wanted. Numerous proposals would have the immigrants bound for a longer indenture,
perhaps three years, possibly five, though there was no firm agreement as to
an exact duration. Such a long term was contrary to the views of Earl Grey,
who had so advised the governor. This put the latter official in an awkward
position. The Colonial Office expected him to influence colonial attitudes in
such a way as to produce legislation in conformity with the wishes of the
imperial government; yet the House of Assembly, jealously guarding its
prerogative, would resent official suggestions as interference by the governor. In an effort to exercise tact, Governor Grey chose the indirect approach. A select committee had been appointed by the assembly to frame a
bill. With David Ewart as intermediary, the governor unofficially communicated to the committee chairman Earl Grey's instructions for contracts not

to exceed one year. Nonetheless, as the bill emerged from the assembly, it provided for three-year contracts. When the governor informed the council of Earl Grey's instructions, that body amended the measure to provide the required one-year maximum for contracts. The bill as amended by the council was accepted by the House of Assembly.[1]

The governor, hard pressed by matters of colonial finance, had no time for a careful scrutiny of the immigration measure. Instead, he relied upon the opinion of the Attorney General. Assured by him of nothing objectionable in it, Sir Charles forwarded to England "An Act to Further Immigration." At the same time he suggested that as Jamaica now met all requirements for receiving liberated African immigrants, there was no longer anything to prevent Earl Grey from issuing directives for them again to be sent there. However, the governor obviously had given only passing attention to the subject. His brief official communication with regard to the immigration act was not even a separate despatch, but merely a postscript to a lengthy communication pertaining to financial matters and a request for a guaranteed loan.[2]

At the Colonial Office, Earl Grey and his staff were also concerned with many problems, including those which were by-products of the campaign to end the slave trade. Africa yards were still overcrowded to the point where continual attention was imperative, with emigration the most logical remedy. As Jamaica was again in a position to accept those who were willing to emigrate, the Secretary of State for the Colonies did not wait either for official analysis or allowance of the Jamaica immigration act.[3] Relying only upon the governor's assurance of its merits, he instructed the Colonial Land and Emigration Commission again to include Jamaica in the list of places to which liberated Africans might be sent.[4] Despite the many years during which the Colonial Office had adamantly required that contracts-for-service not exceed twelve months, Earl Grey now modified his attitude and no longer adhered so rigidly to the rule. In fact, he had recently agreed to some exceptions for other West Indian colonies, and seemingly was willing to do the same for Jamaica.[5]

1. C. E. Grey to Earl Grey, Feb. 6, 1850, in no.1773 Jamaica, CO 137/306.
2. Ibid.
3. Minute to the Board of Trade, May 29, 1850, in no.3999 Jamaica, CO 137/306.
4. Earl Grey to C. E. Grey, Apr. 12, 1850, in no.1773 Jamaica, CO 137/306.
5. Ibid.

Meanwhile, soon after the Legislature passed the immigration act, planters became impatient to know its fate in England. They needed laborers, and they would like to be sure of getting them.[6] Applications were filed for seven thousand immigrant laborers, but there was no definite word as to when or in what numbers they would arrive. In reality, when Earl Grey directed restoration of Jamaica to the list of receiving colonies, the CL&EC had found it necessary to revise immigration plans. Some of the smaller West Indian colonies (Granada, St. Lucia, St. Kitts, Tobago) as well as British Guiana and Trinidad had been included as recipients. With the addition of Jamaica, it meant a total of seven colonies who would share immigrants. To have some logical basis for apportionment, the commissioners selected three criteria: (1) average exports for the years 1845, 1846, and 1847, (2) rate of wages, and (3) "other considerations." Jamaica's exports for the selected years had exceeded those of any other West Indian colony; but, concluded the commissioners, her wage scale (lower than in British Guiana or Trinidad) indicated a labor shortage less acute then in the other two colonies. The commissioners determined, on the basis of these exports and wages, that her immigrants be at a ratio of seven to twenty.[7]

As to what immigrant ships Jamaica could expect, and when, the commissioners were somewhat indefinite. Perhaps the *Glentanner* (with a capacity of 284 adults) would arrive approximately July 12; or perhaps the *Fame* (capacity 318 adults) about August 10. The *Clarendon,* which had definitely been assigned to transport immigrants to Jamaica, might appear about August 1.[8] While planters waited, distress mounted. Weather conditions were favorable for a good cane yield, but labor was urgently needed. In at least two parishes (St. Mary's and Metcalfe) the creoles took three and one-half weeks holiday in August to commemorate their freedom, thereby almost entirely stopping work during a month critical for sugar-making. In five more parishes[9] estates were showing neglect because not enough laborers could be found to maintain them properly. Planters complained that because of the Sugar Duties Bill and the subsequent fall in the price of their sugar, they were unable to afford wages high enough to attract the creoles, who were turning to production of other commodities.[10]

6. C. E. Grey to Earl Grey, Apr. 19, 1850, no.36, CO 137/306.
7. CL&EC to Herman Merivale, May 6, 1850, in no.337, *PP,* 1852-1853, LXVII:216-217.
8. Ibid., 217-218.
9. Westmoreland, Hanover, St. James, Trelawney, and St. Ann's.
10. Henry Westmoreland to Thomas F. Pilgrim, Aug. 27, 1850; William Hosack

July, August, and September passed without the arrival of a single immigrant ship. Not until November 1 did the CL&EC offer an explanation. Unknown to the commissioners, orders for the first ship had been changed by the governor of Sierra Leone, who sent it to Demerara. Assuming the first ship sailing from Sierra Leone was proceeding to Jamaica, the commissioners changed orders for the second ship, and directed it to go from St. Helena to Demerara. The third ship was delayed in England; then its orders were changed. After an unsuccessful attempt to secure immigrants at Sierra Leone, it proceeded to the Kru Coast to recruit for Tobago. The CL&EC gave assurance that the *Glentanner,* when it returned to Sierra Leone in October, would recruit immigrants for Jamaica, and could be expected to arrive there in early November with two or three hundred Africans. Furthermore, it promised, additional immigrant ships would be sent to Jamaica to compensate for the many errors.[11]

Recruiting for the *Glentanner* was slow, and when the ship left Sierra Leone it carried far less than a capacity load. On reaching Jamaica it called at Port Royal, spent two nights there and finally arrived at Lucea late in November.[12] By then the island had been struck by further disaster in the form of cholera. The ship's master, anxious to avoid the disease, quickly discharged his 178 passengers and departed for Sierra Leone without complying with the customary formalities. He did not even conduct any business at the Immigration Office or communicate with the Jamaica agent of Messrs. Hyde, Hodge, and Company, the firm which owned the *Glentanner* and most of the immigrant vessels. The master's haste and neglect of formalities made it impossible for the AGI to fulfill his own duties, which included reporting the state of the ship upon its arrival, preparing a report for transmission to England, and sending duplicates of that report to the governors of both Sierra Leone and St. Helena.[13]

There was no difficulty, of course, in finding employment for the

to [T. F. Pilgrim], Aug. 27, 1850, enc. in C. E. Grey to Earl Grey, Sept. 9, 1850, in *PP,* 1852-1853, LXVII:54-55.

11. Extract from a Report of the CL&EC to Merivale, Nov. 1, 1850, in no.384, *PP,* 1852-1853, LXVII:255.

12. Report by David Ewart, "Return of Immigrants . . . into Jamaica, Feb. 1-Dec. 31, 1850," *Votes,* 1850-1851, Ap. 77, p.271; C. E. Grey to Earl Grey, Dec. 27, 1850, "Report on Immigration by the Ship *Glentanner,*" no.98, *PP,* 1852-1853, LXVII, p.57.

13. Ewart to C. E. Grey, Dec. 25, 1850; C. E. Grey to Earl Grey, Dec. 27, 1850, in no.687 Jamaica, CO 137/307.

immigrants who arrived on the *Glentanner.* All of them were assigned in the parish of Hanover, over fifty percent of them to two employers (Henry Brockett and Isaac Jackson). The remaining 78 were distributed among seven employers.[14] No other immigrant transport arrived in Jamaica in 1850, although during the course of the year 61 *emancipados* were brought from Cuba.[15]

While Jamaica was impatiently awaiting immigrants from the Africa yards, it suddenly became host to Negroes freed directly from a slave ship. The *Clementine,* a Brazilian brig with a cargo of slaves, was sighted off the Isle of Pines in May, 1850. After a 48-hour chase in the Gulf of Mexico, it was captured by HMS *Bermuda* (Archibold D. Jolly, Commander) and taken as prize to Port Royal.[16] It was so extraordinary for a slaver to be brought into Jamaica as prize that no one was quite prepared to deal with it even though there was a Vice-Admiralty Court at Spanish Town. The colony had no established organization or personnel to provide care for the slave cargo, and while emergency measures were being developed the Africans were kept on board. They were in bad condition when captured; 40 died before the vessel anchored at Port Royal; 14 more were to die before adjudication was completed.[17]

When the *Clementine* was brought into port, the immediate problem was food. There was none on board; no one was willing to supply it. The commander of the capturing vessel requested the collector of customs at Kingston to take charge of the "cargo."[18] The latter was not unwilling but lacked authorization. Something had to be done, however, and done at once. The collector, J. G. Swanson, went to Spanish Town for an interview with the governor and was officially assigned care and custody of the captured Negroes.[19] It was further agreed during the course of the conference that Fort Augusta, just across the harbor from Port Royal, was the best place to land and maintain the Africans until adjudication.

14. "Return of First Employers of African Immigrants . . . ," Dec. 21, 1850, *Votes,* 1850-1851, Ap. 77, p.274.
15. "Return of Immigrants and Liberated Africans Introduced into the West Indies . . . ," Eighteenth Annual Report of the Emigration Commission, *PP,* 1857-1858, XXIV:493.
16. C. E. Grey to Earl Grey, June 4, 1850, in no.5456 Jamaica, CO 137/306.
17. "Remarks," Return of Vessels Adjudicated in the Vice-Admiralty Court of Jamaica . . . , in no.6492 Jamaica, CO 137/307.
18. A. D. Jolly to Collector of HM Customs, May 22, 1850, in no.5456 Jamaica, CO 137/306.
19. J. G. Swanson, Collector, to Pilgrim, May 23, 1850, ibid.

Having officially been given responsibility for care of the recaptured Africans, Swanson lost no time. Immediately after his interview with the governor, he appointed two men[20] to go on that very day to Fort Augusta, where late that evening (and three days after the prize was brought into port) they received all Africans from the slave ship. The officer in charge of the *Clementine* requested, and was given, a receipt for the number landed[21] which at the time of debarkation was 244—160 males, 84 females. They were described as in a weakened condition, and without food or clothing. Both were immediately provided, and "wholesome" food was distributed twice a day. Despite efforts by a Kingston doctor who visited the Africans daily during their detention, several died there at Fort Augusta.[22] In order to have some sort of account of these people, officials caring for them prior to their adjudication recorded name, sex, and estimated age of each one.

Not until June 17 was the case heard before the Vice-Admiralty Court at Spanish Town. The judge, holding the *Clementine* to have been employed in illegal transportation of Negroes for slavery, ordered the ship broken up and the parts sold separately. He pronounced the slaves found on board as forfeited to the use of the Queen.[23]

The Negroes from the slaver now were officially liberated Africans and as such became the responsibility of the AGI, who found employment for them as free laborers or apprentices, depending upon their age. In lots varying in size from one to ten, Ewart assigned them to thirty-five different employers in eleven parishes. Many of the employers were of politcal prominence or from families who were.[24] The records do not indicate age, sex, or name of those assigned to a given employer. However, of the 240 landed at Fort Augusta, 126 were recorded as eleven years of age or less, with many of them between the ages of three and six. Nothing suggests they were children accompanying their mothers. In a time when the need was for instant labor, employers who accepted the very young apprentices might

20. C. F. Bruce, the Tide Surveyor at Port Royal, and John Davis, Island Clerk to the Collector.

21. Swanson to Pilgrim, May 27, 1850, in no.5462 Jamaica, CO 137/306.

22. Bruce and Davis to the Collector of Customs, May 25, 1850, in no.5456 Jamaica, CO 137/306.

23. Copy, Interlocutory Decree, the Queen *vs.* the Brazilian Brig *Clementine,* in no.6492 Jamaica, CO 137/307;

24. The employers included Hinton Spalding, George Geddes, P. A. Espeut, William Hosack, J. R. Hollingsworth, Baron Kettelhodt, George Price, Gilbert Shaw, John Ewart. "Return of Employers of Captured Africans, per slaver *Clementine,*" Ap. 6 of the Report of the AGI, Feb. 1, 1851, *Votes,* 1850-1851, Ap. 77, p.275.

well be credited with humanitarian as well as economic motives. Total cost to the island government was £269 6*s*. 5*d*. which the governor estimated as 9*d*. per day, including clothing, for each African.[25]

The prize *Clementine* was a boon to Jamaica, but to Britain it was another matter. As that country was maintaining a naval patrol along the West Africa coast in order to stop the African slave trade near its source, the appearance of a slave ship in the western Atlantic meant there had been successful evasion of the royal navy. Worse yet, it was not one but two ships which had eluded the British patrol. One slaver, the *Brazil,* was large, heavily armed, and had a "cargo" of some 600 Africans which it landed in Cuba. It was embarassing to Her Majesty's ministers, who had some questions for which they needed answers. How had this evasion been possible? Where had it occurred? No one knew even from what part of Africa these people had been taken.

Detailed information was difficult to obtain, for the Africans from the *Clementine* spoke a dialect unlike any of those commonly heard in Jamaica. The "cargo," it seemed, was from the Bight of Biafra. At least part of the slaves had been kidnapped by fellow Africans: two boys had been seized while they were asleep, were bound and gagged, then carried to a boat; one man told of having been caught and sold to the Spanish. Apparently the cargo had been collected a few at a time, for "No. 35" mentioned having been put on a ship which already had slaves on board when it arrived at Gaboon. Both the *Clementine* and the *Brazil* had collected in small, out-of-the-way places, but left with a short cargo because a British steamer reportedly had come into the neighborhood.[26] If slave ships continued to elude the Royal Navy and make their way to the western Atlantic, it might mean that more "recaptures" would be landed directly in Jamaica for adjudication there.

Meanwhile Jamaica was swept by a new and terrible disaster in the form of cholera, the disease which had so terrified the master of the *Glentanner.* The first recorded fatality occurred on October 7 at Port Royal. Within three weeks 150 had died there. The disease appeared in Kingston only a week later than in Port Royal, and within two weeks between 100 and 150 persons had died. It soon struck Spanish Town, where within a six-mile radius 50 died during one week. The Legislature met briefly on

25. C. E. Grey to Earl Grey, Aug. 5, 1850, in no.7258 Jamaica, CO 137/307.
26. C. E. Grey to Earl Grey, Oct. 11, 1850, in no.9142 Jamaica, CO 137/307.

October 22, but because of the epidemic was adjourned until November 19.[27]

Port Royal, where cholera had first occurred, was reputedly a filthy town. In an effort to check the spread of the disease, island authorities decided to limit contact with that port town, by restricting the vessels which had called there. By Order in Council, any ship which arrived from Port Royal or Kingston within less that five days after departure from the pest-ridden port must be sent to quarantine.[28] When news of the Order in Council reached the Secretary of State, there was a curious reaction. He was sympathetic, but regretted imposition of quarantine, which would not halt the epidemic, yet would hinder trade and industry, thereby causing great distress. The proper remedy, he implied, was cleanliness and ventilation.[29]

Jamaica was relatively inexperienced with cholera and knew little about it. Reportedly the disease was communicated not by living persons, but by the corpses, bed-clothes, and body clothes of those who had died. It was assumed, on this basis, that cholera was spread by those who attended funerals or wakes. To add to the horror, there was difficulty in getting the dead buried. On one day, November 9, Kingston had accumulated no less than one hundred unburied corpses.[30] Although the disease fell most heavily upon the laboring (and less sanitary) class, it was no respecter of persons. The governor's secretary was ill, but recovered; Dr. Macfayden, acting president of the Board of Health and a botanist, was among the less fortunate.[31] The disease, spreading rapidly to other parts of the island, became a frightful epidemic. Within three months an estimated 10,000 had died.[32]

The Legislature met briefly in December. The members were all too aware of peril to both their own and Jamaica's health, welfare, and economy. The colony was now losing by disease more than the total number of Africans who had immigrated since 1840. Decimation of the labor force endangered not only the current sugar crop, but, far worse, the continued cultivation of the soil, which was the keystone of Jamaica's economy.[33]

27. C. E. Grey to Earl Grey, Oct. 26, 1850, in no.9381 Jamaica, CO 137/307.
28. Order in Council, in no.9381 Jamaica, CO 137/307.
29. Minute by Earl Grey, to no.86, C. E. Grey, Oct. 26, 1850, in no.9381 Jamaica, CO 137/307.
30. C. E. Grey to Earl Grey, Nov. 11, 1850, in no.10,080 Jamaica, CO 137/307.
31. C. E. Grey to Earl Grey, Nov. 28, 1850, in no.231 Jamaica, CO 137/307.
32. C. E. Grey to Earl Grey, Jan. 11, 1851, in no.1056 Jamaica, CO 137/310.
33. C. E. Grey to Earl Grey, Dec. 13, 1850, in no.235 Jamaica, CO 137/307.

Despite their haste to be gone from Spanish Town because of the disaster, the House of Assembly and the Council took time to ask (by means of memorials to the Queen) that all captured Africans be sent to Jamaica, and that the imperial government adopt measures to encourage free Africans to come as immigrant laborers. The Council went a step further to touch upon the humanitarian note by referring to Jamaica's ability to offer employment to the many Africans who had been doomed to slavery until rescued by Her Majesty's Squadron.[34] Despite the calamity in Jamaica, the imperial government could not comply with the request, for to do so would exclude the other West Indian colonies, also in need of labor, from any share in the liberated Africans.[35]

Planters were becoming desperate because of financial conditions. The imperial government stubbornly refused to equate reduction in income from sugar with decreased ability to pay taxes. Trouble was everywhere: credit was difficult if not impossible to obtain; cholera continued to reduce the population; vagabondage was becoming serious. Africans as well as coolies tended not to renew their contracts; instead, when the original term of service was completed, they left the estate, often merely to wander about the countryside. Finally, ill and destitute, they became public charges, sometimes committed to the public hospital. Africans could be absorbed quite easily into the peasant population, but Jamaica authorities professed to fear the consequences. One service period of twelve months, they argued, was not sufficient time to impart civilization to the newly liberated Africans. By their speedy departure from estates these Africans, who were not yet integrated into creole culture, seemed to threaten retrogression for the peasant population. If this could be halted by extending the term of service, presumably the Africans and creoles would benefit more than planters. It was a rationale likely to appeal to those who might still be interested in the "great experiment" of emancipation, and brought response from some in high places.

Earl Grey, at the Colonial Office, concluded that if sugar cultivation should come to an end in Jamaica so would the presence of the planting interests whose withdrawal, he feared, would halt the progress which was being made by those who had been slaves. Efforts made to procure free

34. Memorial to the Queen by the House of Assembly, *Votes,* 1850-1851, pp.49-50; Memorial to the Queen by the Council, in no.683 Jamaica, CO 137/307.
35. Earl Grey to C. E. Grey, Feb. 15, 1851, no.398 in *Votes,* 1850-1851, p.283; minute to no.94 in no.235 Jamaica, CO 137/307.

emigrants from Africa had failed, and current reports, he warned, did not indicate any prospect for a change in that quarter. He had a scheme, however, which he believed could provide a solution; but before proposing it to Jamaica he sought and secured approval by the West India Committee which had so often tried to influence the West India policies of the government.[36] While emphasizing relief for Jamaica as the responsibility solely of the assembly, the Colonial Secretary suggested means which might be used, if authorized by island legislation. These included: (1) Importation by private enterprise of laborers from areas other than Africa—particularly of freed Negroes from the United States—without cost to the government. There should be "some simple law" by which those who advanced passage money to immigrants would be guaranteed repayment. Although he was vague as to how this would be possible, he said he would not oppose contracts for three years. (2) Passage of a law to permit introduction at public expense of laborers from Europe, America, or China. Funds for this could be advanced from the colonial treasury and be recoverable by it, as a debt, from the immigrant. (3) A reduction of import duties which, theoretically, would reduce the price of foodstuffs, thus making it more profitable for laborers to hire out for wages than to cultivate their own provision grounds. Loss of revenue from import duties might be met by a land tax. He apparently expected this to become permanent, and thus a step toward continuing appropriations, which was a major objective of his office.[37] Earl Grey's long exposition of February 15 touched upon many subjects, and officially was a reply to the memorials of December. Although application of Colonial Office theories might not be practical, tact as well as protocol required their submission for consideration by the House of Assembly.[38]

Such was the situation when late in the session the assembly began the annual task of drawing an immigration measure. As Earl Grey had written, " . . . if the legislature of Jamaica should see fit to pass a law for this purpose [i.e., legalizing contracts for three years, and with immigrants from the United States] I should not consider it necessary to advise her majesty to withhold her sanction from it." Committeemen framing the bill and members of the Assembly alike may have seized upon the quoted part of the statement. Certainly they ignored two qualifications: (1) Earl Grey's

36. Minute by Earl Grey, C. E. Grey to Earl Grey, Dec. 13, 1850, in no.235 Jamaica, CO 137/307.
37. Earl Grey to C. E. Grey, Feb. 15, 1851, no.398, CO 137/307.
38. Message by the Governor, *Votes*, 1850-1851, p.281.

expression of "strong opinion as to the extreme impolicy" of such contracts;[39] and (2) omission of Africa from the list of recruiting areas where three-year contracts-for-service might possibly be made.[40] Bearing a lengthy title, "A Bill to Provide for the Reception and Care of Captured Africans, *Emancipados,* and other African Laborers, introduced into this colony by Her Majesty's government, or otherwise to encourage voluntary immigration into this island from foreign countries, and to legalize contracts for service by immigrants for any period not exceeding three years," the proposed measure was introduced in the House of Assembly on April 24.[41]

While the bill was under consideration, the annual report of the AGI was laid before the assembly.[42] Written nearly three months prior to its presentation, its contents undoubtedly were already known to many or all of the gentlemen concerned with the welfare of the colony. Ewart referred to problems relating to the liberated Africans, such as obeah, myalism, and alcohol. Because he was known to have had the privilege of studying recent despatches from Earl Grey, who had proffered advice for dealing with the problems, the report and suggestions of the AGI would seem to have more significance than if made by most island officials.

Although the AGI report antedated by a fortnight the February 15 despatch of Earl Grey, the assemblymen might have overlooked that fact as, pressed by many problems, they worked hurriedly in late April. Presumably the governor, too, had not then read the report very carefully. Mauritius and Trinidad, so Ewart understood, had enacted laws which accorded with the Colonial Office views and had been sanctioned by Her Majesty's government. Their provisions, Ewart stated, included the following: (1) For a liberated African above eighteen years of age, a government officer could conclude a contract of twelve months, no longer. At the end of twelve months, the African should not leave his first employer until he had made a contract with some other employer. This could be for three years, if the African gave his consent. The lengthened service presumably would lessen the chance of his becoming the victim of a practitioner of obeah. (2) All Africans under eighteen must be apprenticed until that age. (3) Contracts for three years should be allowed in the case of all immigrants introduced at the expense of the colony. Ewart repeated his own suggestion, made on previous occasions:

39. Earl Grey to C. E. Grey, Feb. 15, 1851, no.398, ibid., p.285.
40. Enc.2 in Earl Grey to C. E. Grey, Oct. 16, 1850, ibid., p.294.
41. Ibid., p.397.
42. Apr. 29, 1851, ibid., p.270.

in order to control alcoholism, withhold wages until the end of the year.[43] Influenced by Ewart's report, on May 12 the assembly gave final passage to an immigration bill which was approved by the Council.

The governor, when proroguing the Legislature a few days later, confounded that body when he announced refusal of assent to the immigration bill. Some of its provisions applicable to liberated Africans, brought at the expense of the imperial government, were at variance, he said, with instructions from the Colonial Office—instructions which he emphasized had been communicated to the House of Assembly both by himself and by the AGI. He suggested its sponsors confer with the latter official, then prepare a measure acceptable at the next session.[44] The governor's reference to the bill was brief, but left no doubt of his irritation with the Legislature because it had passed such a measure.

Governor Grey did not explain the situation promptly to the Colonial Office, but merely sent a copy of his prorogation speech, which was a routine procedure. This meant that the Colonial Office was kept waiting all summer for both a copy of the bill and a detailed explanation by the governor. So long as it was uninformed, it could do little but concur with the views of Sir Charles.[45]

Some West Indian interests in Britain, however, wanted prompt action. Lack of labor, they asserted, had compelled them to curtail or give up cultivation of their properties in Jamaica. Now that the Legislature had passed a bill which would encourage proprietors to import laborers at their own expense, the governor, they complained, was preventing its implementation. They wanted the Secretary of State for the Colonies to direct Sir Charles to give his assent to the measure. There is nothing to indicate that any changes were effected by the would-be pressure group.[46]

It was late September before Governor Grey's detailed report arrived at the Colonial Office. His objections to the immigration bill were many: (1) It made no distinction between liberated Africans, brought in at imperial expense, and those Africans who had never been slaves and whose transportation costs had not been assumed by Great Britain. (2) All would be

43. Ewart to C. E. Grey, Feb. 1, 1851, *Votes,* 1850-1851, Ap. 77, pp.262-270.
44. Speech by the Governor, May 23, 1851, *Votes,* 1850-1851, pp.585-586.
45. Minute by H. T., July 14, to C. E. Grey to Earl Grey, June 11, 1851, in no.5853 Jamaica, CO 137/309.
46. Memorial, West India Association of Glasgow, July 24, 1851, in no.398 Earl Grey to C. E. Grey, Feb. 15, 1851, *PP,* 1852-1853, LXVII, Part 2:213.

assigned as contract servants to planters according to priority of application by the planters. (3) Every assignment would be for a three-year term. (4) No money wages would be paid during the first twelve months. (5) No provision was made for inspection of the Africans' treatment on the estates. (6) All contracts made out of the colony were to be valid, West Coast Africa not excepted. The measure had been drawn for immigration in general, with some of the provisions doubtlessly intended for application to North America, but it had been so badly worded as to apply to liberated Africans. The governor gave vent to his irritation by concluding his despatch with a blistering denunciation of both planters and assembly.[47]

Despite the governor's withholding approval of the bill, many gentlemen, whether resident in Jamaica or in Britain, continued their efforts to promote immigration. Meeting at the West India Committee rooms in London, they drew up a set of resolutions aimed at enabling Jamaica to obtain laborers from various parts of the world. Specifically, they wanted authorization for contracts made out of the colony if they did not exceed a three-year period and were not made in Africa or India. They also asked for promotion of immigration at public expense, with reimbursement to the public treasury by annual payments per capita from employers of the immigrants so introduced. Again there was a casual suggestion of securing free immigrants from the United States. The real objective, however, was immigration assisted by an imperial loan of £100,000, with security based on a proposed export tax. A delegation appointed to seek a conference with the Colonial Secretary included William Beckford and men prominent in Jamaican affairs, including Edward Thompson and Henry Westmoreland.[48] In view of the governor's denunciation of the assembly, it was fortunate for the colony that these men were on the London scene and could serve as unofficial agents of their colony.

The immigration act which the governor had rejected was an astonishing measure. In addition to the defects already noted, it adhered closely to Ewart's report of the Trinidad and Mauritius laws, and included such provisions as: (1) Liberated Africans brought to Jamaica were to be assigned by the AGI to a planter for twelve months service. Prohibited from leaving the estate without a pass, they would be paid wages only "from time to time"

47. C. E. Grey to Earl Grey, Aug. 16, 1851, in no.8060 Jamaica, CO 137/310.
48. At a Meeting of Gentlemen Interested in the Island of Jamaica . . . , Oct. 14, 1851, *Votes,* 1851-1852, Ap. 33, pp.73-74.

and as the AGI "thought fit." (2) The original twelve-month period of service would be extended automatically for an additional twelve months unless the liberated African had previously entered into a contract with another employer. (3) An immigrant who refused to enter into a written contract must pay 15*s*. quarterly. (4) An employer must pay to the island treasurer 10*s*. for each liberated African assigned to him.[49]

When a copy of Jamaica's immigration bill eventually arrived in London, the Colonial Office not only agreed with the objections of the governor, but found serious additional faults. Although Earl Grey had said he would accept a bill which legalized contracts for a three-year period, the Jamaica bill had the effect of requiring them, and of denying the immigrant an opportunity to make any other arrangement during the three years. Moreover, "distribution according to priority" for the employers had the effect of nullifying the principle of assignment according to what was best for the immigrant. There were too many regulations, too many penalties aimed at ensuring the immigrant's working after his arrival. Earl Grey was completely out of patience with the Legislature for having passed such a measure.

At this point the planters who were seeking the loan found themselves able to serve the colony in an unanticipated way. They explained the bill as resulting from a combination of haste on the part of those present in the assembly and inexperience by those who had drawn the bill. Such tasks were usually performed by experts, but in this instance the members of the assembly who were specialists in these matters had been unable to attend.[50] Earl Grey was soothed sufficiently to put aside the suspicion that Jamaica had been trying to flout imperial advice. Nonetheless, he informed both the governor and the Jamaica delegation that an acceptable immigration act was a *sine qua non* for a loan to promote immigration.[51]

Meanwhile, dissatisfaction long simmering among planters had come to a boil. Throughout the entire period of African immigration, offers of employment had consistently exceeded supply. Seldom had a vessel carried its full complement of passengers; occasionally, and presumably for good reason, it discharged passengers in a port other then the one designated by the AGI. Ewart, as the chief official in charge of immigration, prided him-

49. Island Act no.322, in *PP*, 1852, LXII:346-354.
50. Earl Grey to C. E. Grey, Nov. 12, 1851, no.453, *Votes*, 1851-1852, pp.297-301.
51. Ibid., p.301.

self on making the most equitable distribution possible within unavoidable limitations. However, some, who were disgruntled because they did not receive as many immigrants as they wished, did not concur with Ewart's claim of his impartiality as AGI.

Absentee landlords who wanted to complain could write directly to the Colonial Office to demand justice—a procedure not permitted landlords in Jamaica. Two in particular gave vent to their anger over failure to obtain the number of African immigrants they wanted. William Beckford, in London, charged discrimination against the parish of Westmoreland. Labor for production of a hogshead of sugar cost him twice as much in Westmoreland as it cost him in St. Thomas-in-the-East. This, he charged, could be accounted for in only one way, that of partiality in distribution of African immigrants and refusal to give the parish of Westmoreland its fair share.[52] From Brussels, Lord Howard de Walden, proprietor of estates in St. Catherine and St. James, protested rather sharply his right to claim the same "advantages" that his neighbors had for hiring laborers.[53]

Ewart and Sir Charles, as the former's superior, were in a position to refute the accusations. Undoubtedly, conceded Sir Charles, St. Thomas-in-the-East did have some advantages over other parishes, and in the earlier period of African immigration, the parish might have obtained an undue share of immigrants; but since 1848, when Ewart became AGI, there had been strict impartiality as indicated by the evidence. The governor stated that on the occasion when a ship discharged passengers at Port Morant, it had been in disobedience to Ewart's orders. Sometimes, at the last moment, applicants for immigrants changed their minds and refused to pay the forty-shilling tax per immigrant. As the latter could not be left to shift upon the world, the immigration official was then forced to find some other employer. Such incidents, by disrupting the scheduled distribution, were a serious inconvenience to the colony. Agents of Beckford and of de Walden had been guilty of refusing at the last moment to accept some immigrants for which they had applied and thereby had deprived their estates of those indentured laborers.[54]

In justification of his policies, Ewart submitted a detailed report for the entire period of his administration. Documentation included: name of

52. William Beckford to Benjamin Hawes, Apr. 29, 1850, *PP*, 1852-1853, LXVII:315.
53. In Earl Grey to C. E. Grey, Oct. 16, 1850, *PP*, 1852-1853, LXVII:211.
54. C. E. Grey to Earl Grey, Aug. 8, 1850, in no.7260 Jamaica, CO 137/307.

ship, with number of immigrants landed alive; name of planter or agent, estate (with number of immigrants to each), and parish of each employer; and total number of immigrants assigned to each parish. Figures clearly showed the parish of Westmoreland as second only to St. Thomas-in-the-East in number of immigrants which had been received.[55] The report was sent to the Colonial Office, where it was carefully studied. Officials there saw no reason for accusation against Ewart. In fact, they noted that he had done "everything in his power" to distribute immigrants fairly.[56]

Planters who were in Jamaica and unhappy could complain directly to the AGI, the governor, or the House of Assembly.[57] Planters of the parish of St. Mary had been particularly jealous of St. Thomas-in-the-East. Some of the members of the Legislature were also among those who had obtained immigrants, but wanted more. They, too, wanted to see Ewart's documented defense of his entire administration. Consequently, the assembly appointed a committee which formally requested the governor to have Ewart provide a copy for them. As submitted, the papers included not only name of planter, estate, and number of immigrants assigned to it, but also notation of the tax levied upon all first employers of African immigrants. This tax, at the rate of £2 for each immigrant above ten years of age, and £1 for each one between the ages of six and ten, was collected for the immigration fund before the immigrant left the depot. Also, while still at the depot, both employer and immigrant-employee were required to sign a contract whose terms were in accord with principles laid down by the Colonial Office.[58] If any members of the assembly had hoped to find a basis for preferring charges against Ewart, they were disappointed. The report clearly demonstrated there was no favoritism in the policy he had followed.

Some of the planting interests not only resented continued assignment of immigrants to the eastern parish, which had obtained more than its share due to its proximity to Africa, but also objected to permitting ships even to call for orders at Port Morant. Consequently, Governor Grey and Ewart determined to have all immigrant ships avoid the entire parish, and instead, proceed for orders to Port Royal.[59] They suggested, too, that with planters

55. Ewart to C. E. Grey, July 6, 1850, in no.7260 Jamaica, CO 137/307.
56. Minute by H[enry] T[aylor], in C. E. Grey to Earl Grey, Aug. 8, 1850, ibid.
57. In the last instance, procedure depended upon whether the planter was a member of the Assembly.
58. "Return of Employers of Captured Africans," *Votes*, 1850-1851, Ap. 780.
59. C. E. Grey to Earl Grey, Feb. 6, 1850, *PP*, 1852-1853, LXVII, Part 2:11.

so urgently in need of labor, it would be unfair to assign an entire shipload of immigrants to one locality. Therefore, to facilitate distribution of laborers, immigrant ships would no longer limit debarkation to one port; rather, on arrival at Port Royal the ship's master would receive orders for the one or two ports to which he should proceed for discharge of passengers.[60] Both governor and AGI were attempting to distribute the limited supply of laborers with a minimum of friction. They reckoned, however, without Messrs. Hyde, Hodge, and Co., a London firm whose ships, by contract with the CL&EC, conveyed the liberated Africans to the West Indies.

The company disliked the whole program and, to defeat it, found many objections with which to bombard the CL&EC. They objected in particular to being forced to sail past Port Morant to pick up orders; waiting in port, at their own expense, until orders arrived; and finally, being sent at their own expense to discharge passengers at more than one port.[61] The CL&EC was sympathetic with the shipping firm, and discretion called for the governor to alter his policy in order to avoid controversy with those officials in London. He agreed that in the future, directions as to port of debarkation would be awaiting each ship when it arrived at Port Morant. However, because planters were currently in desperate need of laborers, it was imperative to distribute the next arrivals in more than one area. It would be inadvisable to send them overland, for if they were marched from one parish to another, every estate along the way would try to secure more than its fair share. Terms of the contract did not bind the shipping firm to send its ships to more than one port for discharge of passengers. In this instance, where facility of conveyance rather than cost was the determining factor, two ports of debarkation were obviously needed. The governor conceded that for the one occasion, the island would have to pay the expense of the additional port.[62]

Despite the clamor for additional laborers, immigrants for Jamaica were few in 1851. Sixty-one who came were *emancipados,* brought a few at a time by the monthly mail packet from Cuba. All of the others were liberated Africans, for whose migration arrangements had been made prior to word that Jamaica's Immigration Act of 1851 was unacceptable. In each

60. C. E. Grey to Earl Grey, Aug. 8, 1850, in no.7460 Jamaica, CO 137/307.
61. Earl Grey to C. E. Grey, Oct. 27, 1851, no.448, CO 137/310.
62. C. E. Grey to Earl Grey, Dec. 15, 1851, in no.679 Jamaica, CO 137/311; Earl Grey to C. E. Grey, Oct. 27, 1851, in no.6296 Jamaica, CO 137/310.

instance, transportation costs were borne by the imperial government. Only four ships came from Africa during the entire year.[63]

The first of these to arrive was the *Glentanner,* March 27, with liberated Africans from St. Helena. After thirty-three days on voyage, it touched only at Kingston, where the passengers were landed. Listed as suitable for a maximum load of 284.5 statute adults, it had departed from St. Helena with 365 (286 adult males, 74 adult females; 8 boys under ten, 2 girls under ten). Eight adults and two children died during the voyage, but cause of death was not recorded. Two more children died after their arrival in Kingston. Twenty-two immigrants, so ill as to require medical care, were placed in the public hospital.[64] The remaining 336, divided into groups varying in number from 10 to 25, were distributed in nine different parishes. In many instances, the employers again were men of importance both agriculturally and politically, among them, Baron Ketelhodt and Henry Westmoreland.[65] The AGI, in making his official report, noted the good order of the ship and a "considerable" surplus of water and provisions.[66] A question might well have been raised as to why a ship with an "admissable" capacity of 284.5 statute adults had been permitted to depart from St. Helena with 360 adults and 10 children. The embarking agent was not under the authority of Jamaica, however, and no notice of the incident was taken by the AGI or by the CL&EC in their annual report.

Occasionally during the course of its efforts to secure African immigrants, Jamaica had undertaken to honor an obligation to offer a free return passage to those who had fulfilled certain conditions, including five years residence in the colony. It did so now since the *Glentanner* would call at Sierra Leone on its eastward passage. Forty-nine Africans who had completed the residence requirements and were entitled to a free passage home elected to take advantage of the opportunity.[67] They were reported as having been in Jamaica approximately six years and were returned at the expense of the Jamaica government.[68]

---

63. "Returns of Immigrants into Jamaica" for quarters ending Mar. 31, June 30, Sept. 30, Dec. 31, 1851, in *PP,* 1852-1853, LXVII:76, 91, 126, 141.
    64. Ewart to C. E. Grey, Apr. 12, 1851, ibid., pp.71-73.
    65. Also, James Porteous, J. R. Hollingsworth, Hinton Spalding, G. W. Gordon, A. Barclay, William Rose, Edward Thompson, and Louis McKinnon. "Distribution List . . . per *Glentanner,*" ibid., p.73.
    66. Ewart to C. E. Grey, Apr. 12, 1851, *PP,* 1852-1853, LXVII:73.
    67. "Return of Immigrants at Public Expense," *PP,* 1852-1853, LXVII:92.
    68. *Votes,* 1850-1851, p.435.

The second immigrant vessel arrived in June from Sierra Leone. As the twenty-nine day crossing had been marred by two deaths from smallpox, when the ship touched at Port Royal it was sent to quarantine for fourteen days. It carried less than half its capacity load of passengers, but if there were other cases of smallpox they were not noted. The 247 liberated Africans (197.5 statute adults) were eventually landed at Rio Bueno, on the north of the island.[69] In late July the third transport, the *Fame,* arrived at Kingston. It had been forty-eight days on voyage from Sierra Leone. With only 68 passengers (53 statute adults) it brought less than twenty percent of capacity load. Six children had died on the voyage, but cause of death was omitted from the records.[70]

Many planters were disappointed by the small number of immigrants brought by the *Fame.* Planters in the parish of St. Mary considered themselves particularly unfortunate, for a recent outbreak of cholera had further depleted their labor force. They had hoped to receive liberated Africans from the *Fame.* When they failed to do so, they ignored the lack of immigrants, and protested the distribution of all Africans who had arrived during the year. They gave vent to their irritation by accusing Ewart of having sent the immigrants to districts comparatively well supplied.[71] The governor undertook to placate them with a reminder that immigrants had been less numerous than anticipated, and an assurance of Ewart's adherence to a policy of strict justice.[72] Ewart proposed to appease these employers by assigning to St. Mary's all of the liberated Africans who arrived on the next ship. The next arrival was the *Glentanner,* in September, from St. Helena. Instead of an overload it brought only about 30 percent of capacity.[73]

Emigration from Africa still was not providing the laborers Jamaica needed. Lack of passengers for the emigrant ships could be attributed in part to a sharp decline in the number of ships captured with slaves on board. At Sierra Leone the number of Negroes liberated from slave ships was only about one-third as many in 1851 as in the preceding year,[74] and they were

69. C. E. Grey to Earl Grey, June 27, 1851, no.52, *PP,* 1852-1853, LXVII: 87-88.
70. Ewart to C. E. Grey, Aug. 23, 1851, ibid., pp.103-104.
71. Memorial from planters and proprietors in the parish of St. Mary, ibid., p.121.
72. C. E. Grey to Earl Grey, Sept. 25, 1851, no.88, ibid., pp.122-123.
73. C. E. Grey to Earl Grey, Sept. 27, 1851, no.41; Ewart to Pilgrim, Sept. 8, 1851; Ewart to C. E. Grey, Sept. 25, 1851; ibid., p.123.
74. Great Britain, Foreign Office, *British and Foreign State Papers,* 1852, XLI: 195-196.

reluctant to leave Africa. With passenger loads uncertain, shipping firms hesitated to continue sending their ships to African ports.

Late in 1851 the CL&EC concluded a new agreement which granted much latitude to the shipping firm, Messrs. Hyde, Hodge, and Co. It could send out vessels when it chose, but was required to give the commissioners three weeks prior notice. Moreover, in view of the growing uncertainty of securing immigrants, the company agents at Sierra Leone and St. Helena might engage shipping on the spot. The lengthy contract stated specifications as to minimum standards for ship, health, and diet. It provided regulations for selection of immigrants, and rate of fare per passenger. All passengers ten years of age or above were counted as adults, for whom a fare of £6 1s. 10d. would be paid from Sierra Leone to Jamaica, and £6 14s. 10d. from St. Helena; but no payment was to be made to the company until after the commissioners received an account of the completed voyage.[75] Even as it was drawn, however, the contract was of no importance to Jamaica.

Immigration of Africans, which by now meant immigration of liberated Africans, and at the expense of Great Britain, had ceased before the close of 1851. The CL&EC thought the chance of its renewal unlikely, and questions pertaining to it not worth further attention.[76]

75. Earl Grey to C. E. Grey, Oct. 13, 1851, *PP,* 1852-1853, LXVII:247-252.
76. Extract of a Report of the CL&EC to Merivale, Feb. 5, 1852, ibid., p.128.

10

Years of Frustration

GOVERNOR GREY'S REFUSAL TO APPROVE THE 1851 immigration act, just at the close of the legislative session, left Jamaica once more without the laws necessary to regulate and protect immigrants. Not until the next regular session (October, 1851-February, 1852) could the House of Assembly again consider the problem. Although Jamaica needed an imperial loan in order to finance immigration, she could not obtain it unless she provided an immigration law and security for liquidation of interest as well as principal of the proposed loan. Both the law and the security must be satisfactory to the imperial government. As it would be helpful for the Legislature to know exactly why the recently proposed immigration act had been rejected and what provisions were recommended as desirable for inclusion, the assembly requested a copy of the correspondence on the subject.[1] At this point there was a curious breakdown in communication. Earl Grey's words to the governor were to send a copy of "this" (Earl Grey's despatch no. 453) "together with a copy of so much as is material of your despatch."[2] To the governor's scathing denunciation (August 16) of assembly and planters, the Colonial Secretary had appended a notation,

1. Message by the Governor, Dec. 19, 1851, *Votes,* 1851-1852, p.294.
2. Earl Grey to C. E. Grey, Nov. 12, 1851, no.453, ibid., p.302.

"This paragraph must not be published,"[3] Yet the governor, instead of presenting to the Legislature only what was "material," included the paragraph so derogatory to assembly and planters.[4]

The papers were replete with both guidelines and Earl Grey's theories relative to immigrants and their wages. Immigrant laborers, unacquainted with either colony or employers, he wrote, were unable to select the most advantageous employment. The choice should be made for them by a government official whose decision ought to be determined not by priority of application, but by probability of best treatment, regular payment of wages, and attention to health, moral, and religious instruction.[5] Although the employer to whom immigrants were assigned should pay full value of the labor he obtained from them, his payments would not necessarily be to the laborers themselves. Rather, a sufficient amount should be deducted from their wages, either directly or indirectly, to repay the colony *in toto* the full cost of their immigration.[6] Grey emphasized that liberated Africans were introduced at the expense of the British government, and should not be taxed to repay the cost of transportation; yet, as some means had to be found to make certain they would work, he suggested taxing them and using the resultant revenue to build schools and hospitals for their benefit.[7] In the interest of uniformity for all classes of immigrants, the Secretary would permit liberated Africans, as well as all other immigrants, to enter into contracts of not less than twelve months until their five-year residence had been completed.[8] He suggested that in lieu of a free return passage, immigrants might be offered the alternative of a plot of land or free transportation to the colony for their wives and families. To aid the assembly in framing a satisfactory bill, he sent a copy of some correspondence with the governor of Trinidad and an immigration ordinance proclaimed there.[9]

The Trinidad ordinance permitted liberated Africans above seventeen years of age to be assigned to plantations for twelve months, but the governor was the official authorized to make the assignment. Ewart's recom-

3. C. E. Grey to Earl Grey, Aug. 16, 1851, in no.8060 Jamaica, CO 137/310.
4. C. E. Grey to Earl Grey, Aug. 16, 1851, no.73, *Votes,* 1851-1852, p.297.
5. Earl Grey to C. E. Grey, Nov. 12, 1851, no.435, ibid., pp.299-300.
6. Some further views which Grey held on the subject may be found in Earl Grey, *The Colonial Policy of Lord John Russell,* Vol 1.
7. Earl Grey to C. E. Grey, Nov. 12, 1851, no.435, *Votes,* 1851-1852, p.300.
8. Earl Grey to C. E. Grey, July 25, 1851, no.438, *Votes,* 1851-1852, Ap. 38, p.28. Special provision was made for Chinese, who would not go without long-term contracts.
9. Earl Grey to C. E. Grey, Nov. 12, 1851, no.453, *Votes,* 1851-1852, p.301.

mendation, accepted by the assembly but denied assent, would have given
that authority to a "government official," not necessarily the governor. The
Trinidad ordinance, favored by the Colonial Office, required the employer
to pay forty shillings for each captured African employed by him, and
levied five shillings per month tax, to be paid in advance, upon every liberated African not under written contract during his "industrial residence." It
also set the workday as nine hours between sunrise and sunset, Monday
through Friday; five or six hours on Saturday; no work on Sunday, Good
Friday, Christmas, and New Year's Day.[10]

If Jamaica hoped to secure an imperial loan to promote immigration,
she must comply with suggestions made by those in high positions. In this
case it was not difficult, for they seemingly would meet the colony's need
for controlling longer and more effectively the liberated slaves who came
from Africa as indentured laborers. Only one feature, the tax on employers,
might be objectionable to planter interests, but for the time being it was
ignored. Curiously, no one raised a voice to recall the recent failure of
immigration or to imply that the whole program might be visionary. The
result was passage of "An Act to Encourage Immigration into This Island
and to Promote the Industry of Immigrants," together with three additional
acts relative to immigration.[11] To all four the governor gave his assent,
although he had some reservations as to their acceptability in Britain.[12]

Jamaica wanted more than a loan and sanction for immigration. She
feared the final results of the equalization of the sugar duties which was
scheduled to be completed in 1854, unless Parliament acted to prevent it.
The price of sugar had fallen sharply since 1846, but reportedly the decline
in price was even more precipitate in 1852.[13] Under these conditions it was
becoming increasingly difficult to secure from London houses the advances
needed to continue cultivation.[14] If Jamaica could persuade Parliament to
arrest equalization, thereby retaining a slight differential against slave-grown

10. Ordinance, Trinidad, no.10 of July 1, 1850, in *Votes,* 1851-1852, Ap. 38,
pp.62-63.

11. "An Act for raising of monies to be applied to the Introduction of Free
Laborers and for other purposes;" "An Act to appoint a board of immigration correspondence in this island;" and "An act for appointing commissioners and authorizing
them to provide for the return passage of certain immigrants . . . " *Votes,* 1851-1852,
p.548.

12. C. E. Grey to Pakington, May 13, 1852, no. 42, CS 102/14, series 1852.

13. "Statement of Facts relative to the Island of Jamaica," Thompson, Smith,
and Girod to Pakington, June 3, 1852, *PP,* 1852-1853, LXVII:307.

14. C. E. Grey to Earl Grey, Mar. 1, 1852, no.18, CS 102/14, series 1852.

sugar, the economy of the sugar colonies might be saved. Jamaica planting interests clung to this hope while, by memorials and delegation, they tried to awaken sympathy in Britain and secure favorable legislation from Parliament.

The assembly and council in Jamaica had sometimes engaged in bitter controversy. Now, however, both were so disturbed by the desperate condition of the island's economy that just before the close of the legislative session (February 26, 1852) they agreed upon both content and wording of a memorial to the Queen. As further and extraordinary demonstration of unanimity they presented it to the governor by a joint deputation headed by the Chief Justice of Jamaica.[15] Stressing the threat of ruin from competition with slave-grown sugar, and claiming, as loyal subjects, the same consideration as those resident in the United Kingdom, they asked the right to send sugar into Great Britain free of duty. It would prevent the total abandonment of numerous estates, they asserted, yet would not raise the cost of necessities of life in Great Britain or cause any noticeable reduction in the national revenue. Unless there was relief, they warned, continued abandonment of estates would reach such proportions as to produce retrogression of civilization, with "religion and morality" replaced by "barbarism and superstition."[16] Yet these very memorialists, who foresaw utter desolation of the colony's economy, were seeking a guaranteed loan, for which, ironically, they would pledge a duty on exports as security for interest and sinking fund.[17]

There were other memorials, among them one drawn in Spanish Town by "The Staple Producing Residents" relative to the "Distressed Condition of the Cultivation of Sugar." Those who signed it were men well known in the economic and political life of the island.[18] Another, from the president and members of the College of Physicians and Surgeons on "The State and Prospects of the Island," warned that prostration of agricultural and commercial interests of Jamaica had nearly dried up the sources of income, and foretold utter decay and ruin if the British colonies were placed on the same

15. C. E. Grey to Earl Grey, Mar. 1, 1852, *PP,* 1852-1853, LXVII:135-137; Grey to Pakington, Aug. 23, 1852, no.13, CS 102/14, series 1852.

16. Memorial to the Queen, Feb. 19, 1852, *Votes,* 1851-1852, pp.533-536.

17. C. E. Grey to Earl Grey, Mar. 1, 1852, *PP,* 1852-1853, LXVII:132-133.

18. Among them were Edward Thompson, William Smith, William Rose, Lucius MacKinnon, Bryan Edwards, J. Davidson, James H. Mitchell, T. H. Dakyns, George Price, and James W. Mitchell. ibid., pp.140-141.

footing with slave-holding colonies.[19] The governor, too, in his official reports, noted the drooping and decaying condition of the planting interests.[20]

The 1851-1852 session of the colonial legislature closed in late February. Only a few days earlier the Russell ministry had resigned. The Earl of Derby became Prime Minister, with Sir John S. Pakington succeeding Earl Grey at the Colonial Office.[21] About a fortnight later, when questioned in the House of Commons, Pakington stated that his government would not interfere in any way with the reduction of the duty on sugar.[22]

The governor had forwarded the four immigration acts promptly after their passage by the Legislature, but he did not get around to writing a detailed commentary on them until May 15. By that time he was reporting to the new Colonial Secretary, and expressed the hope that if the acts were not acceptable in their current form, Her Majesty's government would suggest some modification which would enable the island to obtain the loan. He added, "If the prospect of getting a large supply of labor is taken from the planters in their present circumstances, their despair will be complete."[23]

Some members of the Legislature, who were not directly connected with planting interests, were becoming reluctant to subject the whole colony to any new taxes which they thought would benefit only the planting class. Within this category they placed expenditures for African or coolie immigration.[24] However, many who favored immigration believed more could be gained for the island by a special delegation to London than by mere petition. When some members of the assembly could not agree on the composition of a committee, private subscription provided the necessary funds for William Smith, Edward Thompson, and William Girod to proceed to England to serve as representatives of the inhabitants of the island. Although technically not delegates, they considered themselves as such.[25] Their mission was to convince Parliament and ministers that, in view of the

19. Ibid., pp.142-143.
20. C. E. Grey to Earl Grey, Mar. 1, 1852, ibid., pp.132-133.
21. Pakington was Colonial Secretary, February-March, 1852.
22. *Hansard*, 3rd series, 139:1037-1038.
23. Grey to Pakington, May 13, 1852, no.42, CS 102/14, series 1852.
24. Grey to Pakington, Aug. 23, 1852, no.73, ibid.
25. Thompson was a planter and proprietor of a large but currently unprofitable estate; Smith, managing director of the Railway Company and Land Company; Girod, editor of the *Colonial Standard* (Kingston), and an advocate of the planter cause. Grey to Pakington, Aug. 22, 1852, no.73, ibid.

prospective dangers which would result from competition between free-labor-grown and slave-grown sugar, the sugar industry could not fairly be brought within the category of free trade. They were prepared to offer specific suggestions for aid to the colony. Cuba, they said, was selling sugar at a low price and in greater quantities than formerly, presumably as the result of a flourishing slave trade there. Messrs. Smith, Thompson, and Girod, as spokesmen for Jamaica, asked removal of all restrictions upon importation of free laborers from Africa to the British West Indies, and replacement of the old one-year term of indenture with three or five years of service to be required of all adult Africans. On the basis of dire need of labor, because of heavy mortality from recent epidemics of cholera and smallpox and the anticipated repatriation of coolies, the three gentlemen asked that all Africans rescued by Her Majesty's cruisers be sent exclusively to Jamaica. Furthermore, on the basis of decrease in island revenues and increased cost of maintaining institutions for the laboring class, they asked for a direct tax on laborers, with vagrancy laws applied against those who would not pay.[26]

Pakington seemingly was sympathetic, yet unwilling to raise hopes which could not be fulfilled.[27] To suggestions that recruiting be permitted anywhere along the coast of Africa, he gave the Jamaica delegation a firm refusal, and repeated the explanation of his predecessors: to permit recruiting where slavery existed would only encourage slave-trading and its accompanying warfare. Neither could all liberated Africans be directed to Jamaica, for it would be unfair to the other colonies.[28] The delegation received encouragement on only two of its requests. The Secretary believed a longer term of service might be beneficial to the Africans, and saw no serious objection to it, provided the term did not exceed three years, and the African was well protected. To ensure his protection, Jamaica must, by law, empower the AGI or some other responsible official to cancel the indenture if the welfare of the African required it. Pakington also saw no objection to a tax, such as a hut tax, upon the immigrant laborer, but the revenue must be used strictly for his benefit.[29]

26. Thompson, Smith, and Girod to Pakington, June 3, 1852, *PP,* 1852-1853, LXVII:304-305.
27. *Hansard,* 3rd series, 122:1180.
28. T. F. Elliot to Thompson, Smith, and Girod, Aug. 25, 1852, *PP,* 1852-1853, LXVII:314.
29. Ibid.

During its most recent session the Jamaica legislature had enacted immigration laws designed to meet the requirements of Earl Grey. As a result of the change in government, final decision concerning them fell to Pakington instead of Grey. Only one of the four bills was permitted to become law as it stood; none of the other three was regarded as beyond correction. One, as previously noted, did not provide adequate security for the proposed loan. Another went beyond imperial law by attempting to use a part of the guaranteed loan for return passage of coolies. The third, for "Encouragement of Immigration and Promoting the Industry of Immigrants" (no.3957) had several objectionable features, most of them pertaining to coolies. Among those relative to Africans was the failure to state that all proceeds of the tax upon liberated Africans must be applied solely to improving their condition, and with expenditure of this fund restricted to the governor alone. The precept of Earl Grey was reiterated by Pakington: as the cost of introducing liberated Africans was paid entirely by the British government, no repayment was due from the Africans to the colonial treasury. Pakington advised Jamaica that if three-year contracts-of-service were to be allowed, certain conditions must be met. Jamaica must by law require the contracts to include provision for lodging, clothing, rations, payment of wages, hours of work, and the usual half-holiday, all of which had been approved by the Secretary of State. Pakington would add to the contracts a statement specifying that after his first year the laborer would receive current wages. To ensure compliance with these regulations, an immigration officer or stipendiary magistrate should have full power to inspect estates where liberated Africans were located, and to hear complaints which they might wish to make.[30]

Part of Jamaica's problem, however, was taken care of by Parliament. It simply removed the contradiction between Jamaican and imperial legislation by amending its own act which had authorized the guaranteed loan. The fund could now be used for general purposes of immigration—a term vague enough to include returning coolies to India, as the imperial government had urged.[31] Technicalities which caused Colonial Office objections to the "Act for Encouragement of Immigration" were remedied by the island Legislature itself. By mid-April, 1853, when the four immigration acts passed by the Legislature in the previous year had been corrected and had

30. Pakington to Grey, Oct. 3, 1852, ibid., pp.315-316.
31. Newcastle to Grey, Jan. 14, 1853, no.2, *Votes,* 1852-1853, p.299.

become law,[32] the island at last met the qualifications for receiving a guaranteed loan. The first half was offered and was quickly subscribed.

Hopes at this time centered upon obtaining Chinese and Madeirans, for Africans seemed impossible to obtain. Although a loan of £100,000 appeared large, its limitations were soon apparent. Cost of repatriation (or compensation) of coolies had been sadly underestimated. Earlier the CL&EC had ordered two thousand Chinese laborers for Jamaica and this costly project had not been countermanded. The two expenditures would require not only all of the first half of the loan, but so much of the total as to leave only about twenty percent for other immigration purposes.[33]

As part of the reorganized program to further immigration, the legislature had created a Board of Immigration Correspondence, charged with finding immigrant labor for Jamaica.[34] It was believed that men resident in Jamaica, knowledgeable, and directly concerned with the planting economy might succeed when others had failed. With Jamaica now meeting imperial regulations for receiving immigrants, the Colonial Office asked to be informed as to how many Jamaica wanted during the next season. The decision was one to be made by the Board of Immigration Correspondence. The original members were in England on business and, as the decision could not be postponed, the governor appointed new members, who met at King's House, in June, to consider the problem and to weigh various proposals made in both Jamaica and Britain. Once again someone who claimed to have traveled widely in the United States gave a glowing report of at least 3,000, perhaps 10,000 Negroes who could easily be persuaded to move to Jamaica.[35] The board was not impressed, for it believed these people would not be willing to come as immigrant laborers, hence would not fall within the terms of the immigration act. Instead, it suggested perhaps the CL&EC could send laborers from Madeira or West Coast Africa, if cost did not exceed £20,000. Aware of the impending cost for repatriation of laborers already in Jamaica, it proposed that no more immigrants be promised the right to a return passage at public expense.[36]

32. Ibid., pp.298, 301, 557.
33. Grey to Newcastle, June 24, 1853, in no.7276 Jamaica, CO 137/317.
34. *Votes,* 1851-1852, p.548.
35. Thrasher Lyons to Mr. Wright, Feb. 22, 1853, in no.7276 Jamaica, CO 137/317.
36. At a Board of Immigration Correspondence, June 16, 1853. Present were the governor, Peter Alexander Espeut, Stephen Weis Mais, and Robert Russell. In no.7276 Jamaica, ibid.

The board found itself pressured also by Messrs. Hyde, Hodge, and Company, ship owners who wanted board members then in London to agree to a contract proffered by their firm. Terms of the contract would have given the company authority to hire African laborers for Jamaica for a three-year term at 10d. per day; sole right to convey immigrants from the Kru Coast to Jamaica; payment for passage at a rate of £7 for each adult (with an adult defined as a person of ten years of age or more) and £3 10s. for each passenger under ten.[37] There is no record to indicate the reaction of the board, for developments within the island precluded its acceptance.

When the Derby ministry resigned, December, 1852, the Earl of Aberdeen formed a ministry, with the Duke of Newcastle at the Colonial Office. Newcastle wanted an amendment to the island act which had authorized the loan, and until that had been accomplished, he opposed raising the second half of the loan. As a result, Jamaica was left in the position of having overspent its immigration fund. By the time the amendment was adopted, there were further difficulties. Board members in England were expected to explain more fully to the company why the proposal made by the shipping firm could not even be considered.[38]

Planting interests had continued to hope for some alteration in the sugar duties,[39] but when in December, 1852, Benjamin Disraeli, then Chancellor of the Exchequer, stated that the government would not intervene to prevent equalization, even a remote possibility for some sort of preference was removed. Certainly there was no reason to expect better treatment by the Aberdeen ministry, which came into office only a few days later. When news of these developments reached Jamaica, if Governor Grey appraised the situation correctly, there was utter despair over unrestricted competition with foreign and slave-grown sugar. Although Grey conceded that the planting interests (which still dominated the assembly) had good reason for wanting to reduce taxes and free public revenue from unnecessary charges, he continued adamantly opposed to any alteration which would then reduce the salary of the governor or of other officials.[40]

In the spring of 1853 the long-standing retrenchment quarrel erupted

37. Hyde, Hodge, and Co. to W. W. Mackeson, May 13, 1853; W. W. Mackeson to Grey, May 16, 1853, ibid.

38. T. F. Pilgrim to W. W. Mackeson, June 9, 1853, ibid.

39. Address of the Assembly, no.11, 1852, *Votes,* 1852-1853, p.26.

40. Grey to Newcastle, May 10, 1853, no. 40, in no.5746 Jamaica, CO 137/316.

to dominate not only everything within Jamaica, but also relations between colony and mother country. The assembly noted on February 4, 1853, that despite the distressed condition of the colony, the imperial government was determined not "to render such material aid as will afford immediate and substantial relief," and then resolved to vote only a sharply reduced supply.[41] Retrenchment, import duties, and rum bills were passed twice by the assembly but rejected by the Council. Blocked in its efforts to reduce expenditures, the assembly on May 4 declared it would not conduct any further business with the Council.[42] As a result of the deadlock, revenues were not collected, civil and ecclesiastical officials could not be paid, and both the economy and prestige of Jamaica were injured.

In October Sir Henry Barkly succeeded Grey as governor of Jamaica. When he convened the Legislature, soon after his arrival, he informed it that the imperial government would offer a loan large enough to cover most of the island indebtedness, but such a grant must be preceded by a reform in the constitution.[43] Suffice it to state here that changes were eventually agreed to, and in April, 1854, a new constitution was approved.[44] The Council, a bit enlarged, became merely a legislative council, whereas formerly it had acted as both legislative and privy council. Members of a small, new executive committee[45] were given exclusive right to introduce monetary bills and might also serve the governor as spokesmen in the legislative branch of the government. In effect, the assembly was appreciably weakened, the executive strengthened. The governor congratulated Jamaica on its new framework of government,[46] and in the following November the colony received a guaranteed loan as promised.[47]

As soon as other duties permitted, Governor Barkly set out on an extensive tour of the island. Formerly a proprietor there, and possessed of an unusual knowledge of soils, climate, and their effect upon sugar production, he was exceptionally well qualified to assess conditions in Jamaica. He found planters to be neither bigoted and violent men, nor stereotyped

41. Ibid. They stated, however, they would honor the interest on the debt.
42. Ibid.
43. Speech by the Governor, Oct. 18, 1853, *Votes,* 1853-1854, pp.3-8.
44. "A Bill for the Better Government of This Island," Barkly to Newcastle, Apr. 7, 1854, no.43, in no.3649 Jamaica, CO 137/323.
45. Composed of one member from the Council, no more than three from the House of Assembly.
46. Speech by the Governor, Apr. 13, 1854, *Votes,* 1853-1854, pp.580-581.
47. Speech by the Governor, Nov. 28, 1854, *Votes,* 1854-1855, p.11.

opponents of progress. They would be "as willing as anyone" to adopt improved methods of agriculture, including the use of machinery, if production were at a higher level. But the limited and uncertain supply of labor, both native and imported, had seriously hampered large-scale agriculture. In fact, the extent of cultivation had been forced down to the level of the labor supply. Aware of creole reluctance to work for wages, yet convinced that only with adequate labor could cultivation be directed toward recovery, the governor, too, advocated importing laborers.[48]

Some laborers were actually departing from Jamaica—coolies who were repatriated to India, a few Negroes who went to Panama to work on the railroad. In the period 1852-1859 Jamaica received few immigrants from anywhere, none from Africa. There were few African immigrants for any of the West Indian colonies: British Guiana received 273 immigrants from the Kru Coast, and only 215 liberated Africans; Trinidad, only 28 liberated Africans, and no Krumen. The prospects for African immigration were still gloomy when in April, 1857 Jamaica for a second time suddenly found itself the locale for a prize court and host to a cargo liberated directly from a slave ship.

HMS *Arab* was on patrol in the Western Atlantic when Lt. Stubbs was ordered to take the pinnace and a small crew to watch Cuban waters for an expected slaver, which he was to detain until the *Arab* arrived on the scene. After several days of watching and waiting, Lt. Stubbs spotted a schooner running for the passage. There was a four-hour chase before he was able to overtake the vessel, name and nation unknown. Before he got alongside, the crew had deserted, but he boarded their escape boat and seized the captain, the cook, and a slave. He then allowed the boat to run ashore while he turned back to the slaver, which had been left running straight for a reef.[49]

Aboard the schooner, Stubbs found a cargo of slaves raging with thirst. The vessel, forty-eight days out of Kabinda, had sailed with a cargo of 500 slaves, 466 men, 44 females. During the brief period when the ship was without crew or the lieutenant, the Africans had broken everything open, eaten large quantities of salt fish and pork, and drunk most of the water. In dire need of water and supplies for the vessel, and uncertain how long it would be until the *Arab* arrived, Stubbs disobeyed orders. He first intended

48. Barkly to Newcastle, May 26, 1854, no.73 in no.6478 Jamaica, CO 137/323.
49. Edward Stubbs, Lt. RN, to Commodore Henry Kellett, Apr. 16, 1857, in no.4594 Jamaica, CO 137/334.

to make for Port Royal; but finding himself off St. Ann's Bay, he put in there to secure essentials. He then reported to Commodore Kellett, senior naval officer at Port Royal, and pursuant to orders, took the prize on toward Port Royal, where it was anchored across the harbor, just off Fort Augusta. Responsibility for the Africans now fell temporarily to Kellett, whose first task was for health's sake to get them landed immediately. Not until he had received official orders from Bell, the lieutenant governor, did Kellett turn them over to the collector of HM customs.[50]

Major General Edward Wells Bell had been sworn in as lieutenant governor when Barkly left Jamaica in May, 1856. Although he could seek advice from various officials in the colony, final decision on many matters pertaining to these Africans fell to Bell. He gave orders for landing the slaves at Fort Augusta, and for providing them with the necessary food and provisions. He also instructed Kellett to care for the schooner and secure all information possible in the event legal proceedings should be instituted. It was Her Majesty's Collector of Customs W. G. Freeman who within the space of twenty-four hours found himself faced with the immediate care of these people. All were young; only twenty-three were estimated to be adults. Supervision by experienced officials was needed. Freeman appointed John Davis (who had supervised the liberated Africans in 1850) as superintendent at Fort Augusta. Two medical attendants were appointed, for some of the Africans were quite ill. The two doctors sent thirty-seven to the hospital, and for the remainder provided a dietary scale which it was hoped would improve their health. Freeman had been concerned, too, because the males were in a state of nudity, and the females were were only partially covered with aprons and handkerchiefs. As there was no further reference to the need for clothes, presumably they were quickly provided.[51]

The attorney general suggested immediate legal proceedings against both vessel and cargo. The case was heard in the Vice-Admiralty Court of Jamaica, May 18, 1857, before Bryan Edwards, judge. The schooner was pronounced condemned and forfeited to the Queen, and was handed over to the senior naval officer of Her Majesty's service; the Africans (310 males, 40 females) were placed in the care of the agent general of immigration, David Ewart, who went to Fort Augusta formally to receive custody of them.[52]

50. Kellett to Lt. Gov. Bell, Apr. 20, 1857, ibid.
51. W. G. Freeman to Walter G. Stewart, Lt. Governor's Secretary, Apr. 23, 1857, ibid.
52. Bell to Labouchere, July 9, 1857, no.48; In the Vice-Admiralty Court of

There was some uncertainty as to what should be arranged for these people. Many were still weak and emaciated; many of them were children considered as unsuited to plantation labor; yet guidelines were needed for determining their assignment in such a way as to avoid local, imperial, and international criticism. Because Jamaica's immigration laws, applicable to laborers arriving as free immigrants or liberated Africans, said nothing about Africans landed directly from a slave ship, Ewart resorted to a search of regulations arising from treaties between Great Britain, Spain, and Portugal, and to various instructions from the Secretary of State for the Colonies. From the treaties he gleaned the following regulations: (1) The period of service should be the same for all Negroes who at the time of hiring were above thriteen years of age. Indenture was for seven years, subject to a three-year reduction upon recommendation of the master and proof that the apprentice was capable of earning an honest living. (2) For an African under the age of thirteen, apprenticeship should be until the age of twenty but might be shortened upon proof of his ability to maintain himself. (3) An African must receive wholesome and abundant food, and such clothes as were "the custom of the country." (4) The African should be taught some useful business or trade by which he could support himself after his service ended. (5) Females must not be employed in agricultural work. (6) The employer must agree to have the African instructed in the Christian religion and in reading, and to have him baptized.[53]

Although Ewart believed the above regulations had never been submitted to the island legislature, from a study of both the laws and correspondence pertaining to employment of liberated Africans[54] he concluded he was expected to do what was best for the immigrants, and to include in their contracts stipulations for lodging, clothing, rations, payment of wages, hours of work, and so on.[55] By act of the Jamaica Legislature[56] the AGI was free to select employers and employment which seemed most advantageous for the African. Seemingly he had found adequate regulations for making assignments.[57] However, a serious defect was discovered in the

Jamaica, May 18, 1857, William Duff, Registrar. Both in no.6989 Jamaica, CO 137/334.
53. Ewart to W. G. Stewart, June 18, 1857, no.58, ibid.
54. Grey to Grey, relative to the Immigration Act of 1850.
55. As suggested by Pakington, Oct. 3, 1852.
56. 12 Vic. c.18.
57. Ewart to Stewart, June 18, 1857, in no.6986 Jamaica, CO 137/334.

island legislation, for it failed to provide guidelines for apprenticeship of Africans under age seventeen. An earlier act (13 Vic. c.30) relative to this type of immigrant, had been repealed (15 Vic. c.38) and obviously had then been overlooked. Some sort of regulation was urgently needed. Consequently, at a conference with the solicitor of the crown and the commissioners of immigration correspondence, it was decided that with the sanction of the governor, the AGI should assign all females and the youngest boys as domestic servants to families of "known respectability."[58]

It is interesting to note that in arriving at this decision, weight was given to the theory of environment as playing a significant role in the early education of a child: best location for an African child to begin his education was in the household of a respectable Jamaica family, who would train him in Jamaican ways more quickly than would his countrymen on a sugar estate. He needed to learn the fundamentals of reading, writing, religion and "moral and social duties"—advantages which the child, when grown, might take back with him to Africa. Whatever the rationale, all of the females and most of the children were assigned, one to a household, to reputable families. All adult males were assigned to agricultural employment.[59]

The incident of the *Arab* and its prize had raised some questions. Freeman wanted nothing more to do with caring for captured Africans brought into the island in vessels taken prize by Her Majesty's cruisers. To have the care of Africans located six miles by water from his office seemed to him incompatible with his position as collector of customs. When imperial law had originally placed Africans under the care of that official, they were not free; but in recent years, those who arrived were free. He suggested that captured Africans awaiting adjudication could be provided for through the island immigration act, and upon arrival be assigned directly to the AGI. Furthermore, as he was no longer collector of Her Majesty's customs, he should not be called upon by imperial legislation to take charge of immigrants arriving in Jamaica and provided for by the island legislature.[60] Both the lieutenant governor and the Colonial Secretary were in agreement with Freeman. Thereafter, it was directed, all slaves who might be captured and taken to Jamaica for adjudication should be delivered to the care and cus-

    58. Ibid.
    59. D. Ewart, Return of Africans Captured by HM Brig *Arab;* and Ewart to Stewart, June 18, 1857, no.58, ibid.
    60. W. G. Freeman to W. G. Stewart, July 17, 1857, in no.6988 Jamaica, CO 137/334.

tody of the AGI who would deal with them in conformity with the immigration acts.[61]

The assembly, on the other hand, reflected the excitement generated by a prize brought into the island. The Secretary of State had approved the procedures relative to the captured Africans, and when the Legislature was convened in November, 1857, the governor, Sir Charles Darling, informed it of the good news.[62] For its part, the assembly proposed to show its appreciation by voting a grant of £200 to Stubbs and £100 to the crew of the pinnace under his command.[63] When Governor Darling, through a member of the executive committee, suggested including a clause to make the award receivable with the approval of the Lords Commissioners of the Admiralty[64] some of the assembly retorted by proposing to request the Admiralty to appoint Stubbs in command of one of the gunboats employed on the coast of Cuba to prevent the slave trade. The proposal was defeated, with only five votes for it,[65] but the awards were confirmed.[66]

The House of Assembly wanted to know more also about the recently released slaves: What disposition was made of them? To whom were they assigned? To this purpose it instructed the AGI to present a detailed report. His account showed fifteen of the Africans were then in the West India Regiment; seventeen had died in the public hospital; one was still there; the remainder had been assigned to employers, but in over fifty percent of the cases, no more than one immigrant was assigned to any one employer. Only about a dozen of the employers were members of the Legislature.[67]

In submitting his report, Ewart undertook to avert any possible criticism by explaining in some detail how the bases for indenture and distribution were determined. He quoted at length from Colonial Office despatches which had been helpful, and cited the island act (16 Vic. c.30) which specified indentures of three years for those above seventeen. He explained that in applying these principles to the Africans captured by the

61. 16 Vic. c.38; 18 Vic. c.35. Bell to Labouchere, July 10, 1857; Labouchere to Darling, Oct. 3, 1857, ibid.
62. *Votes,* 1857, p.12. Darling, one-time AGI, had returned to Jamaica as Governor, July, 1857.
63. Ibid., p.80.
64. Ibid., p.132.
65. Ibid., p.154.
66. Ibid., p.163.
67. Return, signed by D. Ewart, AGI, Dec. 2, 1857, *Votes,* 1857, Ap. 11, pp.56-57. The Reverend W. G. Gardner is listed as an employer of one African.

Arab, most of the children were allotted to householders because it seemed the best employment to improve their health. His explanations were ones which could not in good grace be challenged. If the members of the assembly were dissatisfied, there is no evidence to suggest it.[68]

The question of return passage continued to plague Jamaica. This time it was the governor of Sierra Leone who had received petitions from some of the inhabitants, begging that their relatives and children in the West Indies be granted a free return passage as they had been promised when they emigrated. The governor of Sierra Leone was unable to locate a record of any agreement, and the petitioners did not know to what colony their absent relatives had gone; but reputable people in the colony, he reported, were certain such had been promised after a service of five years. The governor, Stephen J. Hill, hoped a query of West Indian governors could be made in an effort to gain some information.[69]

At the Colonial Office it was decided to comply with the request by sending a circular despatch, together with the names of the forty-three Africans, to British Guiana, Trinidad, and Jamaica. While recognizing that these immigrants could not legally claim back passage except within two years after expiration of their five-year residence, the secretary intimated the wisdom of supplying it if there was to be any encouragement of immigration.[70]

The AGI in Jamaica compared the list with his roster of immigrants. He found 231 Africans had applied for repatriation in 1849. (The immigration law then applicable directed every immigrant entitled to return passage to give six months prior notice of his intention to demand it.) Of these 231 applicants, 27 bore names identical to those currently being sought by relatives in Sierra Leone. All 27 had arrived on the *Glen Huntley* when immigration was under imperial supervision. Absolute identification merely by name was difficult, however, for certain names, such as John Davis, were exceedingly popular.[71] No provision for returning these Africans had been made until 1851, when the commissioners of public accounts authorized sixty to be sent back to Sierra Leone on the *Glentanner.* Notice for the

68. Ibid., p.58.
69. Stephen J. Hill to Labouchere, June 30, 1857, *PP* (Lords), 1859, IV: 421-422.
70. Circular to the Governors, British Guiana, Trinidad, Jamaica, Sept. 8, 1857, *PP* (Lords), 1859, IV:421.
71. Ewart to Austin, Dec. 23, 1857; Darling to Labouchere, Mar. 19, 1858; both in no.3681 Jamaica, CO 137/336.

voyage was short, however, for not until the ship arrived in Jamaica were authorities there informed that Sierra Leone would be its next port of call. Only 49 Africans accepted the offer—some, perhaps, because of the brief notice; others because they did not wish to leave. Ewart simply noted that none of the 27 was then "ready to leave" when the ship was ready to sail.[72]

Seemingly no other Africans were repatriated until 1856-1857. Although no merchant ships were then available, thirteen Africans were returned to Sierra Leone in HMS *Perseverance.* For their provisions the colony was charged with 501 seaman's rations and paid £537 16s. 9d.[73] The Board of Immigration Correspondence, when asked in September, 1857, to authorize return passages, resolved that such applications could not be considered, as under existing conditions there was no opportunity to provide them.[74]

While the incident of the *Arab* had raised hopes of similar prizes being brought into Jamaica ports, it had also pointed up a need for regulations. The Legislature passed an act (1857) to "Authorize the Indenturing of Persons Condemned as forfeited to Her Majesty under the Statutes for the Abolition of the Slave Trade." It provided for an indenture of not more than seven years, and ratified the contracts which had just been made for the African children freed from the slaver.[75] When Labouchere, at the Colonial Office, wanted to know the form of indenture for those Africans, and if they had been separated from their parents, the governor replied they were all parentless, and their assignment was legal under the provisions of the local "Act for the Apprenticeship of Minors." He enclosed a copy of the form of indenture by which the employer agreed to provide clothing, food, and the like; medical attention by a qualified medical practitioner; Divine Service; Sunday and one-half day per week without work; and to permit the AGI from time to time to inspect the condition of the Africans.[76] But Labouchere was not satisfied, and wanted to know the term for which these Africans were indentured, because the Jamaica law might possibly require a

72. Ewart to Austin, Dec. 28, 1857. But Darling, who stated that none claimed passage, also referred to the incident as having occurred in April, 1852 rather than in 1851. Darling to Labouchere, Mar. 19, 1858, no.45; both in no.3681 Jamaica, CO 137/336. See ch.8.

73. Darling to Labouchere, Dec. 24, 1857; Stanley to Darling, Apr. 4, 1858; both in no.691 Jamaica, CO 137/335.

74. Extract, Minutes of the Board of Commissioners of Correspondence, Sept. 4, 1857, in no.3681 Jamaica, CO 137/336.

75. Enclosure in Darling to Labouchere, Feb. 8, 1858, in no.2264 Jamaica, CO 137/336.

76. Darling to Labouchere, Oct. 31, 1857, no.31 and enclosure, CO 137/334.

longer period than the home government advocated.[77] As a matter of fact, the term was for seven years, although the act seemingly would permit the governor to make modifications, if they should be needed.[78]

Stanley, who succeeded Labouchere at the Colonial Office, February 18, 1858, objected to the act, which authorized an indenture of seven years for all liberated Africans, whatever their age might be, and encouraged reindenture. Great Britain sanctioned an indenture of no more than three years or until the African reached the age of eighteen. It was emphasized again that liberated Africans were not introduced at the expense of the colony and must be dealt with according to principles which the British government had laid down for their protection. Jamaica was notified that for these reasons the act would be disallowed, and the Africans from the slaver could not be indentured for a period longer than the one permitted by Great Britain.[79]

Planting interests continued to complain of labor shortages and of the need for importing workers as the means of increasing the supply. Stipendiary magistrates, making reports for their parishes, emphasized that conditions could be remedied only by additional laborers. The governor observed that some of the stipendiary magistrates who formerly had opposed immigration changed their attitude and were now definitely supporting it. Many others no longer opposed it.[80] There was, however, in the assembly a powerful party which considered itself the protector of the native population, and had long opposed applying public revenue to the importation of competitive labor. If their opposition was to be avoided, it would be advisable to place upon the employer the entire cost of immigration.[81] With hope now turning toward India as a source for labor (and possibly to China) the Legislature turned to the task of framing a new immigration measure, entitled an act "to amend the Law as relating to Agricultural immigration, and for raising funds to defray the expenses tendant upon their introduction and subsequent colonization in the island."

The act placed upon the employer most, if not all, of the cost of bringing an immigrant to Jamaica; but to ease the burden, it authorized

77. Labouchere to Darling, Dec. 23, 1857, no.52, in no.10890 Jamaica, CO 137/334.
78. Darling to Labouchere, Feb. 8, 1858, in no.2264 Jamaica, CO 137/336.
79. Stanley to Darling, May 15, 1858, no. 17, *Votes,* 1858-1859, Ap. 13, p.62.
80. Extracts, Darling to Labouchere, Mar. 19, 1858, no.47, ibid., pp.56-59.
81. Darling to Labouchere, Feb. 8, 1858, in no.2264 Jamaica, CO 137/336.

payment by semiannual instalments spread over a period of three years. Very few of the provisions of the bill applied specifically to Africans. It permitted voluntary immigrants to be brought from Africa with the consent of the imperial government, and sanctioned ratification of contracts made out of the island by either Africans or Asiatics.[82] To prevent the Jamaica treasury from being drained by demands for return passage to Africa, the House of Assembly inserted in the bill a more stringent regulation for claiming it. Africans who had served a five-year indenture and had reindented for another five years of service, might under certain circumstances claim a return passage, but only if Britain would not authorize a grant of ten acres of land in lieu of repatriation.[83] Most of the act was expected to apply primarily to coolies, but the Colonial Office saw serious faults in length of indenture, as well as in provisions for their return passage.[84] The act was disallowed, but notification of this did not reach Jamaica immediately.

While Jamaica was awaiting official approval of the recent legislation, prospects for immigrants from Africa suddenly became more encouraging. Early in 1858 a large number of Africans were taken into Sierra Leone and placed with the resident population. As in former times, if liberated Africans who were brought to Sierra Leone could be persuaded to emigrate to the West Indies it might benefit everyone concerned, including Great Britain and the treasury.

The Colonial Land and Emigration Commissioners, pursuant to instructions from the Colonial Office, again undertook to arrange for transporting Africans, whether free or liberated, to the West Indies, if they were willing to go. The firm of Hyde, Hodge, and Co. would transport Africans who might be liberated there if guaranteed a fare of five pounds per adult.[85] The governor of Sierra Leone was instructed to encourage emigration and to explain to both free and liberated Africans that when they arrived in the West Indies, they must enter into contracts for three years of service, or, in the case of children, until the age of eighteen.[86]

Jamaica was informed of the plan, and asked if she wished to share in

82. Report of the Attorney General, ibid., CO 137/336.
83. Darling to Labouchere and enclosure, ibid.; *Votes*, 1858-1859, Ap. 13, pp.48-49.
84. Stanley to Darling, Apr. 16, 1858, no.17, in no.2264 Jamaica, CO 137/336; ibid., pp.58-65.
85. Contract with Hyde, Hodge, and Co. was made in February. Murdock to Newcastle, Aug. 6, 1858, *Votes*, 1858-1859, Ap. 13, pp.54-55.
86. Labouchere to Darling, Feb. 25, 1858, ibid., pp.49-50.

these benefits, should they materialize. If so, she must furnish a statement of wages and other advantages enjoyed by laborers in Jamaica, and provide for paying £5 for passage and $1 (4s.) fee to the embarking agent for every adult African from Sierra Leone. Labouchere seemingly was quite pleased to be able to offer the West Indian colonies these "benefits" from operations of Her Majesty's cruisers.[87]

Official communication had not been as rapid as the grapevine. Even before Labouchere's despatch arrived, Jamaica knew (through a private communication from London to a member of the executive committee) of the recaptured Africans in Sierra Leone and of the contract with Hyde, Hodge, and Co. Already many prospective employers were filing applications for their services. Jamaica not only wanted them, but through the governor requested a "fair" share, and stressed the superior advantages that the colony could offer by reason of the new immigration act with its provision for settling Africans upon lands.[88] A few days later, when transmitting the half-yearly reports of the stipendiary magistrates, the governor called attention to frequent references to the prosperity of "small-holders" (owners of plots of land from one to fifteen acres), as well as to the employers' need for laborers. He also stressed the absence of crime in Jamaica, and the orderly conduct of the laboring population.[89]

Information with regard to working conditions was provided by the AGI. Wages varied considerably, depending upon type of work and of contract; labor was still usually paid by the piece or job, by which the laborer could earn from 2s. to 3s. per day. If he preferred day wages, he would receive about 1s. per day with house and grounds and medical attention.[90] The estimate of advantages had been hastily drawn in order to accompany the governor's despatch of the same date. Ewart took the time, however, to wonder if liberated Africans thereafter were to be allotted on the same basis as the free immigrants from Sierra Leone. If so, the form of contract provided by the Immigration Act of 1857 could probably be applied to both groups.[91] He later submitted a more detailed estimate of wages and cost of

87. Ibid., p.50.
88. Darling to Labouchere, Mar. 10, 1858, Jamaica no. 36, Executive, ibid., pp.55-56.
89. Extract from Darling to Labouchere, Mar. 19, 1858, *Votes,* 1858-1859, Ap. 13, pp.56-57.
90. Ewart to Austin, Mar. 25, 1858, no.54, ibid., p.51.
91. Ibid.

living. Industrious laborers, he suggested, could expect to receive 1s. 6d. for nine hours of steady work; young people, 6 to 9d. per day. Although the price of some items had changed since his last report, many were still the same. For instance, bread was still 3d. per pound; a man's work clothes, 3s. 6d.[92]

The Immigration Act of 1857 was disallowed, and the CL&EC, on the scene in London, knew of it before official notification reached Governor Darling. The commissioners had not liked the act, partly because of the latitude seemingly given to the AGI, and had advised against the bill when it was referred to them.[93] Conveyance of both liberated and free Africans had been authorized by the governor, in accordance with the powers conferred upon him during the period when the 1857 immigration act was law in Jamaica.[94] But the CL&EC now asserted it must have authorization from "the colonial government" before it could promise the shipping firm five pounds for each African landed in Jamaica.[95] Once again Jamaica was being excluded from receiving immigrants from Africa. Exasperation could be detected in Darling's tart suggestion: "It may prevent the occurrence of any new grounds for withholding immigrants from Africa if the emigration commissioners would be good enough to inform me . . . what classes of persons the colony will be permitted to receive and under what conditions their reception can be accomplished."[96]

The agencies and laws which had been displaced by the Immigration Act of 1857 were automatically revived by disallowance of the measure. As time was required to get the old machinery back into operation, Darling was not able to bring the Board of Immigration Correspondence together until July.[97] Then it returned to the task of trying to secure immigrants. After setting aside £20,000 for bringing in Chinese, it then assigned the balance of the loan to be used in importing Africans and other laborers. The board also sanctioned the arrangements made by the CL&EC with Messrs. Hyde,

92. D. Ewart, "Statement of Wages . . . " May 25, 1858, ibid., p.76.
93. T. C. Murdock and Frederic Rogers to Herman Merivale, May 10, 1858, ibid., p.52.
94. Darling to Stanley, June 25, 1858, Jamaica no.94, Executive, ibid., pp.52-53.
95. Murdock and Rogers to Merivale, May 10, 1858, ibid., p.52.
96. Darling to Stanley, Jamaica no.94, Executive, ibid.
97. They met at King's House. In addition to the Governor, those present were Edward Jordon, George Price, P. A. Espeut, S. W. Mais, and the AGI, David Ewart. "At a meeting of the board of immigration correspondence," *Votes*, 1858-1859, Ap. 13, p.87.

Hodge, and Co. for bringing Africans from Sierra Leone. As Jamaica's attempt to establish a long indenture had been both disallowed and denounced, the board now assumed that contracts would be legal for one year only.[98]

Jamaica awaited immigrants. Not until September did the Secretary of State for the Colonies, now Sir E. Bulwer Lytton, direct the CL&EC to include Jamaica in the arrangements for sending both liberated and free Africans from Sierra Leone to the West Indies. At the same time, he found an opportunity to lecture Jamaica on the subject of return passage. Charging the colony with having been quite tardy in sending back its immigrants who wanted to return home, he warned that repetition of noncompliance with the promise of return passage would necessitate excluding Jamaica from receiving immigrants.[99]

Darling was irritated. There had been repeated references to bad faith by Jamaica and implications of indifference on the part of the governor. He reminded his superior that prior to the arrival of Barkly, the financial and political situation had made it inexpedient to attempt repatriation at the expense of the colonial treasury; but since the adoption (in 1854) of the new form of government, efforts had been made to remedy the situation and to prevent a recurrence. Darling suggested that it would be a more generous policy to regard the new constitution as marking a new era, and to judge the reformed Legislature of Jamaica by its own acts, not by those of the past.[100] It was a sharper reply than a governor usually made to criticism from the Colonial Office.

And what of the immigrant laborers who might come from Sierra Leone? Again there was disappointment for Jamaica. A flood of liberated Africans was no longer flowing into that African colony, and without them there was no assurance of any large number who would emigrate. Messrs. Hyde, Hodge, and Company would not send vessels to the coast of Africa merely for possible emigrants from among the resident population of Sierra Leone. If by chance there should be Africans who wished to emigrate to Jamaica, there would be no ships to bring them.[101]

98. Darling to Lytton, July 8, 1858, no.99, Executive; Minutes, Hugh W. Austin, Secretary to the Board of Immigration Correspondence, July 6, 1858, ibid., pp.85-87; no.7592 Jamaica, CO 137/338.
99. Lytton to Darling, Sept. 10, 1858, Jamaica no. 27, *Votes,* 1858-1859, Ap. 13, pp.85-87.
100. Darling to Lytton, Sept. 24, 1858, no.118, CO 137/346.
101. Murdock to Merivale, Aug. 6, 1858, *Votes,* 1858-1859, Ap. 13, pp.54-55.

During the months when the fate of the 1857 Immigration Act was still unknown, some of the people who opposed it expressed their views in writing. From three different parishes came memorials which were identical and suggested a common origin. Each one was signed by only the chairman "on behalf of the meeting." The memorialists all referred to themselves as a "large body of lately emancipated Africans," and expressed surprise and alarm over the Immigration Act of 1857 which they claimed had been passed very quickly. (Introduced on November 17, it had received the governor's approval on December 15, 1857.) They begged the monarch to withhold her consent to the act. To support their request they asserted that: (1) No labor shortage existed except during certain seasons of the year. (2) Tribal wars and a semislave trade would be revived in Africa if Jamaica permitted immigrant laborers to be transported from Sierra Leone. (3) The morals of the Jamaica people would be injured by the introduction of many "heathen and pagan foreigners" with their "religious superstitions and wickedness."[102] Memorials expressing similar views were presented by the London Missionary Society in Jamaica and by the Jamaica Baptist Union at Falmouth, which warned that sanction of this act would tarnish the honor of England.[103] Formerly many who opposed immigration had stressed their opposition to the use of public funds for that purpose; now when public funds would not be involved, they asserted the introduction of "heathens" would have a detrimental effect upon the population. Disallowance of the Immigration Act of 1857, although on grounds far different from those of the memorialists, was a cause of satisfaction to them but not to employers of labor.

The Legislature was not sitting when news of the disallowance reached Jamaica. Planter and local officials, dismayed by the rejection, had wanted the legislative body summoned at once in order to take immediate action, but their wishes were ignored. Not until November was it convened. When the governor met the Legislature he promised to provide full information of the grounds on which the act had been disallowed, and gave assurances that a new bill would be introduced promptly.[104] He had already received infor-

---

102. Memorials to the Queen from the parishes of St. James, Hanover, Trelawney, enc. in Darling to Stanley, April 7, 1858, no.56, in no.4336 Jamaica, CO 137/337.
103. Darling to Stanley, May 4, 1858, no.69, enc., in no.5217 Jamaica, CO 137/337; same to same, May 1, 1858, no.70, in no.5218 Jamaica, CO 137/337.
104. *Votes*, 1858-1859, pp.8-9.

mation that if the island met certain conditions, it would be included in the renewed coolie immigration.[105]

The subject of immigration was dealt with by a series of four bills. "An Act to authorize the indenturing of persons condemned as forfeited to Her Majesty under the statutes for the abolition of the slave trade in certain cases" was passed by the Legislature, assented to by the governor, and on November 26 was forwarded to the Colonial Office.[106] It authorized the AGI, subject to the governor, to be responsible for persons brought directly from a slave ship, and limited the period of indenture to three years, or until the age of eighteen. As in 1857, the governor was authorized to borrow a sum not to exceed £50,000 per annum for immigration purposes.[107] Provision was made for the introduction of Chinese, regarded as another possible supplement to the labor force.[108] The terms of indenture, reindenture, and guarantee of return passage were modified to comply with suggestions from the Colonial Office.[109] The act "To amend the Law Relating to Immigration" (22 Vic. c.V) limited indenture to three years (except for Indians and Asians); required the employer to make annual returns; authorized the governor to make regulations binding upon the employer in matters of food, clothing, and medical care; and made return passage (for coolies) a guarantee upon the general revenue. At the close of his indenture, an immigrant could demand a "certificate of industrial residence," which would indicate fulfillment of his indenture, and permit him to leave the island if he wished. Again, as in the 1857 act, the employer would pay all, or most, of the expense of bringing in the immigrant whom he employed, and the payment could be spread over six semiannual instalments.[110]

These bills, designed to comply with the wishes of the imperial government, were passed without a division, and without any petition against them.[111] In many instances they specifically referred to coolies, for Jamaica was now looking to India for labor. Africans were not excluded, but there seemed to be little reason to hope for any.

105. Darling to Lytton, Oct. 11, 1858, no.128 in no.1145 Jamaica, CO 137/339.
106. Darling to Lytton, Nov. 26, 1858, no.150, and enc., no.12818 Jamaica, CO 137/340.
107. No.4239 of 1858, *PP* (Lords), 1859, IV:555-556, 557.
108. No.4240 of 1858, ibid.
109. Darling to Lytton, Nov. 26, 1858, no.152, in no.12820 Jamaica, CO 137/340.
110. Ibid., and no.4238 of 1858, *PP* (Lords), 1859, IV:537-554.
111. Darling to Lytton, Nov. 26, 1858, no.152, in 1280 Jamaica, CO 137/340.

11

A Brief Revival of African Immigration

JAMAICA CONTINUED TO NEED IMMIGRANTS TO WORK
in the fields. When importation of contract laborers was renewed in 1860,
they were brought primarily from India rather than from Africa, as had
been foreshadowed by the Immigration Act of 1858.

There was also a revival of the African slave trade, and corre-
spondingly, a renewal by Britain of efforts to extinguish it. Once more,
slavers were captured with slaves on board; again Britain was confronted
with the problem of what to do with these hapless people after the courts
had pronounced them as forfeited. She returned to the policy of transporting to the West Indies any who were willing to go. It was a procedure which
seemed in the best interest of all—Great Britain, Africans, and the West
Indies.

Yet only a few of the Africans rescued from slave ships now came to
Jamaica. The number emigrating tended to vary in direct ratio with the
number in the Africa yard. Occasionally they were sufficiently numerous to
warrant hiring a ship exclusively for their conveyance. In those instances all
expenses prior to arrival at a Jamaican port were still borne by Great
Britain. As a rule, however, so few would go that it was impractical to
make special arrangements for their transportation. The economy of

Jamaica could not be saved by a small number of African emigrants.

With the focus now upon Indian coolies, African immigration to Jamaica in the period 1860-1863 became both incidental to the coolie trade and a by-product of it. If a ship, sailing from Calcutta with coolies for Jamaica, lacked a capacity load or had lost passengers by reason of deaths en route, it might call at St. Helena and persuade some of the liberated Africans to come aboard and sail as immigrants to Jamaica. Such Africans constituted only a small percentage of the passenger list of a coolie ship.

Only forty-seven African immigrants entered Jamaica in 1860. All had been rescued from slave ships and liberated at St. Helena. They agreed to go to Jamaica, and were taken aboard the coolie ship *Themis* when it called at St. Helena on the voyage to Jamaica. (The ship needed these additional passengers because many of the coolies had died since leaving Calcutta.) The Africans, like the coolies, were expected to agree to work for a certain number of years; but unlike the coolies, they were not promised return passage and were expected to remain in Jamaica.

The ship arrived at Savanna-la-Mar on May 29 with 276 coolies and the 47 liberated Africans embarked at St. Helena.[1] Much desirable information is unavailable because records were not kept with as great detail as formerly. For instance, clothing was supplied before the ship sailed from St. Helena, but the type and amount are not specified; number of days on voyage is not given, although reportedly all 47 Africans were pronounced in good health when they arrived in Jamaica. There was no difficulty in finding someone who would accept them. They were assigned, in groups varying in size from 2 to 12, to seven employers, some of whom were politically prominent.[2]

The Africans on the *Themis* were not brought in at the expense of the imperial government, but under terms of the 1858 immigration act, which made total cost payable within the colony. Passenger fares from St. Helena to Jamaica came to £352 10s.; in addition, there was a 10s. fee per passenger for the ship's surgeon, a sum charged for clothing supplied at St. Helena, and a fee of 6s. per head to the subagent of immigration. This Jamaica official was expected to visit the estates where immigrants were employed in order to muster and inspect them periodically during their three-year indenture. There was also a new charge for insurance to cover risks from death

1. Darling to Newcastle, June 6, 1860, in no.6415 Jamaica, CO 137/350.
2. Report by Ewart, Nov. 17, 1860, *Votes,* 1860-1861, Ap. 7, pp.71-72.

"and otherwise" during the indenture term, and so large in amount that it equaled one-third of the passage-money. For the forty-seven Africans the total cost of importation was £598 3s. 10d., averaging £12 14s. 6½d. per African. By law, in this instance, the employer was liable for two-thirds of the cost, £8 9s. 9d., to be paid in semiannual instalments over a period of three years.[3]

The Immigration Act of 1858 had defects which soon became apparent to the employers of immigrant laborers. It placed the entire cost (or in some cases, only two-thirds) of importation upon the individual employer, who was expected to file an offer of employment in advance of the laborer's arrival. At the same time, he must agree to pay transportation costs, which had not then been determined. To remedy the situation, the Legislature in 1861 undertook to shift the expense from individual planters to employers in general. By "An Act to make further provision for Immigration into this Island" it made two-thirds of the cost chargeable to an immigration loan, repayable from proceeds to be derived from a tax on the chief exports. (These were stated as sugar, rum, coffee, arrowroot, beeswax, honey, coconuts, and mahogany.) In other words, the tax would be paid by the class of planters who exported their products, and would not be restricted to sugar producers. The remaining one-third would be defrayed from the general revenue. There would be a tax also upon the employer of an immigrant, but only 20s. per year for each adult immigrant indentured to him, 10s. for each nonadult, with a maximum indenture of five years. Although the act was designed for immigrant laborers expected primarily from India and China, it might be applicable to those who came from Africa.[4]

There were some in Jamaica who opposed the act. They disliked on principle the assumption of a loan for immigration purposes, and they objected to the method of financing the loan because it would place the burden on many who would not benefit from it. Their views were expressed by means of memorials, which were forwarded to London. On the other hand, the governor gave his assent to the measure and forwarded to his superior a somewhat detailed explanation of its merits.

At the Colonial Office, where the information for and against the measure was weighed, it was decided not to oppose the loan if certain

3. Report by Ewart, AGI, ibid.
4. Darling to Newcastle, Aug. 7, 1861, in no.4854 Jamaica, CO 137/354.

conditions were met. Jamaica was told she must limit debentures for immigration purposes to a maximum of £50,000 in any one year, and a total of no more than £150,000, repayable within fifteen years from date of issue. In addition, she must provide security for repayment by increasing the annual tax paid by the employer of an indentured immigrant. Newcastle preferred a rate of 40s. for each adult and 20s. for each nonadult, but would accept 30s. to 15s.[5] Such measures would, of course, have to be approved by the legislature.

A general election, held in the preceding year, had produced a notable alteration in the composition of the House of Assembly. One-third of the members were men who had not sat there before, and the section connected with trade was materially strengthened.[6] Jealous as always of its rights and privileges, the assembly was no more willing than had been its predecessors to accept outside suggestions for levying additional taxes. So strong was the opposition to any additional payment that the executive committee had to abandon any thought of a one hundred percent increase in the employers' tax. It also agreed to draw Colonial Office attention to the economic condition of the island. The assembly then levied a 30s. to 15s. employers' tax, to be paid on each indentured immigrant, but set no limit to the amount which Jamaica might borrow for immigration purposes. The bill, as finally passed, was entitled, "An Act to Amend the Laws Relating to Immigration and in respect to contracts made in China by Chinese Immigrants." Intent upon showing its displeasure, the assembly attached a suspending clause to the section relating to Chinese immigrants;[7] and to dispel any possible doubt as to its sentiments, it resolved that Newcastle's proposal for the tax was "an invasion of the privilege of self-government."[8]

When Newcastle received the transcript of the measure, he officially ignored the bad temper of the assembly, and concluded that with one exception Jamaica had enacted the necessary amendments. The omission of a limitation on borrowing was no great handicap, however, for constitutionally the power to raise loans still resided with the governor, with the advice of the executive council. The Secretary now used the simple device of directing the governor not to approve any loan which would raise above

    5. Murdock to Elliot, Nov. 1, 1861, in no.9808 Jamaica, CO 137/358; Newcastle to Darling, Nov. 30, 1861, no.380, CO 138/73.
    6. Darling to Newcastle, Aug. 20, 1862, in no.8960 Jamaica, CO 137/350.
    7. Statement by the Executive Committee in no.2171 Jamaica, CO 137/369.
    8. Eyre to Newcastle, Feb. 7, 1862, in no.2171 Jamaica, CO 137/364.

£150,000 the total borrowed by Jamaica. At the same time, he notified the governor that the Jamaica Immigration Act of 1861, as amended, would be approved.[9]

Immigration of liberated Africans into Jamaica increased somewhat during 1861. Most of them were brought in ships sailing directly from African ports; a few came by way of coolie ships which called at St. Helena en route to Jamaica. Information provided about these people by the different agencies concerned with immigration varied slightly. The Jamaica Blue Book for 1861 recorded 649 African immigrants for the year, all from St. Helena.[10] Statistics published by the Colonial Land and Emigration Commission give the same total, but indicate that 390 of them came from Sierra Leone, 259 from St. Helena.[11] Those figures coincide with the ones provided in the "Returns" submitted to the Assembly.[12] The agent general for immigration, David Ewart, in his annual report dated November 30, 1861, stated that Jamaica had received "by direction of the Secretary of State" one "cargo" of liberated Africans from St. Helena. They had sailed on July 23, spent thirty-seven days on voyage, and arrived in Jamaica August 29. Two immigrants had died during the crossing, but 259 were landed (205 adult males, 54 adult females, and two children).[13] Ewart mentioned that two more transports which had been promised from Africa, one from Sierra Leone, one from St. Helena, were expected at any moment.[14]

One of the promised ships arrived with African immigrants before the year 1861 came to a close. The *Patterson*, after a thirty-day crossing on which five died, discharged its 390 passengers in Jamaica on December 28, 1861. Two more immigrant ships arrived within approximately one week. One, from Calcutta, brought only coolies. The other, the *Clarendon* from St. Helena, completed the voyage in twenty-two days, with two deaths. It landed 219 immigrants (197 adults, of whom 162 were men). A short time later the *Scoresby* arrived from India, and, along with the coolies, brought 22 liberated Africans who had been taken aboard at St. Helena. These were

9. Newcastle to Darling, March 28, 1862, no.432, CO 138/73.

10. Jamaica Blue Book, 1861, in Eyre to Newcastle, Oct. 1, 1862, no.1156 Jamaica, CO 137/367.

11. "Return of Immigrants and Liberated Africans into the West Indies," *PP*, 1865, XXXVII:521.

12. Return of Immigrants and Liberated Africans introduced into the West Indian colonies, 1843 . . . 1864. *Votes*, 1864, Ap. 4, p.80.

13. Appendix A to the Annual Report of the AGI, Nov. 30, 1861.

14. *Votes*, 1861-1862, Ap. 5, section 60.

all males, twelve years of age, or more.[15] Passage-fare for the immigrants brought by the *Patterson* and the *Clarendon,* which had sailed directly from an African port, was paid in England from the British treasury.[16] The *Scoresby,* however, had not sailed directly from Africa, and the £208 2s. 6d. charged for its African passengers was paid its owners by Jamaica.[17]

There is little information available about either the immigrant ships or the passengers who arrived in late December and early January. Ewart made only a brief report immediately following their arrival, and promised a more detailed account when he had received further information from the subagents.[18] His later report, though listed in the calendar, is missing from the despatches.[19]

Despite the acquisition of some African immigrant laborers in 1861, Jamaica was beset by the spectre of some two hundred earlier arrivals who now asked for free return passage to Africa. Some based their claim on a written certificate; others merely asserted they had been given an oral promise, but nothing in writing. Despite doubts about the validity of their claims, maintenance of good public relations made it necessary to honor them. To do otherwise would probably subject Jamaica to criticism by the imperial government and to loss of confidence of the Africans. Either eventuality would be hazardous to the African immigration which the colony was still trying to promote. In August, 1861, a ship (the *Clarendon,* recently arrived from Calcutta) was hired and provisioned in accordance with the regulations for immigrant ships, with seven weeks allowed for the voyage to Sierra Leone. At the last moment 109 of the claimants decided to accept a six-pound bounty in lieu of the trip back to Africa. A total of 70 statute adults finally embarked. (There were 38 men, 28 women, 5 boys, 3 girls.) It was hoped that with the sailing of the ship from Kingston on August 13, 1861, the last of the African immigrants who had a claim to return passage had been accomodated, either by being sent back to Africa free of charge or by receiving compensation money.[20]

15. "Return of the Number of Immigrants imported into Jamaica during the season 1861-1862," by David Ewart, Nov. 10, 1862, *Journals of the Legislative Council,* 1862-1863, pp.16-17.
16. Ibid.
17. Enc. in Darling to Newcastle, Feb. 7, 1862, no.2170 Jamaica, CO 137/364.
18. Enc. in Darling to Newcastle, Jan. 8, 1862, in no.999 Jamaica, CO 137/364.
19. CO 137/364.
20. Darling to Newcastle, Aug. 21, 1861, and encs., no.8197 Jamaica, CO 137/356.

Jamaica was subjected to a further disadvantage in her struggle to secure African immigrants, for the Colonial Office was moving toward an important change in its system of financing immigration from Africa. Although the old arrangement (whereby Britain hired and paid for voyages when the passengers were all liberated Africans sailing directly from Africa) had enabled the imperial government to lessen to some degree the overcrowding of the Africa yards, it was costly. If part or all of the charges could be shifted to the colony receiving these Africans, the home government would thereby effect a small saving for itself, while continuing to remove some of the liberated Africans to areas where they would have employment. The current policy, Newcastle noted, had been adopted as a relief measure when the sugar colonies were suffering a severe depression "occasioned in part by imperial legislation" [i.e., the Sugar Duties Act] ; but their need for that had passed, he said, and they were now well able to share the cost. He announced that Her Majesty's government would continue to bear all costs prior to embarkation [i.e., collection costs] ; but the receiving colony would become responsible for the other expenses. These would include the usual fee[21] to the emigration agent who embarked the people, freight charges for the vessel, and payment to the surgeon and officers of the ship. The liberated Africans would still be a bargain, suggested Newcastle, for the colony would pay no collection fees, and there would be no promise of a return passage to be borne by the colony.[22]

The Secretary of State, who seemed to believe that planters could easily assume additional financial burdens, was confident they would agree to do so in order to secure laborers. He did not foresee any difficulties, even though it meant an increase in Jamaica's expenditures. Newcastle gave instructions for the necessary funds to be provided in the same way as for the coolies, with one-third of the gross cost placed upon the general revenue, and the remaining two-thirds on the planting interests. The employer could pay a part of his contribution at the time of the allotment and the balance by semiannual payments within three years. The term of indenture must be no more than three years, he emphasized, because transportation costs were less for a liberated African than for a coolie.[23]

There was a note of urgency in the directive to the governor, who was

21. $1.00 or 4*s*. per head.
22. Newcastle to Darling, Nov. 7, 1861, Circular, *Votes,* 1861-1862, pp.200-201.
23. Darling to Newcastle, ibid.

to obtain the legislation necessary for implementing the change, and then report promptly to the Secretary. Explanation lay, perhaps, in the fact that April 1, 1862, had already been fixed as the date when the new plan would become effective. Colonial cooperation was imperative if the plan was to succeed. Newcastle was also eager to determine the portion of immigrants which each colony would receive. He must know, therefore, which colonies would participate, and must be informed no later than January of each year how many Africans each colony would accept. He frankly doubted that supply would equal demand. But he gave cause for wonder as to how much he understood about financial difficulties within the colony. While emphasizing there would always be uncertainty as to when these ships would arrive, he nonetheless warned the colony to have funds constantly available to meet the freight charges, which would be payable within the colony whenever the ship might come into port.[24]

The governor, early in January, 1862, sent Newcastle's despatch to the House of Assembly.[25] There a bill to implement the Colonial Office directive was promptly introduced by a member of the executive committee. It was hurried through the various stages and signed by the governor within the month.[26] Entitled "An act to provide for the payment of the expenses of introducing Africans after April 1 next," it provided for an annual payment of 30s. by the employer of each adult African immigrant brought in after that date, and 15s. if the African was under eighteen years of age.[27] When a transcript of the act arrived at the Colonial Office, Newcastle pointed to an inconsistency. The Act to Amend the 1861 Immigration Act, passed a few days later, provided for a 30s. tax per annum payable by employers of Africans twelve years of age or more (except liberated Africans transported at the cost of Great Britain). Newcastle ruled that the later act superceded the earlier one, which meant that the 30s. tax per annum should apply to all Africans above twelve introduced after April 1, 1862.[28] The legislation adopted by Jamaica and approved by the Colonial Office enabled the island to remain on the list of colonies eligible to receive liberated Africans. Would the Africans arrive?

One ship, for which Jamaica paid transportation costs, came with

24. Newcastle to Darling, ibid., pp.201-202.
25. *Votes*, 1861-1862, p.61.
26. Ibid., pp.217, 225, 268.
27. Ibid.
28. Newcastle to Darling, Mar. 28, 1862, no.432, CO 138/73.

liberated Africans before the AGI wrote his report for the year ending September 30, 1862. There was a slight decrease in the year's total. Only 608 arrived, all from St. Helena.

Months elapsed without the arrival of many Africans. Disappointed, and resentful of what they thought was a large number sent to British Guiana, members of the assembly became impatient. They requested the lieutenant governor, Edward John Eyre,[29] to draw the attention of his superiors to the inequitable distribution of liberated Africans. They also asked him to forward to the Colonial Office their own request that in the future Jamaica be allotted the same number of immigrants as British Guiana.[30]

The message from the assembly was referred to the CL&EC where, five years earlier, the principle for distribution of Africans had been determined. Now, because her exports of sugar had increased, Jamaica was asking for a larger share. The commissioners conceded an increase in Jamaica's sugar exports, but pointed to a greater increase in the amount of sugar sent out from British Guiana. They concluded that Jamaica was not warranted in asking for an adjustment.[31]

The assembly, reluctant to let the question rest, next suggested total exports rather than sugar alone as the basis for determining the distribution of liberated Africans.[32] The Blue Book of 1862 indicated that Jamaica's exports included many products not derived from sugar cane—such as pimento, coffee, ginger, logwood, coconuts, and beeswax. Their total value amounted to about half that of sugar. Eyre used these statistics (showing the export value of each product) when he requested the Colonial Office to consider total exports in determining need for laborers.[33] This time he was successful. Jamaica was notified of a modification in her favor, with a ratio of 6.5 for Jamaica against 8 for British Guiana.[34] Nonetheless, the counting still was unfavorable to Jamaica, for the Africans landed directly from the

29. Darling left Jamaica in February, 1862. Eyre then became lieutenant governor, but was not made governor until July 1, 1864.
30. Eyre to Newcastle, May 20, 1863, in no.5829 Jamaica, CO 137/372; *Votes,* 1862-1863, p.140.
31. Murdock to Rogers, June 29, 1863, *Votes,* 1863-1864, pp.109-110; Walcott to Rogers, Extract, ibid., p.111.
32. Eyre to Newcastle, Aug. 17, 1863, in no.8978 Jamaica, CO 137/374.
33. Ibid.
34. Newcastle to Eyre, Jan. 20, 1864, and enc., *Votes,* March-May, 1863-1864, pp.20-22.

slaver in 1857 were subtracted from her allotment. Jamaica was informed that in the period 1859-1863 she actually had received more than British Guiana.[35] Only two ships arrived from St. Helena prior to April, 1863; thereafter, none came with Africans. Immigration of Africans had come to a standstill.

Immigration of coolies had also been halted. When planters learned they would be charged the new 30s. to 15s. tax on coolies, for whom they had applied at the old 20s. to 10s. rate, they simply refused to accept them and pay the new rate.[36] Both the House of Assembly and the Legislative Council tried to restore the old tax, but the lieutenant governor opposed their action and went out of his way to assure Newcastle that the measure had not been "government sponsored."[37] The immigration agent in India was instructed not to send any more coolies.

Information pertaining to Africans who came to Jamaica in the 1860-1863 period is quite limited, and is to be found primarily in reports of the subagents of immigration. Each subagent, who was in charge of one or more parishes, was now required to make quarterly reports on such matters as wages, health, living conditions, and hospital and medical facilities for immigrants. He must give an overall account of his district, as well as a separate one for each estate under his jurisdiction. The subagents' reports were then briefed by the agent general of immigration, who sent his own report, together with the briefs, to the lieutenant governor. With so much copying and recopying, errors could easily creep in. There seems to be a discrepancy in at least one summary by the AGI, who reported the highest wage for a given estate as 11s. per week, yet mentioned a weekly savings of £10 and £12.

Most reports relative to the condition of immigrants dealt primarily with coolies, or with coolies and Africans together. Seldom was there any differentiation. Wages tended to vary from one estate to another, and from parish to parish, but there is nothing to indicate the types of work for which the wages were paid, although presumably it was all field work of different kinds. The lowest wage recorded, 1s. to 1s. 6d. on a single estate in the Port Maria area, brought from Eyre a demand for investigation and correction of

35. Ibid.; Murdock to Rogers, Jan. 9, 1864; ibid., pp.21-22.
36. Murdock to Rogers, Jan. 12, 1863, no.300 Jamaica, CO 137/377.
37. Eyre to Newcastle, May 8, 1863, in no.5233 Jamaica, CO 137/372; *Votes, 1863-1864*, p.157.

what was less than a "subsistence wage." The highest wages, paid on several estates, were 11s. and 12s. per week with corresponding lows of 3s. 6d. and 3s. Most frequent highs were about 6s. with average weekly earnings about 3s. Hours spent in work were not long by standards of either the area or the era. The work week on some estates was limited to five days; on some, the work per day was no more than five or six hours; on others, if the immigrants worked one day, they sometimes remained in their cottages the next. One subagent commented that there was not much incentive to expend energy when natural wants could be satisfied so easily from the abundance which nature provided in Jamaica. But despite the somewhat limited amount of work, if the subagents' reports are to be taken at face value, part of the immigrants were able to accumulate savings and were encouraged to deposit them in the Kingston Savings Bank or one of its branches.[38]

When there were specific references to the Africans, their health and "social condition" were frequently described as very good; sometimes they were "well clad" and "interested in their appearance." Many of the recent arrivals were located in the parish of Westmoreland or near-by—47 from the *Themis,* 22 from the *Scoresby,* and 225 from the *Wentworth,* the last of the ships to arrive with Africans. Many of the last group were reported as young, eight to fifteen years of age, but "remarkably healthy and much liked by the Planters." In St. Thomas-in-the-East, the locale for the initial experiment, there were no immigrants except Africans, and the feeling between them and their employers was reported as one of the "luke warm" mutual satisfaction. Some were not too well pleased with the location of their living quarters, close to the residence of the manager. They preferred separate dwellings with a bit of ground where they could have a garden and keep a pig and a few chickens. For that reason, and for the purpose of encouraging the Africans to remain after their indenture had ended, a few employers were moving toward a system of detached dwellings in a sort of colony. Socially, some of the immigrants went into the Negro villages where they fraternized with both creoles and older Africans, although they seemed to prefer the latter. Apparently, however, they remained with the estate, for there are no references to desertion by these immigrants. As references to

38. No.8986 Jamaica, CO 137/374, upon which this account of conditions of African immigrants is based, is a very large collection containing despatches of Eyre to Newcastle, of the Governor's Secretary to Ewart, of Ewart to the Governor's Secretary; reports of subagents of immigration; and the AGI's briefs and report to the Governor. The citation will not be repeated except for one specific reference.

schools and attendance at Sunday services are noticeably lacking, it may be concluded they were no longer of concern.

Despite the advantage of available labor, many employers felt the costs were exceedingly high. Care of the sick became a subject of great controversy. The governor had demanded that each planter construct or set aside a building to be fitted up for use exclusively as a hospital. Adequate medical attendance must also be provided despite the increasing difficulty of finding qualified medical men. Employers of twenty or thirty Africans considered that maintaining one building exclusively as a hospital for those who might possibly become ill was too heavy a financial burden. Although hospital accomodations were sometimes reported as adequate, quite often they were described as not meeting requirements set by Eyre, who became increasingly irritated with both planters and subagents of immigration.

Subagents of immigration held that office as a poorly paid one, which was often thrust upon them in addition to a regular full-time position. Estates under their supervision might be as much as twenty miles distant from the residence of the subagent, and accessible only by horseback over poor and rugged roads. Because time, energy, and health would not permit frequent visits to many or distant estates, these officials tended to depend upon accounts given to them, rather than on their own on-the-spot inspection. When one subagent neglected to follow up reports of an excessively high death rate on a single estate, the lieutenant governor demanded explanations, which eventually led to charges of gross neglect of duty and dismissal of both subagent and David Ewart, agent general of immigration.[39] Newcastle then insisted that Jamaica must provide an adequate salary for an AGI, who would not be permitted to hold any other office.[40] When the Legislature seemed hesitant, the colony was again removed from the list of those eligible to receive liberated Africans.[41] Within a few months Jamaica complied with the demand, and was restored to the list—information which the governor conveyed to the Legislature soon after it convened in November, 1864.[42] In reality it mattered little, for captures of slavers with slaves

39. Austin to Ewart, Aug. 24, 1863; Eyre to Newcastle, Aug. 24, 1863; both in no.8986 Jamaica, CO 137/374.
40. Message from the Lt. Governor to the Assembly, *Votes,* 1863-1864, pp.317-318.
41. Cardwell to Eyre, Apr. 16, 1864, *Votes,* 1864-1865, p.17.
42. *Votes,* 1863-1864, p.74; Cardwell to Eyre, Aug. 19, 1864, *Votes,* 1864-1865, p.32; Message from the Lt. Gov., ibid; p.310.

on board had ceased. And so had the immigration of liberated Africans.[43]

In review it may be said that some 7,500 immigrants had come voluntarily from Africa to Jamaica in the period 1840-1865. Unable to pay their own passage, they had agreed to make reimbursement by working for a given number of years at a stated wage. The terms under which they came might be described as Jamaica's version of "indentured labor" and "assisted migration" then widely used elsewhere for Europeans who were migrating. Although these African immigrants were eligible for citizenship, in some instances they were also entitled to claim a free return passage to their port of embarkation if they first fulfilled certain conditions. For various reasons, however, most of them remained in Jamaica.

Initiative in the project to recruit Africans as indentured laborers had been taken by Jamaica itself. Planning, recruiting, supervision—all had been by the island government and island agents who acted with at least the tacit consent of the imperial government. In the early stages of the program an emphasis was placed upon provisions for the health and welfare of these immigrant laborers. Certainly the imperial government stressed these aspects; seemingly the island government earnestly attempted to do so. Jamaica had the leading role, however, only during the early period of the drama. When it appeared that something more was needed to stimulate a flow of immigrants, and supervision was therefore taken over by the home government, the importance of Jamaica's part diminished—gradually at first, quite rapidly after 1848. As its economy declined and Jamaica abandoned all hope that Britain would aid by modifying the free trade policy, planting interests became desperate in their efforts to save the industry upon which the island's former prosperity was based. In their frantic attempts to bolster a crashing industry, they seized upon any possible labor for the cane fields, and gave less thought to the condition of the immigrant laborers.

With the new constitution of 1854 and the strengthened executive, initiative passed from the elected House of Assmebly to the governor, who represented Her Majesty's government. The island's part in promoting African immigration then became merely whatever was assigned to it, and of little significance until the immigrant arrived in a Jamaican port.

A change may be detected also in the attitude and policy of the imperial government, which remained committed to the social well-being of

43. "Twenty-eighth General Report" of the CL&EC, Ap. p.61, *PP,* 1867-1868, XVII.

the individual as long as the liberated Africans were not too numerous. But British colonies where the prize courts were located eventually became filled to overflowing with these freed men. At that point the imperial government was concerned primarily with relieving the overcrowding and became less careful about the immigrants after they left the confines of the African colony.

For more than two decades Jamaica had tried to attract large-scale migration of Africans in the form of indentured laborers. Sadly, the hopes generated by success of the first year recruiting under the supervision of Alexander Barclay were never realized. Regardless of who directed it, voluntary African immigration never became large scale; no picture which the recruiter drew of a "better life" across the water could be sufficiently attractive to induce Africans to do anything but remain where they were.

But what of those 7,500 Africans who had come voluntarily as indentured laborers? During their term of service their work was particularly important at crop time, when the creole laborer might decide to spend his time exclusively on his own grounds. On estates fortunate enough to have them, the Africans had been an important factor in the continuance of sugar production. These immigrants were never sufficiently numerous, however, to meet all of the demands. And once their indenture had been satisfied, they were free to leave the estate owner.

What became of these voluntary African immigrants after completion of their indenture? A few claimed a free return passage to Africa and departed; most of these immigrants remained in Jamaica; some were able to acquire land of their own; some accumulated savings. It is possible that others became prosperous traders. Almost none of them seem to have remained with the estates. There is no doubt that these Africans who had come as immigrants became a part of the population, with the same rights as those who were born in the island—including the same right to choose between self-employment and working for wages. African immigrants had been wanted in part because they "blended" so well with the creole population. For that very reason they became virtually unidentifiable. Unfortunately it is impossible to determine their contribution to the island once their indenture ended and they became a part of the mainstream of Jamaican life.

Appendix

SECRETARIES OF STATE FOR WAR AND THE COLONIES

(until June 10, 1854)

1839

Constantine Henry, Marquis of Normanby, Feb. 20

Lord John Russell (afterward Earl Russell), Aug. 30

1841

Hon. Edward Henry Stanley (afterward Earl of Derby), Sept. 3

1845

William Ewart Gladstone, Dec. 23

1846

Henry, Earl Grey, July 3

1852

Sir John Pakington, Feb. 27

Henry, Duke of Newcastle, Dec. 28

(Note: The Secretaryship was divided, effective June 10, 1854.)

SECRETARIES OF STATE FOR THE COLONIES

1854

Sir George Grey, June 10

1855

Hon. Sidney Herbert (afterward Lord Herbert of Lea), Feb. 8

Lord John Russell, May 1

Sir William Molesworth, July 21

Henry Labouchere (afterward Lord Taunton), Nov. 21

1858

Hon. Edward Henry Stanley, Feb. 26

Sir Edward George Bulwer Lytton (afterward Lord Lytton), May 31

1859

Henry Pelham, Duke of Newcastle, June 18

1864

Edward Cardwell (afterward Viscount Cardwell), April 4

Bibliographical Note

THE MORE USEFUL SOURCES FOR THIS BOOK HAVE
been government publications and documents of both Jamaica and Great
Britain. These include:

Jamaica, *Votes of the Honourable House of Assembly of Jamaica,*
1791-1865, published in St. Jago de la Vega. The series provides day-by-day
procedures of the assembly, but includes the sessional papers of the colony.
These papers contain reports of island officials, and of select committees of
the assembly. For this work the author has consulted the volumes covering
the years 1840 through 1865. Files of correspondence between the governor
and the Colonial Office, which are also found in the Public Records Office,
London, (usually file CO 137), are sometimes included in the sessional
papers of Jamaica. In that event, the two have been compared, but citation
has usually been to *Votes* because that was the copy available in Jamaica.
Jamaica, *The Journals of the Honourable Legislative Council,* 1855-1865,
published in St. Jago de la Vega, have not been cited unless the document
was unavailable in *Votes of the Assembly.*

The *Governor's Letter Books* (CS 102) in the Jamaica Archives in
Spanish Town provide a copy of correspondence from the governor to the
Secretary of State for the Colonies. CO 137 in the Public Records Office,

London, more often provides a file of correspondence attached to a single letter from the governor.

The Parliamentary Papers of Great Britain include reports of select committees of Parliament, files of correspondence, and annual reports of the Colonial Land and Emigration Commissioners. Statistics for Jamaica, as provided by the reports of the CL&EC, seldom are the same as those given in the Annual Reports of the agent-general of immigration for Jamaica. The CL&EC used the twelve-month period of January 1-December 31; the AGI, the period October 1-September 30. Great Britain, Parliament, *Parliamentary Papers* (House of Commons) has been cited as *PP*; Great Britain, Parliament, *Parliamentary Papers* (House of Lords) has been cited as *PP* (Lords).

Some volumes of Great Britain, Parliament, *Hansard's Parliamentary Debates* (3rd series), have been useful for pronouncements of party and government policy on subjects which affected Jamaica. These volumes have been cited as *Hansard.*

Useful secondary accounts have been cited in the text.

Index